Lecture Notes in Computer Science

Edited by G. Goos and J. Hartmanis

156

Mark H. Overmars

The Design of Dynamic Data Structures

Springer-Verlag
Berlin Heidelberg New York Tokyo 1983

Author

Mark H. Overmars
Department of Computer Science, University of Utrecht
Princetonplein 5, P.O. Box 80.002, 3508 TA Utrecht, The Netherlands

CR Subject Classifications (1982): 68 C 05, 68 C 25

ISBN 3-540-12330-X Springer-Verlag Berlin Heidelberg New York Tokyo
ISBN 0-387-12330-X Springer-Verlag New York Heidelberg Berlin Tokyo

Library of Congress Cataloging in Publication Data. Overmars, Mark H., 1958–
The design of dynamic data structures. (Lecture notes in computer science; 156)
Bibliography: p. Includes index. 1. Data structures (Computer science) I. Title.
II. Series., QA76.9.D35O93 1983 001.64 83-12433
ISBN 0-387-12330-X (U.S.)

© by Springer-Verlag Berlin Heidelberg 1983
Printed in Germany

Printing and binding: Beltz Offsetdruck, Hemsbach/Bergstr.
2145/3140-543210

PREFACE

An important topic in the area of the design and analysis of algorithms is the
construction of efficient data structures. When solving problems by means of a computer, one often needs to store sets of objects in appropriate data structures to
be able to answer specific types of questions about the objects. The data structures
are either static, i.e., build for a fixed set of objects, or dynamic, i.e., it is
possible to insert or delete objects efficiently. Clearly it is in general harder
to construct dynamic data structures than it is to construct static structures.
Especially in such areas as Computational geometry, Database design and Computer
graphics, numerous static data structures are designed that tend to be hard to dynamize (i.e., make dynamic). This text concerns itself with general principles of
constructing dynamic data structures. It describes a number of techniques for turning
static data structures into dynamic data structures, that are applicable when the
known static data structures or the problems they are constructed for satisfy suitable
properties. It shows that dynamic data structures can often be obtained by applying
standard methods rather than by engineering individual problems and static structures.
The dynamization techniques described form a "tool-box" for those who have to design
dynamic data structures for specific problems.

Although this text was originally written as a Ph.D. Thesis and thus aimed at
presenting original research, I have tried to present the material in the style of
a monograph covering the area of dynamization of data structures. Hence, some results
of other researchers are included as well, with due credit given in the bibliographical comments following each chapter. Moreover I have tried to write the monograph
in such a way that I believe it to be readable for everyone that has some elementary
background in the design and analysis of algorithms and data structures.

There are a number of people I would like to thank for their help while preparing
this text. First of all I would like to thank Jan van Leeuwen who introduced me to
this interesting area of research. A large number of the results in this monograph
resulted from the many interesting discussions we had. Many thanks are due also to
Herbert Edelsbrunner, Kurt Mehlhorn and Derick Wood with whom I collaborated on parts
of the research presented. Thanks also to Joke Pannekoek for turning my ugly hand-
writings into beautifully typed text, to Fer-Jan de Vries for helping me with the
terrible job of proof-reading and to Thomas Ottmann who pointed out a number of
errors in the first version of this text. This work was made possible through the
support of the Netherlands Organization for the Advancement of Pure Research (Z.W.O.).

.

CONTENTS

CHAPTER I

INTRODUCTION

Ever since computers are used for solving problems, people have tried to write programs that solve these problems as efficient as possible. Two types of efficiency are particularly important: (i) the amount of time required for running the program and, hence, for solving the problem, and (ii) the amount of storage required. In the early years of computing, efficiency was generally obtained by "clever" programming and coding tricks. Soon people became aware of the need for systematic methods for solving problems and for a mathematical apparatus for analysing such methods and solutions. The field of "Algorithm design and analysis" was born.

In order that algorithms can be designed and analysed, it is important to establish a proper model of computation. Numerous models of computation have been proposed and studied, from realistic random access machines (RAMs) to more theoretical models such as Turing machines and, recently, several models of parallel computation and VLSI circuit design. In this text we use a random access machine with real-arithmetic as the model of computation (as in e.g. Aho, Hopcroft and Ullman [AhHU]), because it is a good approximation of any present day general purpose computer.

An important topic in algorithm design is the construction of data structures to store sets of objects such that questions about these (sets of) objects can be answered efficiently. Data structures are used to store intermediate results while solving a problem and to store large files of information (databases) that are often searched in. Traditionally these structures have been static, i.e., constructed for a fixed set of objects with no immediate provision for updates. The complexity of such a data structure is measured by three bounds: the building time, the amount of storage required to store the structure and the query time, i.e., the amount of time required for answering a question on it. In more recent years, in particular because of the increased interactive use of computers, there has appeared a need for dynamic data structures that can be updated efficiently. The complexity of a dynamic structure is measured by the update time, the amount of storage required and the query time. An early example of a dynamic data structure, the AVL-tree, was devised in 1962. It had the property that it could handle both insertions and deletions of objects in time proportional to the logarithm of the number of objects present in the structure (Adel'son - Vel'skii and Landis [AdVL]). The early static and/or dynamic data struc-

tures were only suited for answering simple questions about a set of objects, like:
"is object x in the set". Especially in the area of database design, where sets of
multi-attribute objects need to be stored and searched in an efficient way, new and
more complex data structures were devised. The techniques used for dynamizing (i.e.,
make dynamic) simple data structures seemed not to be applicable and, hence, these
more complex searching problems appeared not to be solvable dynamically in an efficient way. Exploiting the connection of multi-attribute objects to objects in multi-
dimensional space, Shamos [Sh1] introduced and investigated a new area in algorithm
design (in about 1975), called "Computational geometry", that deals with all computational problems about sets of points, lines, etc. in multi-dimensional space. To solve
these problems numerous "multi-dimensional" data structures were needed. Shamos and
numerous researchers after him showed by systematic analysis that such solutions could
be made surprisingly efficient. Computational geometry provided the abstraction required for a clearer understanding of the algorithmic structure of multi-dimensional
searching problems. Still multi-dimensional data structures appeared to be very hard
to dynamize. New techniques for turning static data structures into dynamic structures
had to be devised.

   This text deals with general techniques for dynamizing data structures. The techniques usually are applicable only to classes of problems or data structures that
satisfy certain mild constraints. The first attempt to devise a general dynamization
technique was made by Bentley [Be3] (see also Saxe and Bentley [SaxB]) and much of
the incentive for the further study of such methods is due to him. Bentley introduced
a class of so-called "decomposable searching problems" and gave a general transformation for turning static data structures for such problems into structures that allow
for insertions, at the cost of only a small loss in the efficiency of query answering.
Soon after his paper, other results on dynamizing data structures for multi-dimensional
searching problems started to appear. This text will give an overview of the dynamization techniques as known at present.

   The text is organised as follows. In Chapter 2 we briefly review the most important types of searching problems considered in the past few years. Most of these problems arose in the study of Computational geometry. The best known results for the
static case are mentioned and sometimes solutions are shown or methods are indicated.
References to papers where the complete solutions can be found will be given. The
problems and data structures treated in Chapter 2 will be used in the chapters that
follow to demonstrate how the dynamization techniques presented can be used in obtaining efficient dynamic solutions to specific searching problems. Knowledge of the
contents of Chapter 2 is not strictly necessary for the understanding of the later
chapters although it will be helpful. Readers familiar with the literature on Computational geometry can skip this chapter.

   Chapters 3, 4 and 5 deal with dynamization methods based on properties of known static solutions for the searching problems that are to be dynamized. In Chapter 3 we consider the well-known technique of "balancing" (here termed "local rebuilding") that maintains data structures in a balanced form by making some local changes only after an update (insertion or deletion) occurs. First, the four main types of balancing are briefly described. Next, a general method is presented that treats many classes of balanced search trees in one integral way. Balancing techniques are mainly used for dynamizing simple (one-dimensional) data structures. At the end of Chapter 3 it is indicated how these techniques can also be used for dynamizing data structures for some multi-dimensional searching problems. In Chapter 4 we consider a new dynamization technique, termed "partial rebuilding" that maintains data structures for searching problems by occasionally rebuilding degenerated parts of the structure into a perfectly balanced form, in this way giving the structure "room" again to accomodate a number of updates without going out of balance again for some time. Hence, occasionally a lot of work needs to be done, but often updates can be performed in little time. The method yields good average update time bounds for some data structures for which previously no good update techniques were known. Chapter 5 deals with another dynamization technique, called "global rebuilding". It is applicable to structures that allow for so-called "weak" updates, i.e., updates that do disturb balance but do not disturb it too drastically. The technique proceeds by sometimes rebuilding the whole structure. As this takes a lot of time the work is spread over a number of subsequent updates to keep the actual update time spent per transaction low.

Chapters 6 and 7 deal with dynamization techniques that are based on properties of the searching problems themselves rather than on properties of known static solutions to the problems. In Chapter 6 we consider "set problems". Set problems are problems in which some question is asked about a set of objects, i.e., it are searching problems in which there is no searching object. It will be shown that set problems that are "decomposable", i.e., that have the property that the answer over a set can be obtained from the answers over two, separated parts of the set, can be dynamized in an efficient way using one general technique. Chapter 7 deals with decomposable searching problems, as introduced by Bentley [Be3]. His techniques and results are extended in a number of ways to allow for deletions, to turn average update time bounds into worst-case bounds of the same order and to obtain different trade-offs between query and update time bounds.

Chapters 8 and 9 deal with two special types of dynamization of data structures. In Chapter 8 we consider so-called "batched dynamic" solutions to searching problems. In this case all insertions, deletions and queries must be given beforehand. Clearly such problems can be handled using a dynamic data structure but in a number of cases one can do better. General techniques for solving the batched dynamic version of decomposable searching problems will be given. Chapter 9 deals with the notion of "searching in the past". A data structure allows for searching in the past when one can ask questions about the data structure as it was at moments in the past. Hence, the structure has to keep track of how the set of objects changes over time when insertions and deletions occur. Constructing dynamic structures that allow for searching in the past is clearly harder than constructing ordinary dynamic data structures. Methods that turn static and dynamic data structures for decomposable searching problems into structures that allow for searching in the past will be considered.

Chapter 10 gives some further comments and lists a number of open problems and possible extensions of the methods presented. In every chapter bibliographical comments and references are normally saved for the end and listed in a separate section.

Some words about our free use of set-terminology might be useful at this place. In this text a SET will generally be a multiset or even a row of objects that stand in a specific order. Hence, it is possible to speak about an ordered set of objects, or about the first or last element in a set. The term "set" is used because this is customary in most of the literature on the subject.

Some caution is also required in the use of the word "average". With AVERAGE update time we mean the following: a data structure is said to allow for updates in an average of $F(n)$ time when with each update there exists some number n' such that the total time needed for this update and the preceding $(n'-1)$ updates is bounded by $n'F(n)$, where n is the current number of points in the set. This definition covers most uses of the phrase "average time" in the literature on dynamic data structures. Some definitions demand that averages are taken over all preceding updates but this is a weaker notion for it forces us to take into account that the structure might have contained many more points in the past than it does at the moment. In some papers the term "amortised time" is used instead of "average time". It should be noted that "average time" is not the same as "expected time".

To estimate bounds the following notations are used. Let $G(n)$ and $F(n)$ be two functions for integers $n \geq 0$.

   (i) $G(n)$ is said to be $O(F(n))$ if there exists a constant c such that
      $G(n) \leq cF(n)$ for all but finitely many values of n,
   (ii) $G(n)$ is said to be $\Omega(F(n))$ if there exists a constant $c>0$ such that
      $G(n) \geq cF(n)$ for all but finitely many values of n,
   (iii) $G(n)$ is said to be $\theta(F(n))$ if there exists constants c_1, c_2 with $c_1>0$
      such that $c_1F(n) \leq G(n) \leq c_2F(n)$ for all but finitely many values of n,
   (iv) $G(n)$ is said to be $o(F(n))$ if for all constants $c>0$, $G(n) \leq cF(n)$ for
      all but finitely many values of n.

Bounds on the efficiency of data structures are in general expressed in terms of n, the number of points currently in the set. Sometimes bounds are also expressed in m, the maximum of points that have ever been in the set, or N, the number of updates that have been performed on an initially empty structure.

CHAPTER II

A CATALOG OF (MULTI-DIMENSIONAL) SEARCHING PROBLEMS

2.1. Introduction.

The design of efficient algorithms often aims at providing solutions to object-oriented searching problems. A searching problem is a problem in which a question (often called a query) is asked about an object (called the query object) with respect to a set of objects (often called points).

Definition 2.1.1. Given a finite set V of elements of type T_1 and an object x of type T_2, a SEARCHING PROBLEM PR(x,V) maps V and x into an answer of type T_3.

The notation PR(x,V) will be used both to denote a searching problem and its answer. The most familiar example of a searching problem is the "member searching problem" (see Section 2.2.) that asks whether or not x∈V. In this case $T_1=T_2$ and T_3 is boolean. Numerous searching problems are "multi-dimensional" searching problems that deal with multi-attribute sets and query objects. These multi-attribute objects can be viewed as points in a multi-dimensional space. Many of the searching problems treated in this chapter are important examples of the enormous class of multi-dimensional searching problems. They appear in such areas as "Computational geometry" and "database design".

An important subclass of searching problems consists of the so-called "set problems". Given a set of points V, a SET PROBLEM PR(V) asks some question about V. Set problems can be considered as searching problems by using a dummy query object x. An example of a set problem is the so-called "maximum problem" that asks for the largest element in a set of numbers.

Solving a searching problem PR(x,V) consists of devising a data structure S to represent the set of objects V and an algorithm, such that queries with different query objects x can be answered efficiently. A data structure can be static, half-dynamic or dynamic. A structure is called STATIC if it is built once for a fixed set of points and is only used for answering queries from that moment on. A structure is called HALF-DYNAMIC if it also allows for insertions of points in the set efficiently. A structure is called DYNAMIC if it supports both insertions and deletions of objects in the set efficiently. (For set problems the static structure usually is a representation of the answer to the problem itself.)

Notation. Let S be a data structure for a searching problem PR containing n points.

$Q_S(n)$ = the time required to perform a query on S,

$P_S(n)$ = the time required to build S (preprocessing time),

$M_S(n)$ = the amount of storage (memory) required to store S,

$I_S(n)$ = the time required to perform an insertion in S (when applicable),

$D_S(n)$ = the time required to perform a deletion in S (when applicable).

All bounds are assumed to be worst-case bounds for a set of n points. When averages are meant we add a superscript "a". We assume that all functions are nondecreasing and that P_S and M_S are at least linear (i.e., that $P_S(n)/n$ and $M_S(n)/n$ are nondecreasing). Moreover, we assume that all functions are smooth. (A function F is called SMOOTH if and only if $F(O(n))=O(F(n))$.)

The "Design of Algorithms" is almost always concerned with searching problems in one way or another. In the following sections we will briefly describe a number of typical searching problems and review the most important (static) methods that are known for solving them.

2.2. Member searching.

One of the most common searching problems is member searching. Given a set of objects V and an object x, the MEMBER SEARCHING problem asks whether or not x∈V. To solve the member searching problem efficiently, we store the elements of V, ordered in some way, in a balanced (binary) search tree T. This can be done in two ways: (i) The elements are stored in the internal nodes of the search tree. In this case we call T a NODE-SEARCH tree. (ii) The elements are stored in the leaves of the tree and intermediate values are stored at the internal nodes to guide the search. Such a search tree is called a LEAF-SEARCH tree. (The terms "node-search" and "leaf-search" are also used for other tree-like structures.) Both for balanced node-search and leaf-search trees the following result is well-known (see e.g. Aho, Hopcroft and Ullman [AhHU] or Knuth [Kn]):

Theorem 2.2.1. There exists a structure T for solving the member searching problem statically such that

$$Q_T(n) = O(\log n),$$
$$P_T(n) = O(n \log n),$$
$$M_T(n) = O(n).$$

There are two important searching problems related to member searching: the Kth ELEMENT SEARCHING problem that asks for the kth element with respect to an ordering of the set of points (where k is the query object), and the RANK SEARCHING problem that asks for the rank of a given object x with respect to an ordering of the set of points, i.e., for the number of points in the set $\leq x$. If points are stored in sorted order in a balanced binary search tree T and if with each internal node α an integer is associated that contains the number of points in the subtree at α, one easily verifies that both k^{th} element queries and rank queries can be performed within $O(\log n)$ steps.

Theorem 2.2.2. There exists a structure T for solving both the kth element searching problem and the rank searching problem such that

$$Q_T(n) = O(\log n),$$
$$P_T(n) = O(n \log n),$$
$$M_T(n) = O(n).$$

Special instances of the kth element searching problem are (i) the MINIMUM problem that asks for the smallest element in the set, (ii) the MAXIMUM problem that asks for the largest element in the set and (iii) the MEDIAN problem that asks for the median of the set. All three problems are set problems and can be solved statically within $O(n)$ time (see Blum e.a. [Bl] for a solution to the median problem).

2.3. Range searching.

An important searching problem, with numerous applications in algorithm design, is range searching. In this case the set $V=\{p_1,\ldots,p_n\}$ consists of some n points in d-dimensional space. Each point p_i is a d-tuple $(p_{i1},\ldots,p_{id})$ in which p_{ij} is the jth coordinate of p_i. The query object x is a d-dimensional rectilinearly oriented hyper-rectangle. We can represent such a hyper-rectangle (or "range") as $([x_1:y_1],[x_2:y_2],\ldots,[x_d:y_d])$ where x_j and y_j are the left and right endpoints, respectively, of the projection of x on the jth coordinate axis. The RANGE SEARCHING problem asks for all points in V that lie within x, i.e., for all points $p_i \in V$ such that $x_1 \leq p_{i1} \leq y_1$ and $x_2 \leq p_{i2} \leq y_2$ and ... and $x_d \leq p_{id} \leq y_d$ (see figure 2.3.1. for d=2). The range searching problem is motivated by questions in the area of database design. Consider e.g. a salary administration in which the information for each registered person includes age and salary. Viewing each person as a point in 2-dimensional space with as first coordinate the age and as second coordinate the salary, a question like: which persons with age between 20 and 25 have a salary between $10.000 and $15.000 a year, is an example of a range query.

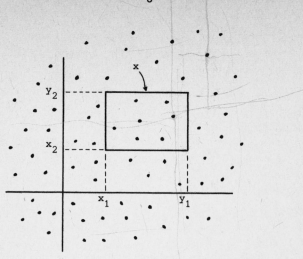

figure 2.3.1.

If we are only interested in the number of points of V that lie within the given range, we call the problem the RANGE COUNTING problem.

The "quad-tree" was introduced by Finkel and Bentley [FiB] as a first data structure for solving the range searching (counting) problem (and many more multi-dimensional searching problems) in an efficient way. A QUAD-TREE of V is a 2^d-ary tree built in the following way. One of the points p_i of the set is taken as the root of the quad-tree. It divides the d-dimensional space in 2^d "quadrants", and therefore splits the set in 2^d subsets. These 2^d subsets will be stored in 2^d subtrees below the root p_i. Each quadrant is split again by taking a point of the subset it contains, and so on, until each subquadrant contains (at most) one point of the set. Figure 2.3.2. shows a quad-tree for a 2-dimensional set of points. Finkel and Bentley [FiB] gave several heuristics to build quad-trees as optimal as possible (i.e., with smallest possible depth), where it is noted that even optimal quad-trees may have depth $\log_2 n$ rather than $\log_{2d} n$, for instance when all points lie on a diagonal line.

Theorem 2.3.1. (Lee and Wong [LeW1] and Finkel and Bentley [FiB]) Storing points in a quad-tree S, the d-dimensional range searching (counting) problem can be solved within
$$Q_S(n) = O(n^{1-1/d}),$$
$$P_S(n) = O(n \log n),$$
$$M_S(n) = O(n).$$

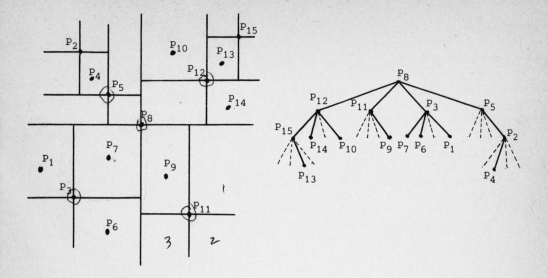

figure 2.3.2.

Although the worst-case query time is not very good, in practice the query time will be much better (see Finkel and Bentley [FiB], Bentley and Stanat [BeSt] and Alt, Mehlhorn and Munro [AlMM]).

A second data structure for solving range queries is the k-d tree. The structure was introduced by Bentley [Be1] as an improvement over quad-trees (see also Bentley [Be2]). A K-D TREE is a binary rather than 2^d-ary search tree, built in the following way. We again take a point p_i of the set that will serve as the root of the tree. It splits the set in two subsets, based on the value of its first coordinate. These two subsets will be stored in the two subtrees below the root p_i. In both subsets we again take a point and split the set with respect to the second coordinate. In the next level we split with respect to the third coordinate etc. After splitting with respect to the dth coordinate we use the first coordinate again. We continue the splitting until each subset contains (at most) one point of the set. See figure 2.3.3. for an example of a 2-dimensional k-d tree.

Theorem 2.3.2.(Bentley [Be1] and Lee and Wong [LeW1]) Using for S a k-d tree, the d-dimensional range searching (counting) problem can be solved within
$$Q_S(n) = O(n^{1-1/d}),$$
$$P_S(n) = O(n \log n),$$
$$M_S(n) = O(n).$$

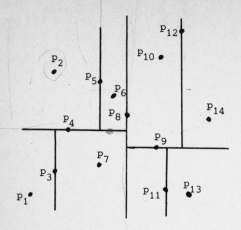 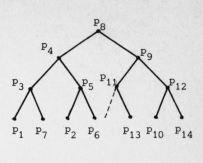

figure 2.3.3.

Also for k-d trees much better bounds can be expected in practice (see Bentley [Be1] and Silva-Filho [SiF]).

Recently, a number of authors independently devised a data structure for range searching yielding much better worst-case query time bounds at the expence of a larger amount of storage (Bentley [Be3], Lee and Wong [LeW2], Lueker [Lu1,Lu2] and Willard [Wi1,Wi2]). We will adopt the term from Willard [Wi2] and call it the SUPER B-TREE. In the 1-dimensional case (i.e., when all points lie on a straight line), the super B-tree consists of a balanced binary leaf-search tree in which points are stored in order of occurence on the line. Moreover, the leaves (points) are linked in that order in a list. To perform a query with a range [x:y] we search with both x and y in the tree for the point nearest after x, respectively y. Starting from the leaf reached by x we walk along the list, reporting the points we pass, until we reach y. The query time is clearly bounded by $O(\log n+k)$, where k is the number of reported answers (points that lie in the range). A d-dimensional super B-tree consists of a balanced binary leaf-search tree T in which the points are stored, ordered with respect to their first coordinate. To each internal node α a d-1 dimensional super B-tree T_α is associated of all points of the set in the subtree rooted at α, taking only the second to d^{th} coordinate of the points into account (see figure 2.3.4.). To perform a range query with range $x=([x_1:y_1],[x_2:y_2],\ldots,[x_d:y_d])$ we begin by searching with both x_1 and y_1 in T. Assume $x_1 < y_1$. For some time the search for x_1 and y_1 will follow the same path, but at some node α we will find that x_1 lies below the leftson of α and y_1 lies below the rightson of α. We must now perform a range

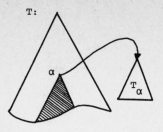

figure 2.3.4.

query with the remaining d-1 coordinates on all points that lie between x_1 and y_1 in T. These are exactly the points that lie below the nodes β_i that are rightson of a node on the path from α towards x_1 or below the nodes γ_j that are leftson of a node on the path from α towards y_1. See figure 2.3.5.

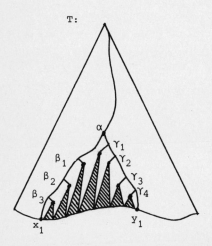

figure 2.3.5.

Because T is balanced, there are at most $O(\log n)$ such nodes β_i and γ_j. One easily verifies that each point of V with its first coordinate between x_1 and y_1 lies below exactly one β_i or γ_j and hence is stored in exactly one T_{β_i} or T_{γ_j}. Hence, to perform a query with the remaining coordinates on these points we recursively perform such a query on each of the T_{β_i} and T_{γ_j}. The answer to the original query is the union of the answers to these queries.

Theorem 2.3.3. Using a balanced super B-tree T, the d-dimensional range searching/
counting problem can be solved within

$$Q_T(n) = \begin{cases} O(\log^d n + k) & \text{for the searching problem,} \\ O(\log^d n) & \text{for the counting problem,} \end{cases}$$

$$P_T(n) = O(n \log^{d-1} n),$$
$$M_T(n) = O(n \log^{d-1} n).$$

Proof

The query time for the searching problem follows from the discussion above. To
obtain the bound for the counting problem we use as a 1-dimensional super B-tree the
structure for k^{th} element searching described in Section 2.2. This structure allows
for range counting queries within $O(\log n)$ time. For the bounds on building time and
storage required we refer to e.g. Bentley [Be3].

□

One can obtain an 'even better bound on the query time for range searching by
using a structure of Willard [Wi3] (also Hart [Ha]) but this method cannot be adapted
to range counting.

Theorem 2.3.4. (Willard [Wi3], Hart [Ha]) There exists a structure S for solving the
range searching problem such that

$$Q_S(n) = O(\log^{d-1} n + k),$$
$$P_S(n) = O(n \log^{d-1} n),$$
$$M_S(n) = O(n \log^{d-1} n).$$

A number of other data structures have been proposed for solving the range
searching/counting problem, yielding different trade-offs between query time, building
time and storage required. The most important techniques can be found in Bentley and
Friedman [BeF] and Bentley and Maurer [BeM1].

A special instance of the range searching/counting problem is the ECDF-SEARCHING/
COUNTING problem. It asks for the points $p_i \in V$ (or their count) that are smaller than
or equal to a given query point x, i.e., the points $p_i = (p_{i1}, \ldots, p_{id})$ such that $p_{i1} \le x_1 \wedge$
$p_{i2} \le x_2 \wedge \ldots \wedge p_{id} \le x_d$. The ECDF-counting problem was treated in Bentley [Be4] and
Bentley and Shamos [BeSh2] but the bounds obtained there are no better than the bounds
for range counting. In fact, one easily shows that ECDF-counting and range counting are
equivalent problems (i.e., can be used to solve each other) and have the same complexity. To solve the d-dimensional ECDF-searching problem one can use the structure of
Willard [Wi3] and Hart [Ha] to obtain a query time of $O(\log^{d-1} n)$, but a much simpler
structure will do to achieve it too. The 1-dimensional ECDF-searching problems asks for
all points in an ordered set that are smaller or equal to a given point. Storing all

points in order in a list, the problem can be solved within a query time of $O(k)$ steps (k the number of answers). Generalizing the structure to the d-dimensional case goes in the same way as for range searching, described above.

<u>Theorem</u> 2.3.5. The ECDF-searching/counting problem can be solved within

$$Q_S(n) = \begin{cases} O(\log^{d-1} n + k) & \text{for the searching problem,} \\ O(\log^d n) & \text{for the counting problem,} \end{cases}$$

$$P_S(n) = O(n \log^{d-1} n),$$
$$M_S(n) = O(n \log^{d-1} n).$$

2.4. <u>Rectangle searching</u>.

There are three important rectangle searching problems. Let V be a set of d-dimensional rectilinearly oriented hyper-rectangles and let x be another such hyper-rectangle.

 (i) The RECTANGLE INTERSECTION SEARCHING problem asks for the rectangles in V that intersect x (i.e., have at least one point in common with x).

 (ii) The RECTANGLE CONTAINMENT SEARCHING problem asks for the rectangles in V that are contained in x.

(iii) The RECTANGLE ENCLOSURE SEARCHING problem asks for the rectangles in V that enclose x.

In the sequel we will write "rectangle" instead of "rectilinearly oriented hyper-rectangle". See figure 2.4.1. for an example for $d=2$. The query rectangle x intersects r_2, r_3, r_4, r_5, r_6, contains r_4, r_5 and is enclosed by r_2. For all problems one obtains the counting variants by asking for the number of rectangles that intersect, are contained in, or enclose x. In particular the rectangle intersection searching/counting problem received considerable attention during the past few years (See e.g. Lee and

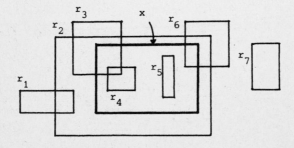

figure 2.4.1.

Wong [LeW3], Vaishnavi and Wood [VaW], Edelsbrunner [Ed1,Ed2] and Edelsbrunner and
Maurer [EdM]). To solve the rectangle intersection searching problem, we will first
consider a special instance of it, the INVERSE RANGE SEARCHING problem: given a set V
of d-dimensional rectangles and a point x, determine all elements of V that intersect
x (i.e., enclose x). The problem is also termed the POINT ENCLOSURE SEARCHING problem.
It was treated in detail in Vaishnavi [Va]. We will only consider the case d=1, in
which we are given a set of segments on a line. The structure we use to store the segments is called a SEGMENT TREE (see Bentley [Be5] and Bentley and Wood [BeW]). Let
$V=\{[a_1:b_1],[a_2:b_2],...,[a_n:b_n]\}$. All begin and end points of segments are stored in
sorted order in a balanced binary leaf-search tree T. With each internal node α the
segment s_α that has the smallest value below α as its begin point and the largest value below α as its end point is associated. Moreover, with α a list L_α is associated
containing all segments that contain s_α but that do not contain $s_{father(\alpha)}$. See figure
2.4.2. for an example of a segment tree containing the segments [0:5],[1:7],[2:4],[3:6]
(only the associated lists are indicated). To perform an inverse range query with a
point x, we search with x down the tree. If we pass a node α, we know that x is enclosed by all segments contained L_α and we report these. One easily verifies that in
this way each segment enclosing x is reported exactly once.

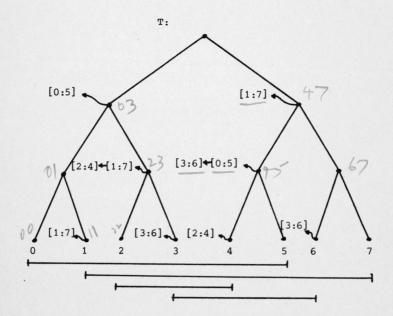

figure 2.4.2.

<u>Theorem</u> 2.4.1.(Bentley [Be5], Bentley and Wood [BeW]) The 1-dimensional inverse range searching problem can be solved within

$$Q_T(n) = O(\log n + k),$$
$$P_T(n) = O(n \log n),$$
$$M_T(n) = O(n \log n).$$

To solve the 1-dimensional rectangle intersection searching problem, note that a segment $[a_1:b_1]$ intersects a query segment $[x:y]$ if and only if either $x \in [a_i:b_i]$ or $a_i \in [x:y]$ (they cannot happen both). Hence we can find all segments of V intersecting a query segment $[x:y]$ by (i) performing an inverse range query with x on V and (ii) performing a range query with $[x:y]$ on the set of begin points of segments in V. A d-dimensional rectangle r_i intersects a query rectangle x if and only if they inter-sect in the projection on each dimension. To solve the d-dimensional rectangle inter-section searching problem we use two structures. (i) A segment tree T_1 in which we store for each element $r_i = ([a_{i1}:b_{i1}],...,[a_{id}:b_{id}])$ the segment $[a_{i1}:b_{i1}]$. With each internal node α we do not associate a list of segments, but we associate a structure T_α for the d-1 dimensional rectangle searching problem on the remaining coordinates of the rectangles corresponding to these segments. (ii) A binary leaf-search tree T_2 in which we store all points a_{i1}. With each internal node α we associate a structure T_α for d-1 dimensional rectangle intersection searching on the remaining coordinates of all rectangles r_i with a_{i1} below α. To perform a query with $([x_1:y_1],...,[x_d:y_d])$ we first search with x_1 in T_1. For each node α on the search path we perform a query with $([x_2:y_2],...,[x_d:y_d])$ on T_α. Next we search with both x_1 and y_1 on T_2. In this way we find nodes β_i and γ_j of which the associated structures contain all rectangles r_i with $x_i \leq a_{i1} \leq y_i$ in the same way as for range searching as described in Section 2.3. For each of these nodes we perform an intersection query with $([x_2:y_2],...,[x_d:y_d])$ on the associated structure. In this way we find all rectangles intersecting x. (The method is adopted from Edelsbrunner [Ed2] where it is spelled out in much greater detail.)

<u>Theorem</u> 2.4.2.(Edelsbrunner [Ed2], Edelsbrunner and Maurer [EdM]) The d-dimensional rectangle intersection searching problem can be solved within

$$Q_T(n) = O(\log^d n + k),$$
$$P_T(n) = O(n \log^d n),$$
$$M_T(n) = O(n \log^d n).$$

It is possible to improve either the amount of storage required or the query time by a factor of $O(\log n)$ (see Edelsbrunner [Ed2], McCreight [Mc]).

Thusfar, we only considered the rectangle intersection searching problem. The structure described above can also be used to solve the rectangle intersection counting problem but better bounds immediately follow from the fact that the d-dimensional rectangle intersection counting problem is equivalent to the d-dimensional range counting problem (Edelsbrunner [Ed3], see also Edelsbrunner and Overmars [EdO1]).

Theorem 2.4.3.([Ed3,EdO1]) The d-dimensional rectangle intersection counting problem can be solved within

$$Q_S(n) = O(\log^d n),$$
$$P_S(n) = O(n \log^{d-1} n),$$
$$M_S(n) = O(n \log^{d-1} n).$$

The d-dimensional rectangle containment searching/counting problem and rectangle enclosure searching/counting problem were recently considered in Overmars [Ov1]. It was shown that both problems were equivalent to 2d-dimensional ECDF-searching/counting (see also Edelsbrunner and Overmars [EdO1]).

Theorem 2.4.4. The d-dimensional rectangle containment searching/counting problem and the d-dimensional rectangle enclosure searching/counting problem can both be solved within

$$Q_S(n) = \begin{cases} O(\log^{2d-1} n + k) & \text{for the searching problems,} \\ O(\log^{2d} n) & \text{for the counting problems,} \end{cases}$$
$$P_S(n) = O(n \log^{2d-1} n),$$
$$M_S(n) = O(n \log^{2d-1} n).$$

2.5. Nearest neighbor searching.

Given a set of n points in d-dimensional space and a query point x, the NEAREST NEIGHBOR SEARCHING problem asks for a point in V nearest to x with respect to some metric. We will only consider the 2-dimensional case. As measure of distance we use the Euclidean metric. A useful structure for solving the nearest neighbor searching problem is the VORONOI DIAGRAM. A voronoi diagram is obtained by dividing the plane in areas of constant answer, i.e., areas such that for all points in an area the answer to the nearest neighbor query with those points is the same. This technique is known as the LOCUS APPROACH. (See Overmars [Ov7] for a number of aspects and applications of the locus approach.) For each point p of the set V the area in which the answer to the searching problem is equal to p is a, possibly open, convex polygon containing p (see figure 2.5.1.). The total number of edges of these polygons is bounded by O(n). Shamos [Sh1] and Shamos and Hoey [ShH1] describe a method for computing the Voronoi diagram of a set of points, using the divide-and-conquer strategy, based on the following result:

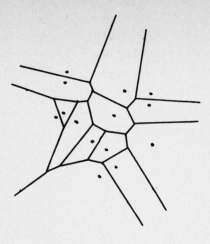

figure 2.5.1.

Theorem 2.5.1.([Sh1,ShH1]) Let $V=\{p_1,\ldots,p_n\}$ be a set of points in the plane, ordered by x-coordinate. Given the Voronoi diagram of $A=\{p_1,\ldots,p_i\}$ and the Voronoi diagram of $B=\{p_{i+1},\ldots,p_n\}$ (some i, $1\leq i<n$), the Voronoi diagram of $V=A\cup B$ can be constructed in O(n) steps.

(It has recently been shown by Kirkpatrick [Ki1] that it is not necessary for 2.5.1. to assume that the pointsets A and B are separated: arbitrary Voronoi diagrams of n and m points can be merged within O(n+m) time.)

The DIVIDE-AND-CONQUER technique proceeds in the following way: (i) split the set into two equal halves, (ii) compute the answers over the two halves of the set, recursively in the same way, and (iii) combine (merge) the two answers into the answer over the total set. When C(n) denotes the amount of time needed for splitting the set of n points and combining the answers over the two halves, the amount of time F(n) needed for solving the problem is given by the following recurrence:

$$F(n) = F(\lceil \tfrac{1}{2}n \rceil) + F(\lfloor \tfrac{1}{2}n \rfloor) + C(n).$$

When divide-and-conquer is used for computing the Voronoi diagram of a set of points V then, after sorting V, C(n)=O(n) due to Theorem 2.5.1. One easily verifies that in this case F(n)=O(n log n). This leads to the following result:

Theorem 2.5.2.([Sh1,ShH1]) The Voronoi diagram of a set of points in the plane can be computed in O(n log n) steps.

Note that the computation of the Voronoi diagram of a set of points is a "set problem".

To locate the nearest neighbor of a query point x it is sufficient to determine the Voronoi region x lies in. The point associated with this region is the nearest neighbor of x.

Theorem 2.5.3. (Kirkpatrick [Ki2]) Given the Voronoi diagram of a set of points, there exists a structure that can be built in $O(n)$ time, using $O(n)$ storage, such that the Voronoi region a given query point lies in can be determined in $O(\log n)$ steps.

Theorem 2.5.2. and Theorem 2.5.3. lead to the following result for nearest neighbor searching:

Theorem 2.5.4. There exists a structure S for solving the 2-dimensional nearest neighbor searching problem such that
$$Q_S(n) = O(\log n),$$
$$P_S(n) = O(n \log n),$$
$$M_S(n) = O(n).$$

There are a number of important set problems that can be solved efficiently using the Voronoi diagram (see Shamos and Hoey [ShH1] and Toussaint and Bhattacharya [ToB]). The ALL CLOSEST POINTS problem asks for each point $p \in V$ for the nearest neighbor in $V \setminus \{p\}$.

Theorem 2.5.5. ([ShH1]) Given the Voronoi diagram of a set of points in the plane, the all closest points problem can be solved within $O(n)$ steps.

The MINIMUM EUCLIDEAN SPANNING TREE of a set of points in the plane is a binary tree connecting all points of the set with minimum total edge length.

Theorem 2.5.6. ([ShH1]) Given the Voronoi diagram of a set of points in the plane, a minimum euclidean spanning tree of the points can be determined in $O(n)$ steps.

A TRIANGULATION of a set of points is a subdivision of the inside of the convex hull (see Section 2.6) of V in triangles with the points of the set as corners (see figure 2.5.2. for an example).

Theorem 2.5.7. Given the Voronoi diagram of a set of points, a triangulation can be constructed within $O(n)$ steps.

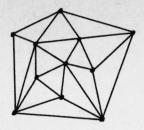

figure 2.5.2.

The LARGEST EMPTY CIRCLE problem asks for a largest circle containing no points of the set whose centre lies inside the set (i.e., inside the convex hull of the set).

Theorem 2.5.8.([ShH1]) Given the Voronoi diagram of a set of points, a largest empty circle can be found within O(n) steps.

2.6. Convex hulls.

The convex hull problem is a prime example of a set problem. Given a set of points V in d-dimensional space, the CONVEX HULL of V is defined as the smallest convex figure containing V. One easily sees that the convex hull is a polyhedron with points of the set as extreme points (corners). See figure 2.6.1. for an example in dimension 2.

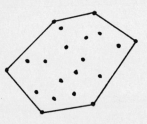

figure 2.6.1.

The convex hull problem, especially in the 2-dimensional case, has a number of important applications in such areas as pattern recognition and computational statistics. It has been a prime topic in the area of Computational geometry in the past few years. Graham [Gr] apparently first showed that the convex hull of a 2-dimensional set of points can be computed in O(n log n) time. Since the appearance of his paper numerous other methods have been proposed for computing the convex hull of a 2- or 3-dimensional set of points in O(n log n) or O(n.k) steps, where k is the number of points of V that appear on the convex hull. See Bentley [Be6] and Toussaint and Akl [ToA] for an overview of the different techniques used. We will describe a method for computing the convex hull of a 2- or 3-dimensional set of points that uses the divide-and-conquer technique of the previous section because of its application in Chapter 6. Without proof we mention the following result:

Theorem 2.6.1. (Overmars and van Leeuwen [OvL1]; see also Gowda [Go] and Swart [Sw]) Let $V=\{p_1,\ldots,p_n\}$ be a set of points in 2-dimensional space, ordered by x-coordinate. Given the convex hull of $A=\{p_1,\ldots,p_i\}$ and of $B=\{p_{i+1},\ldots,p_n\}$ (some i, $1 \leq i < n$), the convex hull of V=A∪B can be computed in O(log n) steps (provided the proper representation is used for A and B).

Using divide-and-conquer, 2.6.1. immediately leads to the following result:

Theorem 2.6.2. Let V be a set of points in the plane. After sorting the points of V with respect to x-coordinate, the convex hull of V can be computed in O(n) steps.

As the sorting of V takes O(n log n) time, 2.6.2. leads to a O(n log n) algorithm for computing the convex hull of a 2-dimensional set of points.

To solve the 3-dimensional convex hull problem, Preparata and Hong [PrH] proved an analog of Theorem 2.6.1.:

Theorem 2.6.3. ([PrH]) Let $V=\{p_1,\ldots,p_n\}$ be a set of points in 3-dimensional space, ordered by x-coordinate. Given the convex hull of $A=\{p_1,\ldots,p_i\}$ and of $B=\{p_{i+1},\ldots,p_n\}$ (some i, $1 \leq i < n$), the convex hull of V=A∪B can be computed in O(n) steps.

Bentley and Shamos [BeSh2] conjecture that it is not necessary for 2.6.3. to assume that the convex hulls of A and B are separated and hence, that the result holds for merging arbitrary convex polyhedra as well. Using the divide-and-conquer technique we obtain:

Theorem 2.6.4. The convex hull of a set of points in 3-dimensional space can be computed in O(n log n) steps.

There also exists a searching variant of the convex hull problem. The CONVEX HULL SEARCHING problem is the following: given a set of points V and a query point x, determine whether x lies inside, outside or on the convex hull of V. One easily verifies that both a 2-dimensional convex polygon and a 3-dimensional convex polyhedron can be represented in such a way that queries of this form can be answered in $O(\log n)$ steps.

Theorem 2.6.5. There exist structures S for solving the 2- and 3-dimensional convex hull searching problem such that

$$Q_S(n) = O(\log n),$$
$$P_S(n) = O(n \log n),$$
$$M_S(n) = O(n).$$

2.7. Common intersection of halfspaces.

In d-dimensional space, a HALFSPACE consists of the region to the left or to the right of some d-1 dimensional hyper-plane. The intersection of n halfspace is bounded by a, possibly open, convex polyhedron. See figure 2.7.1. for an example of a set of 6 halfspaces in the plane. The shaded region is the intersection.

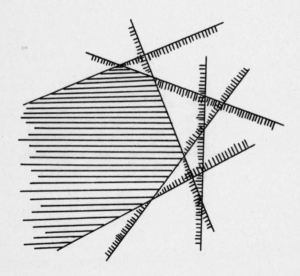

figure 2.7.1.

Shamos and Hoey [ShH2] apparently first showed how the intersection of n halfspaces in the plane could be found in $O(n \log n)$ time. We will describe here a method based on a result of Overmars and van Leeuwen [OvL1].

Theorem 2.7.1.([OvL1], see also Gowda [Go]) Let $V=\{h_1,\ldots,h_n\}$ be a set of halfspaces in the plane, ordered by slope of the boundary line. Given the intersection of $A=\{h_1,\ldots,h_i\}$ and of $B=\{h_{i+1},\ldots,h_n\}$ (some i, $1\le i<n$), the common intersection of the elements in $V=A\cup B$ can be found in $O(\log n)$ steps.

Using divide-and-conquer this immediately leads to the following result:

Theorem 2.7.2. Let V be a set of halfspaces in the plane. After sorting the halfspaces by slope of the boundary line, the intersection can be found in $O(n)$ steps.

As the ordering of V takes $O(n \log n)$ steps, 2.7.2. shows that the intersection of n halfspaces in the plane can be computed in $O(n \log n)$ time.

It was noted by Preparata and Muller [PrM] and Brown [Br1,Br2] that, by means of dualization, the problem of finding the intersection of a set of halfspaces can be transformed into the problem of finding the convex hull of a set of points. This transformation takes $O(n)$ time. Using the result and Theorem 2.6.4. we immediately get a solution to the problem of finding the intersection of a set of halfspaces in 3-dimensional space.

Theorem 2.7.3. Let V be a set of halfspaces in 3-dimensional space. The common intersection of the elements of V can be computed in $O(n \log n)$ time.

The searching variant of the problem asks whether a query point x lies inside or outside the common intersection of n halfspaces. As the intersection is bounded by a convex polyhedron, the following result is immediate:

Theorem 2.7.4. There exist structures S for solving the 2- and 3-dimensional case of the searching problem that asks whether a query point lies inside the common intersection of n halfspaces such that

$$Q_S(n) = O(\log n),$$
$$P_S(n) = O(n \log n),$$
$$M_S(n) = O(n).$$

2.8. Maximal elements.

Another problem related to the convex hull problem concerns the computation of the maximal elements of a set of points in d-dimensional space. For $p_i=(p_{i1},\ldots,p_{id})$ and $p_j=(p_{j1},\ldots,p_{jd})$ we write $p_i\le p_j$ if and only if $p_{i1}\le p_{j1}$ and $p_{i2}\le p_{j2}$ and ... and $p_{id}\le p_{jd}$. A point p_i is called a MAXIMAL ELEMENT of a set V when $p_i\in V$ and no $p_j\in V$ exists with $p_i<p_j$ (i.e., $p_i\le p_j$ and $p_i\ne p_j$). See figure 2.8.1. for an example in dimen-

sion 2, in which the maximal elements are connected by horizontal and vertical lines. This "staircase" bounds the set of points from one side in a way related to the convex hull.

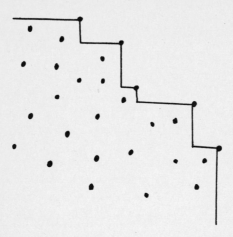

figure 2.8.1.

The problem of finding the maximal elements of a set of points in d-dimensional space was treated by Kung, Luccio and Preparata [KuLP] (see also Bentley [Be4]). Their main result was the following:

Theorem 2.8.1.([KuLP]) The maximal elements of a set of points in d-dimensional space can be computed in $O(n \log n + n \log^{d-2} n)$ time.

2.8.1. shows that $O(n \log n)$ solutions exist in 2- and 3-dimensional space. We will describe another $O(n \log n)$ solution for computing the maximal elements of a 2-dimensional set of points because of its use in Chapter 6.

Theorem 2.8.2.(Overmars and van Leeuwen [OvL1]) Let $V=\{p_1,\ldots,p_n\}$ be a set of points in the plane, ordered by x-coordinate. Given the contour of maximal elements of $A=\{p_1,\ldots,p_i\}$ and of $B=\{p_{i+1},\ldots,p_n\}$ (some i, $1 \leq i < n$), the maximal elements of $V=A \cup B$ can be computed in $O(\log n)$ steps.

Using divide-and-conquer this leads to the following result:

Theorem 2.8.3. Let V be a set of points in the plane. After sorting the points by x-coordinate, the maximal elements of V can be computed in $O(n)$ steps.

There also exists a searching variant of the maximal elements problem. Given a set of points V and another point x, we ask whether x is maximal with respect to V.

__Theorem__ 2.8.4. (Bentley [Be4]) There exists a structure S for solving the d-dimensional maximal element searching problem such that

$$Q_S(n) = O(\log^{d-1} n),$$
$$P_S(n) = O(n \log n + n \log^{d-2} n),$$
$$M_S(n) = O(n \log^{d-2} n).$$

2.9. __Union and intersection of segments on a line.__

Given a set V of segments on a line, one can ask for the union of these segments. Clearly, this union consists of a set of nonintersecting segments. See figure 2.9.1. for an example.

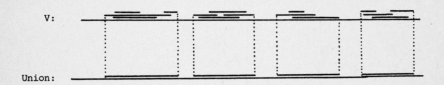

figure 2.9.1.

The problem was treated in Overmars [Ov2].

__Theorem__ 2.9.1. ([Ov2]) Let $V=\{s_1,\ldots,s_n\}$ be a set of segments on a line, ordered by left endpoint. Given the union of the segments in $A=\{s_1,\ldots,s_i\}$ and of the segments in $B=\{s_{i+1},\ldots,s_n\}$ (some i, $1 \leq i < n$), the union of the segments in V=AUB can be computed in $O(\log n)$ steps.

Using divide-and-conquer this leads to the following result:

__Theorem__ 2.9.2. Let V be a set of segments on a line. After sorting the segments by left endpoint, their union can be found in $O(n)$ steps.

It follows that the union of a set of segments on a line can be computed in $O(n \log n)$ time.

The intersection of a set of segments on a line consists of one, possibly empty, segment. One easily verifies:

Theorem 2.9.3.([Ov2]) Let $V=\{s_1,\ldots,s_n\}$ be a set of segments on a line. Given the intersection of the segments in $A=\{s_1,\ldots,s_i\}$ and of the segments in $B=\{s_{i+1},\ldots,s_n\}$ (some i, $1\leq i<n$) the intersection of the segments in $V=A\cup B$ can be computed in O(1) steps.

This immediately leads to:

Theorem 2.9.4. The common intersection of a set of n segments on a line can be determined in O(n) steps.

Both problems can be generalized to higher-dimensional space in which case we are interested in the union and intersection, respectively, of a set of rectilinearly oriented hyper-rectangles.

Also searching variants exist in which we ask whether or not a given query point lies in the union or intersection of a set of segments (rectangles).

2.10. Views of line segments.

An important problem from the area of "Graphics" asks for the "view" of a set of objects from some direction in 2- or 3-dimensional space. A VIEW consists of those object (or parts of them) one can see (partly) looking from the given direction towards the objects. We will only consider the 2-dimensional case and restrict the objects to nonintersecting line segments. In this case, a view consists of a line, divided in a number of segments corresponding to line segments or to places where one can look through the set of objects. See figure 2.10.1. for an example.

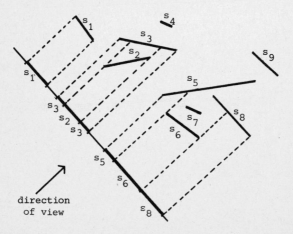

figure 2.10.1.

When one asks for the view from one particular direction, the problem is a set problem. On the other hand, one can also regard the direction as being the query object. Both versions of the problem were treated in detail in Edelsbrunner, Overmars and Wood [EdOW]. We will recall some of their results here.

Theorem 2.10.1. ([EdOW]) Let $V=\{s_1,\ldots,s_n\}$ be a set of nonintersecting line segments in the plane. Given the view from some fixed direction of $A=\{s_1,\ldots,s_i\}$ and of $B=\{s_{i+1},\ldots,s_n\}$, the view from that direction of $V=A \cup B$ can be computed in $O(n)$ steps.

Using divide-and-conquer this leads to:

Theorem 2.10.2. Given a set of n nonintersecting line segments in the plane, the view from some fixed direction can be computed in $O(n \log n)$ time.

For the searching variant of the problem, in which the direction of view is the query object, the following result has been shown:

Theorem 2.10.3. ([EdOW]) There exists a structure S for solving the view searching problem such that
$$Q_S(n) = O(n),$$
$$P_S(n) = O(n^2 \log n),$$
$$M_S(n) = O(n^2 \log n).$$

Generalizations of the problem in which the set consists of "simple" objects rather than just line segments, and views are taken from points rather than from directions, are also treated in [EdOW].

2.11. And many more.

The searching problems and set problems described in the previous sections are just some examples of many that have been studied in the context of multi-dimensional data structuring. We describe some more of the numerous searching and set problems that exist in this section, without giving solutions.

Many searching problems belong to the so-called intersection searching problems. In the most general setting an intersection searching problem is the following: given a set of objects V in some multi-dimensional space and another object x, determine those objects in V that intersect x (or their number). By putting restrictions on the objects in V, the query object and the dimension of the space we obtain numerous searching problems. A number of examples we already considered. When both the objects in V

and the query objects are points, we obtain the member searching problem. When the set
objects are points and the query object is a rectilinearly oriented hyper-rectangle,
we obtain the range searching problem, and when the set objects are rectilinearly oriented hyper-rectangles as well, we obtain the rectangle intersection problem. Three other
important special instances are the polygon retrieval problem, the polygon intersection
searching problem and the circular range searching problem. The POLYGON RETRIEVAL problem asks for the points in a 2-dimensional set of points V that lie in some given query
polygon with a constant maximal number of edges. The problem was treated in Willard
[Wi4]. The POLYGON INTERSECTION SEARCHING problem is the following: given a set V of
simple polygons with a constant maximal number of edges and another such polygon x,
report all polygons in V that intersect x. This problem was considered in Edelsbrunner,
Kirkpatrick and Maurer [EdKM] but no really efficient solutions were given. The CIRCULAR
RANGE SEARCHING problem asks for the points in a 2-dimensional set of points that lie
in a given query circle. Also numerous enclosure searching problems and containment
searching problems can be defined.

"Another large group of searching problems is denoted by the name "closest point
problems" (not to be confused with the closest points problem in Section 2.5.). It are
problems in which we ask for an object in a set V that is, in some way, nearest to a
given query object. The nearest neighbor problem is the most important example. A lot
of work has been done in solving versions of the nearest neighbor problem in which some
other measure of distance is used, for example the L_1 or L_∞ metric, or when other objects instead of points are used for query and/or set objects. Recently, some research
is done in solving the version of the problem in which points in the set get associated
an "intensity" and the distance from a query point to a set point is the actual distance
divided by the intensity of the set point.

A polygon can be viewed as a set of edges. Although there is some relation between
the edges (i.e., the set is not just a random collection of elements of some type) problem with polygons can in general be viewed as set or searching problems. Some examples
are (i) the searching problem that asks whether a given query point lies inside, outside or on the boundary of some polygon, and (ii) the set problem that asks for the
KERNEL of a polygon, i.e., the region of all points inside the polygon from which the
entire polygon can be seen (see figure 2.11.1.). The kernel problem was treated in
Lee and Preparata [LeP2] who showed an O(n) solution to the problem.

There are also a number of searching and set problems related to the view problem
described in Section 2.10. Some examples of them are (i) the set problem that asks
given a set of nonintersecting line segments in the plane whether there is a direction
from which we see all segments separately, and (ii) the STABBING LINE problem that asks
for a line that encounters all segments (see Edelsbrunner e.a. [EdMP]).

Some set and searching problems are very hard to solve. There are for instance
numerous NP-complete searching (set) problems. One example is the traveling salesman

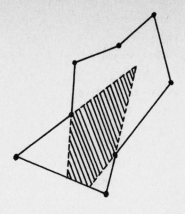

figure 2.11.1.

problem: given a set of points in the plane, find a path that encounters all points and has minimal length (see e.g. Garey and Johnson [GaJ] and Supowit [Su]).

2.12. <u>Composition of searching problems</u>.

There is an immediate, general way in which searching problems can be obtained by combining other searching problems.

<u>Definition</u> 2.12.1. Let $PR:T_1 \times 2^{T_2} \to T_3$ and $PR':T_1' \times 2^{T_2'} \to T_3'$ be two searching problems and let $T_3 \subseteq 2^{T_2'}$, the COMPOSITION of PR and PR', $PR' \circ PR: (T_1 \times T_1') \times 2^{T_2} \to T_3'$ is the following searching problem:

$$PR' \circ PR(x,y,V) = PR'(y,PR(x,V)).$$

An example of a composed searching problem is the following: given a set V of rectangles and two other rectangles x and y, report all rectangles that intersect both x and y. It is the composition of the rectangle intersection searching problem with itself. A second example: given a set V of points in the plane and a point x, determine the point on the convex hull of V nearest to x. It is the composition of the convex hull problem and the nearest neighbor searching problem.

A special type of composition is the ADDITION OF RANGE RESTRICTIONS to a searching problem $PR: T_1 \times 2^{T_2} \to T_3$. Let $T_2' = T_2 \times \mathbb{R}$, i.e. each element from T_2' consists of an element of T_2 and a real. Let $V \in 2^{T_2'}$, i.e., V consists of a set of tuples (p, f_p). Let PR' be the special version of the range searching problem: given a range, report all points p such that $(p, f_p) \in V$ and f_p lies in the range. When we compose PR' with PR we get the following problem: given a set V of pairs (p, f_p) with $p \in T_2$ and f_p real, and two query objects $x \in T_1$ and a range $[a:b]$, report $PR(x, \{p \mid (p, f_p) \in V \text{ and } a \le f_p \le b\})$. This is called the addition of range restrictions to PR. For example, the set consists of cities and with each city its population is given. A query can be: what is the city nearest to a given location x with population between say, 50.000 and 100.000. It is an instance of the addition of range restrictions to the nearest neighbor searching problem. The addition of range restrictions to searching problems was treated in Bentley [Be3] and Lueker [Lu2].

Bibliographical comments.

This chapter only highlighted the searching and set problems most relevant to this text. Each of these searching problems was treated very briefly and only the most important references were mentioned. Readers who want to know more about some specific searching problem are suggested to look at the references of the articles mentioned. An overview with a lot of references can also be found in Toussaint [To]. An extensive bibliography of articles on searching problems (and related topics), containing over 600 entries can be found in Edelsbrunner and van Leeuwen [EdvL].

CHAPTER III

LOCAL REBUILDING (BALANCING)

3.1. Introduction.

        In this chapter we present a new perspective on a well-known dynamization tech-
nique, called "local rebuilding" or "balancing", that is especially applicable to tree
structures for the member searching problem. The technique applies to tree structures
for other 1-dimensional searching problems as well, like kth element searching, rank
searching and 1-dimensional range searching/counting. Even some multi-dimensional
searching problems can be dynamized using local rebuilding. For the sake of simplici-
ty, we will only consider the technique as it is applied to member searching in detail.
        When dynamizing a search tree, it has to remain in some near optimal form, such
that the query time does not change in order of magnitude.

Definition 3.1.1. Assuming the degree of nodes is bounded, search trees are called
BALANCED if the maximum path-length from the root to any leaf is less than c.log n,
where n is the current number of objects in the search tree (i.e., in the set) and
c a constant depending on the type of search tree only.

Clearly balanced search trees have a query time of $O(\log n)$ when used for member
searching.

Definition 3.1.2. A class of balanced search trees is called $O(\log n)$-MAINTAINABLE
if both insertions and deletions of objects can be performed on trees from that class
in $O(\log n)$ time (n the size of the tree) such that the resulting trees are again in
the class.

A first $O(\log n)$-maintainable class of balanced search trees is the class of AVL-trees
(Adel'son - Vel'skii and Landis [AdVL]). In AVL-trees the depth of the left and right
subtree of each internal node differ by at most one (see Section 3.2.1.). Since then,
numerous other criteria of balance have been proposed, that could be maintained in
$O(\log n)$ steps per update. In all these classes, trees are maintained by making some
local changes of the tree structure along the search path to the inserted or deleted
object. In Section 3.2. we will give a brief overview of the most common $O(\log n)$-

maintainable classes of search trees and demonstrate the local rebuilding techniques used.

The many known O(log n)-maintainable classes of balanced search trees are often very different and hard to relate to one another, yet their maintenance algorithms all seem to rely on a very limited number of different techniques. One might hope that out of all these different designs for balanced trees some sort of unifying theory could be distilled to treat many classes in an integral manner.

An interesting attempt at providing a uniform theory for the implementation and study of balanced trees was presented by Guibas & Sedgewick [GuS] in their "dichromatic" framework. They consider binary trees in which every node is allowed to carry one bit (its "color", say, red or black) to store balance information. They characterize a small number of local balancing transformations and argue that various known classes of trees, including AVL- and B-trees, and their maintenance algorithms can be embedded in the dichromatic framework by enforcing conditions on the occurrences of red and black nodes along the search paths. While the desired generality is achieved, the embeddings do not seem to preserve the own identity of classes of balanced search trees in an easily recognizable form.

In Section 3.3. we shall develop a different perspective on balanced trees. We will enforce a certain regularity, called stratification, on trees, that need not be present in all trees of a given type, but that identifies a subclass of that type. We prove that all stratified trees (of a certain type X) are balanced and can be maintained (as stratified trees of the same type X) by means of one master update algorithm in O(log n) steps whenever elements are inserted or deleted.

Most applications of the theory concern the issue of density. For trees DENSITY normally refers to the minimal number of elements that will be packed in a tree of given height. The resulting idea of packing nodes to highest degree was exercised e.g. in the class of "dense multiway trees" proposed by Culik, Ottmann and Wood [CuOW]. While succesful in updating these trees in O(log n) steps under insertions, they report an intuition that routines for deleting elements may need to be more complex if a sufficient degree of density is to be maintained. The theory we present will show that virtually every type of height-balanced trees can be constrained to an arbitrary degree of density, while both insertions and deletions can still be processed in O(log n) steps at a time.

Finally, in Section 3.4. we show how balancing can be used for dynamizing data structures for some other searching problems. First we consider some 1-dimensional searching problems like k^{th} element and rank searching and show how O(log n) update time bounds can be obtained for these problems as well. Next we consider the super B-tree used for range searching. We will briefly show how $O(\log^d n)$ update time bounds can be obtained for this structure (d the dimension of the problem).

...defined in 1962, numerous other O(log n)-
...rees have been introduced. The most important

...ees
...trees

(xii) right brother trees

(xiii) k-right brother trees

(xiv) 2-3 brother trees

(xv) height-balanced 2-3 trees

(xvi) neighbour trees

(xvii) k-neighbour trees

(xviii) αBB-trees

(xix) BB[α]-trees

Readers interested in the precise definitions of these classes and the maintenance
routines used are referred to the open literature or to e.g. Olivié [Ol]. We will
only highlight the four main types of balance criteria used: height-balancing, weight-
balancing, degree-balancing and path-balancing.

3.2.1. Height-balancing.

A class of search trees is called HEIGHT-BALANCED if balance is obtained by
enforcing and maintaining a suitable condition on the height of the subtrees at each
individual node. Search trees (i) - (v) are examples of height-balanced trees. We
shall only consider AVL-trees in some detail, as we shall use this type of tree in
later chapters.

Definition 3.2.1.1. A binary tree T is called an AVL-TREE if for each internal node
α of T the height of the left subtree of α and the height of the right subtree of α
differ by at most 1.

An AVL-tree can be used as a leaf-search tree or as a node-search tree. We will only consider the use as a leaf-search tree. To insert a new point p in an AVL-tree we search for the leaf containing the smallest point p'<p. This leaf we replace by a node with p' as left and p as right son. To delete a point p we search for the father of p in the tree and replace it by the brother of p. In both cases it is very well possible that the resulting tree is no longer an AVL-tree, i.e., that it contains nodes α at which the height of the left and the right subtree differ by more than 1. Such nodes must lie on the search path towards the inserted or deleted point. To recover the balance at such nodes we have to make some local changes, by means of a single or double rotation (see figure 3.2.1.1.), depending on the way in which balance is disturbed. Details can be found in e.g. Knuth [Kn].

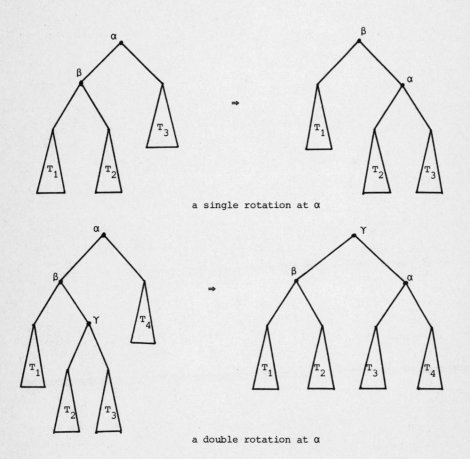

a single rotation at α

a double rotation at α

figure 3.2.1.1.

As both single and double rotations take O(1) time each and only need to be performed at nodes along the search path, both insertions and deletions take O(log n) time. Hence, the class of AVL-trees is O(log n)-maintainable. A very detailed analysis of the maintenance algorithms for AVL-trees was recently given in Mehlhorn and Tsakalides [MeT].

Get!

3.2.2. Weight-balancing.

A class of search trees is called WEIGHT-BALANCED if balance is obtained by enforcing and maintaining conditions on the number of points in the subtrees at each individual node. The class of BB[α]-trees, as introduced by Nievergelt and Reingold [NiR] (see also [ReND]), is a prime example of a class of weight-balanced trees.

Definition 3.2.2.1. Let α be a positive real, with $0 < \alpha \leq \frac{1}{2}$. A binary tree T is called a BB[α]-TREE if for each internal node β, the number of leaves in the left subtree of β divided by the total number of leaves below β lies in between α and $1-\alpha$.

It has been shown that for $2/11 < \alpha \leq 1-\sqrt{2}/2$, balance in BB[$\alpha$]-trees can be maintained after each update by means of single and/or double rotations at nodes along the search path towards the inserted or deleted point. Hence, for each α with $2/11 < \alpha \leq 1-\sqrt{2}/2$, the class of BB[$\alpha$]-trees is O(log n)-maintainable. (See Blum and Mehlhorn [BlM].)

3.2.3. Degree-balancing.

We call a class of search trees DEGREE-BALANCED if all leaves of a tree in the class have the same depth and balance is maintained by varying the degree of internal nodes (i.e., the number of sons) between some fixed bounds. (vi) - (xiv), (xvi) and (xvii) are examples of degree-balanced search trees. As an example we consider the class of 2-3 trees (see Aho, Hopcroft and Ullman [AhHU] or Knuth [Kn]).

Definition 3.2.3.1. A tree T is called a 2-3 TREE iff all leaves of T have the same depth and each internal node has two or three sons.

2-3 Trees can be used as leaf-search or node-search trees. We will only consider the case of leaf-search 2-3 trees.

To insert a point p in a 2-3 tree we search for the position of p among the leaves and add p as a leaf to the appropriate node α. If α had two sons it has room for a third and we are finished. Otherwise, we split α in two nodes α^1 and α^2 both having two two sons, and replace α by α^1 and α^2 as sons of the father of α. Hence, we have propagated the insertion of a node one level higher. This might continue up to the root (if all nodes on the search path have three sons). When the root has two sons we are done.

Otherwise we split the root in two nodes and add them as sons to a new root.

To delete a point p we search for p and delete it. If the father α of p had three sons, he has still got two sons left and we are done. Otherwise we look at the brother β of α. If β has three sons we redistribute them among β and α, leaving both nodes with two sons. Otherwise we take α and β together, in this way propagating the deletion one level higher. This might continue up to the root. If the root had three sons, it will end with two and we are done. Otherwise we discard the root, leaving its one son as a new root. (We have omitted the details of how to fill in or change the search criteria to guide the searching at the nodes along the search path. See e.g. [Kn] or [AhHU] for details.)

As the local changes take at most $O(1)$ per node and need only be performed at nodes on the search path towards the inserted or deleted point, updates clearly take $O(\log n)$ time. Hence, 2-3 trees are $O(\log n)$-maintainable.

3.2.4. Path-balancing.

A class of search trees is called PATH-BALANCED if balance is obtained by en-forcing conditions on the length of the longest and shortest path from individual nodes to leaves in a tree. A prime example is the class of αBB-trees (see Olivié [Ol]).

Definition 3.2.4.1. A binary tree T is called an αBB-TREE if for each individual node β the length s_β of the shortest path from β to a leaf and the length l_β of the longest path from β to a leaf satisfy: $s_\beta/l_\beta \geq \alpha$ if $l_\beta \geq 1/(1-\alpha)$ and $s_\beta \geq l_\beta - 1$ other-wise.

Olivié [Ol] shows that for $\alpha = 1/2$, αBB-trees can be maintained in $O(\log n)$ time per update by means of single, double and triple rotations (see [Ol] for a description of a triple rotation). An important property of these trees is that the total number of rotations needed after an update is bounded by a constant.

In some classes of search trees balance is obtained by a combination of the different criteria of balance described. For instance in (xv), height-balanced 2-3 trees, a combination of height-balancing and degree-balancing is used.

3.3. A general approach.

In this section we will develop a general theory concerning balancing that seeks to identify some common properties of numerous known and unknown classes of balanced search trees (even regardless of whether they are $O(\log n)$-maintainable). It will appear that many such classes contain subclasses of trees that can be maintained at the cost of $O(\log n)$ per update, by means of one master update scheme. While it is not strictly necessary for our theory, we shall adapt the convention that data elements are stored only at the leaves of a search tree, i.e., that the trees are used as leaf-search trees. We shall not explicitly distinguish between search trees (with stored data) and their underlying graphical structure, when we discuss classes of search trees and their properties.

3.3.1. Proper classes of trees and varieties.

Let us assume that some class X of (balanced) trees is given. It is not necessary that an efficient updating algorithm is given with it, although we do assume that trees in X are meant for use in a dynamic environment. For each k, let X_k be the subclass of trees in X of height k. We shall allow that trees of small height (for small sets) are a bit irregular, but we do want X to behave well for larger size sets. Let α be a positive integer.

Definition 3.3.1.1. X is called α-PROPER if and only if for each $t \geq \alpha$ there is a tree in X with t leaves.

If X is α-proper, then each set of size $\geq \alpha$ can be accommodated for by a tree in X. Virtually all known classes of balanced trees are 1-proper, hence α-proper for any $\alpha \geq 1$.

Disturbances of balance in a tree are normally resolved by suitably restructuring subtrees of some bounded size along a search path. It implies that there is some notion of a "good" subtree. Let Z be a set of trees of the same height β. Let l_Z and h_Z be the smallest and largest number of leaves, respectively, that members of Z can have. Note that we do not require that $Z \subseteq X_\beta$!

Definition 3.3.1.2. Z is a β-VARIETY if and only if the following conditions are satisfied:

       (i) all trees in Z have height β,
      (ii) $1 < l_Z < h_Z$,
    (iii) for each t with $l_Z \leq t \leq h_Z$ there is a tree in Z with exactly t leaves.

It should be clear that β-varieties are very easy to construct. For many known classes of balanced trees X is X_β a β-variety, for every β greater than or equal to 1 or 2.

Given a β-variety Z and a α-proper class of trees X, we should like to express that the trees of Z can figure as "good" subtrees in trees of X.

37

<u>Notation</u>. Let $T_1,\ldots,T_t$ be trees and let T be a tree with leaves $x_1,\ldots,x_t$ from left to right. By $T[T_1,\ldots,T_t]$ we shall denote the tree obtained from T by grafting T_i onto x_i for every i with $1 \le i \le t$. See figure 3.3.1.1.

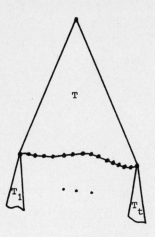

figure 3.3.1.1.

<u>Definition</u> 3.3.1.3. Let X be α-proper. Z is a REGULAR β-VARIETY for X if and only if the following conditions are satisfied:

     (i) Z is a β-variety,

     (ii) for each $t \ge \alpha$ and $T \in X$ with t leaves and all $T_1,\ldots,T_t \in Z$ is
         $T[T_1,\ldots,T_t] \in X$.

If $T \in X_k$, then in (ii) $T[T_1,\ldots,T_t]$ will be in $X_{k+\beta}$.

<u>Example</u>. Let X be the class of AVL-trees. X is α-proper for every $\alpha \ge 1$. For each $\beta \ge 2$ is X_β a regular β-variety for X, considered as a 1-proper class.

<u>Example</u>. Let X be the class of trees with a root of degree d (d fixed) and all other internal nodes of degree 2. Let Z be the set of binary trees of height 2. X is d-proper and Z is a regular 2-variety for X.

3.3.2. <u>Stratification</u>.

    Let X be an α-proper class of trees. Assume there is a regular β-variety Z for X. We will show how to obtain a subclass of very special trees in X, essentially by "layering" trees from Z. Let $K=\max\{\alpha l_Z, \left\lceil \frac{l_Z-1}{h_Z-l_Z}\right\rceil l_Z\} - 1$ and let γ be the smallest integer such that for each t with $\alpha \leq t \leq K$ there is a $T \in X$ of height $\leq \gamma$ with exactly t leaves. (γ exists.)

<u>Definition</u> 3.3.2.1. The class of Z-STRATIFIED TREES (in X) is the smallest class of trees satisfying the following properties:

  (property I) each $T \in X$ of height $\leq \gamma$ for which the number of leaves t satisfies $\alpha \leq t \leq K$ is Z-stratified,

  (property II) if T is Z-stratified and has t leaves and $T_1, \ldots, T_t \in Z$, then $T[T_1, \ldots, T_t]$ is Z-stratified.

<u>Notation</u>. The class of Z-stratified trees (in X) will be denoted as $S(X,Z)$.

<u>Lemma</u> 3.3.2.2. $S(X,Z) \subseteq X$.

<u>Proof</u>

By induction on the definition of Z-stratified trees. Note that each Z-stratified tree has $\geq \alpha$ leaves. Applying property II to any tree in X with $\geq \alpha$ leaves keeps the result in X, by the definition of Z.

$\square$

It should be clear that a tree $T \in S(X,Z)$ if and only if T can be decomposed into the form shown in figure 3.3.2.1. with each of the component trees in the layers chosen from Z. Each layer added corresponds to yet another application of property II.

<u>Lemma</u> 3.3.2.3. $S(X,Z)$ is α-proper.

<u>Proof</u>

Consider Z-stratified trees as they are decomposed into layers. We shall prove the following claim by induction on s:

<u>Claim</u>: $\alpha \leq t \leq Kh_Z^s \leftrightarrow$ there is a $T \in S(X,Z)$ with t leaves and $\leq s$ layers.

The $\Leftarrow$-part is obvious.

The $\Rightarrow$-part is immediate for s=0. Let the claim be true for s. Consider any t with $\alpha \leq t \leq Kh_Z^{s+1}$. Since all t with $\alpha \leq t \leq Kh_Z^s$ are covered by the induction hypothesis, we only need to consider t with $Kh_Z^s+1 \leq t \leq Kh_Z^{s+1}$. By induction we know that for each y with $\alpha \leq y \leq Kh_Z^s$ there is a $T \in S(X,Z)$ with y leaves and at most s layers. We shall argue that the range left for t can be covered by adding one more layer to these trees.

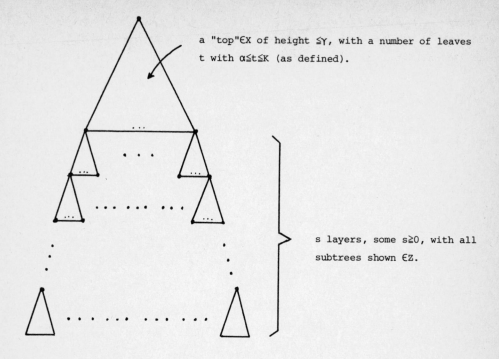

a "top"$\in X$ of height $\leq Y$, with a number of leaves t with $\alpha \leq t \leq K$ (as defined).

s layers, some $s \geq 0$, with all subtrees shown $\in Z$.

figure 3.3.2.1.

Adding a layer to a tree with y leaves yields trees that can have any number of leaves t with $yl_Z \leq t \leq yh_Z$. In this way one can cover all intervals $[yl_Z, yh_Z]$ for t, for y ranging from α to Kh_Z^s. If $(y+1)l_Z \leq yh_Z+1$, then the interval for y interlaces with the next one. Only when $(y+1)l_Z > yh_Z+1$, i.e., when $y < \frac{l_Z-1}{h_Z-l_Z}$, will there be a gap in between.

We note that in this case

$$(y+1)l_Z-1 \leq (\lceil \frac{l_Z-1}{h_Z-l_Z} \rceil -1+1)l_Z-1 \leq K \leq Kh_Z^s$$

and, hence, the t-values in the gap are contained already in the range covered by the induction hypothesis. Observe next that the first interval (with $y=\alpha$) starts exactly at the beginning of the range for t or earlier, as $\alpha l_Z \leq Kh_Z^s+1$. (For s=0 it follows by the choice of K, for $s \geq 1$ by a growth argument.) The last interval (with $y = Kh_Z^s$) ends exactly at Kh_Z^{s+1}, the end of the range of t under consideration. It follows that the joint intervals cover all t with $Kh_Z^s+1 \leq t \leq Kh_Z^{s+1}$ and, hence, that all t-values in this range can appear as the number of leaves of some Z-stratified tree with at most s+1 layers.

□

We conclude that in order to represent sets of size $\geq \alpha$ we can replace X by its subclass $S(X,Z)$. It remains to be seen whether the use of trees of $S(X,Z)$ has a reasonable efficiency. First we consider searches in Z-stratified trees.

Theorem 3.3.2.4. Any Z-stratified tree with n leaves has height $O(\log n)$.

Proof

Let $T \in S(X,Z)$ have n leaves and s layers. It follows that $\alpha 1_Z^s \leq n$, hence $s \leq (\log n - \log \alpha)/\log 1_Z$. The height of T is bounded by $\gamma + s.\beta$, thus by $\frac{\beta}{\log 1_Z}.\log n + c$ for some constant c.

$\square$

It follows that representing sets by trees in $S(X,Z)$ is acceptable as far as the resulting complexity of searches is concerned. We consider the possibility of dynamically maintaining Z-stratified trees in the next section. We note that no maintenance algorithm may actually be known for the class X itself.

It is useful to observe at this stage that there is a resemblance between Z-stratified trees and B-trees. B-trees are a generalization of 2-3 trees in which all internal nodes except the root have a number of sons varying between fixed bounds l and h, where it is normally required that $h \geq 21-1$ (see Bayer and McCreight [BayM], also [Kn]). The root of a B-tree may have a degree between 2 and h. Considering the representation of Z-stratified trees as displayed in figure 3.3.2.1., one could collapse the distinguished subtrees of any $T \in S(X,Z)$ into single nodes and obtain a multiway tree in which all internal nodes except possibly the root have a degree d with $1_Z \leq d \leq h_Z$, i.e., a kind of B-tree, but without the assumption that $h_Z \geq 21_Z - 1$. The maintenance algorithms for Z-stratified trees as presented in the next section combine and extend the techniques used for updating B- and B*-trees (cf. Knuth [Kn]), as was done to some extend also in the study of dense multiway trees by Culik, Ottmann and Wood [CuOW].

3.3.3. Maintenance of stratified trees.

Let X be α-proper, Z a regular β-variety for X and $S(X,Z)$ as defined in the previous section. We shall assume that Z-stratified trees are presented in storage in such a manner that a decomposition as in figure 3.3.2.1. is at hand. This causes no difficulty, because all building blocks (the top and the subtrees from Z) are of bounded size and can be delineated by suitable markings.

Theorem 3.3.3.1. Insertions in Z-stratified trees can be processed in $O(\log n)$ steps.

Proof

Let $T \in S(X,Z)$ and suppose we must insert a new point p. If T currently stores
$t \leq K$ items, then we insert p "manually" at the proper place among the leaves and rebuild T as a Z-stratified tree on t+1 leaves. By Lemma 3.3.2.3. this can be done and
leads to a tree with at most one layer. The amount of work required is $O(K)$, hence
$O(1)$.

Let T currently have more than K items. Thus T will consist of a "top" T_0 of the
necessary specifications and $s \geq 1$ layers below it. Search with p down T to find where
p must be inserted among the leaves. Let the blocks passed by the search path be T_0,
$T_1, \ldots, T_s$, where T_1 to T_s are trees from Z. If T_s has t leaves and $t < h_z$, then it is
sufficient to place p in the right order among the leaves and to rebuild T_s as a
Z-tree on t+1 leaves. (This can always be done and keeps T stratified.) If $t = h_z$, then
we have to do more work and may be forced even to "split off" a new Z-tree in the
current layer which, consequently, must be inserted in T_{s-1}. And this can propagate
through several more layers upwards. Very generally, let us consider the insertion
of a "leaf" in T_i for i>1. Let T_i currently have t leaves.

If $t < h_z$, then we can rebuild T_i as a Z-tree on t+1 leaves and are done.

If $t = h_z$, then we shall examine the "brothers" of T_i to see if we can move elements over and make room for the element to be inserted. Note (see figure 3.3.3.1.)
that T_i is a "leaf" of T_{i-1} and that there are at least l_z-1 neighboring leaves
(Z-trees). If one of them still has room, i.e., less than h_z leaves itself, then we

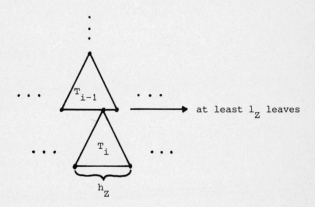

figure 3.3.3.1.

can shift elements over and redistribute them over l_z subtrees such that, with the
new element included, no subtree needs to have more than h_z leaves. It requires the
reconstruction of up to l_z subtrees as Z-trees (and a revision of the search queries
at their nodes), but it is still $O(1)$ steps of work.

If all of these l_Z-1 neighboring brothers are full, i.e., have h_Z leaves, then consider the entire row of $(l_Z-1)h_Z+h_Z+1 = l_Zh_Z+1$ elements we must accommodate. Clearly l_Z subtrees are not sufficient, but l_Z+1 are, because of the following inequality:

$$(l_Z+1)l_Z \leq h_Zl_Z < l_Zh_Z+1 < l_Zh_Z+h_Z = (l_Z+1)h_Z$$

It easily follows that the l_Zh_Z+1 elements (roots of subtrees) can be put together in l_Z+1 Z-trees in this layer, one more Z-tree than we had. Thus we succeed, provided we carry out an insertion in T_{i-1}.

So the procedure repeats, until it eventually gets to T_1 (if it didn't halt before that). For an insertion into T_1 we can not follow the same procedure, because T_0 is not a Z-tree. (In particular, T_0 need not provide l_Z-1 brothers.) Consider T_0 and the entire first layer (see figure 3.3.3.2.). Let the first layer have a total of t leaves, hence $t \leq Kh_Z$. Insert the new node at the proper place and rebuild the

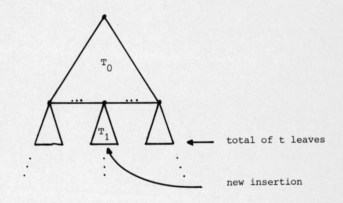

total of t leaves

new insertion

figure 3.3.3.2.

entire portion of the tree as a Z-stratified tree on t+1 elements. By Lemma 3.3.2.3. one can do so, with a resulting tree of at most 2 layers. The amount of work required is $O(Kh_Z)$, thus $O(1)$. Appending the lower layers (automatically as the subtrees of the t+1 elements accomodated for) maintains the conditions of a Z-stratified tree.

The total amount of work adds up to $O(s)$, which is $O(\log n)$.

□

It is noted that the insertion in the top of the tree could have been dealt with more easily (and, perhaps, more efficiently,), had we assumed that $\alpha \geq l_Z$. This not being the case, a rather massive reconstruction is required to carry the proof through.

<u>Theorem</u> 3.3.3.2. Provided the total number of elements remains $\geq \alpha$, deletions in Z-stratified trees can be processed in $O(\log n)$ steps.

Proof

Let $T \in S(X,Z)$ and suppose we must delete a point p. If T currently has $t \leq K$ elements, then we just delete p "manually" and rebuild T as a Z-stratified tree with $t-1$ elements (provided $t-1 \geq \alpha$). This can be done and requires no more than $O(K)$ steps of work.

Let T currently have more than K items. Thus T will consist of a top T_0 and $s \geq 1$ layers attached to it. Search with p down T to find where it is located among the leaves. Let the blocks passed on the way down be $T_0, T_1, \ldots, T_s$, where T_1 to T_s are Z-trees. As for insertions, deletions can propagate upwards. We shall consider the deletion of a leaf node from T_i for $i>1$. Assume that T_i currently has t leaves.

If $t > 1_Z$, then we can perform the deletion and rebuild T_i as a Z-tree on $t-1$ leaves. It requires $O(1)$ steps of work and we are done.

If $t = 1_Z$, then we shall examine the "brothers" of T_i (as Z-trees) to see if one of them has an element to spare, i.e., if one has $>1_Z$ elements. Note that T_i has (at least 1_Z-1 brothers (as in the proof of Theorem 3.3.3.1.) and if one of them has $>1_Z$ elements, then we can shift over and redistribute elements so that, after the desired deletion has been performed, all of these 1_Z subtrees still have $\geq 1_Z$ leaves each. It requires that up to 1_Z subtrees are reconstructed (as Z-trees), but this takes only $O(1)$ steps of work.

If all of the 1_Z-1 neighboring brothers are "minimally filled", i.e., have 1_Z elements, then consider the entire row of $(1_Z-1)1_Z+1_Z-1 = 1_Z^2-1$ elements that must be accomodated. Clearly they do not fit into 1_Z Z-trees anymore, but they do in 1_Z-1, as the following inequality lets us conclude:

$$(1_Z-1)1_Z < 1_Z^2-1 = (1_Z-1)(1_Z+1) \leq (1_Z-1)h_Z$$

The construction of 1_Z-1 Z-trees takes again $O(1)$ steps of work, but note that it gives us one component less than the number we had. Thus to succeed, we must continue and carry out a deletion on T_{i-1}.

So the procedure repeats, until eventually it gets to T_1 (if it didn't finish before). If the first layer has a total of t leaves then do the necessary deletion in T_1 and, like we did in the proof of 3.3.3.1., rebuild T_0 and the entire first layer as a Z-stratified tree on $t-1$ leaves. (Note that $t \geq \alpha 1_Z > \alpha$, which shows that the reconstruction can be carried out.)

The total amount of work is again $O(s)$, which is $O(\log n)$.

$\square$

In the proofs of Theorem 3.3.3.1. and 3.3.3.2. the details of how to modify the assignments of search criteria to guide the searching at the nodes have been omitted. The changes are all local and are left as an easy exercise to the reader.

The maintenance routines for stratified trees described above prove the results we were after, but they are not necessarily practical. For specific classes $S(X,Z)$ one may wish to inspect fewer brothers of the components and use a simpler procedure at the top of the tree.

3.3.4. Applications.

We shall apply the idea of stratification to distinguish some remarkable subclasses of common classes of balanced trees.

The results of Sections 3.3.2. and 3.3.3. can be summarized into the following statement.

Theorem 3.3.4.1. Let X be α-proper and Z a regular β-variety for X. Then $S(X,Z)$ is an α-proper and $O(\log n)$-maintainable subclass of X.

It follows that in order to distinguish interesting subclasses of a given class X (which need not be $O(\log n)$-maintainable itself), it suffices to find suitable regular varieties for X.

Height-balanced trees

Let X be the class of AVL-trees. We know that X is 1-proper, thus we can take $\alpha=1$. Observe that every X_β ($\beta\geq 2$) is a β-variety. The following observation is crucial:

Lemma 3.3.4.2. If Z is a β-variety of AVL-trees, then Z is a regular β-variety for X.

We can immediately use the lemma to stratify with e.g. X_2, to obtain the following class of trees. Let a node be at level j if and only if the longest path from the node to a leaf has j edges.

Proposition 3.3.4.3. There exists a $O(\log n)$-maintainable class of AVL-trees in which every odd-numbered level, except perhaps the root-level, consists of nodes that are in perfect balance.

Proof

Consider the distinct members of X_2 (see figure 3.3.4.1.). Clearly X_2 is a 2-variety and hence, by Lemma 3.3.4.2., a regular 2-variety for the class of AVL-trees (X). Take $Z=X_2$ and consider $S(X,Z)$. The odd-numbered levels of Z-stratified trees, except perhaps those at the top, precisely contain the nodes of the middle level (pointed at by the ← in figure 3.3.4.1.) of each component X_2-tree. It is easily seen that they are in perfect balance the way they occur in the trees. At the top, just

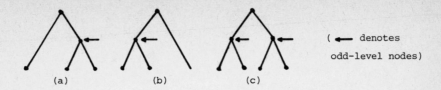

(← denotes
odd-level nodes)

figure 3.3.4.1.

note that K=max{1.3, $\left\lceil\frac{3-1}{4-3}\right\rceil$3}-1 = 5. Thus the top-portions of Z-stratified trees must include the trees displayed in figure 3.3.4.2. (only non-isomorphic copies are shown). Alle nodes, except the root in case (e), that will occur in odd-numbered levels, will

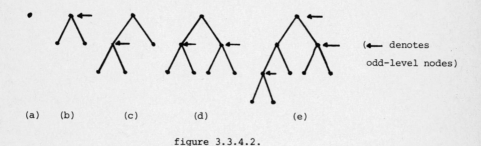

(← denotes
odd-level nodes)

(a)   (b)   (c)   (d)   (e)

figure 3.3.4.2.

be in perfect balance. Thus S(X,Z) is the class as desired.

□

This result can be generalized to obtain a strong density result for AVL-trees.

Theorem 3.3.4.4. For each ε>0, there is a O(log n)-maintainable class of AVL-trees in which the proportion of nodes that are not in perfect balance is less than ε (provided the number of leaves is sufficiently large).

Proof

Determine k such that $\frac{1}{2^k-2}$ < ε. Consider the set Z consisting of perfectly balanced trees on 2^k-1 and 2^k leaves, respectively, as displayed in figure 3.3.4.3. While Z consists of only 2 trees, it is a valid k-variety, hence a regular k-variety for the class of AVL-trees. Consider trees in S(X,Z). If its number of leaves is large enough, then the top of a Z-stratified tree is small compared to the size of the layers. In each component of a layer at most one (the node pointed at by ← in figure 3.3.4.3.) of at least 2^k-2 internal nodes can be out of balance. Thus the proportion of nodes

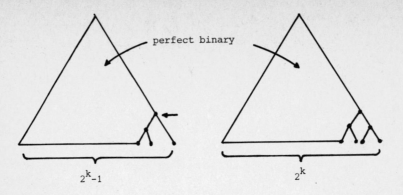

figure 3.3.4.3.

that are not in perfect balance is $\leq \dfrac{1}{2^{k-2}} < \varepsilon$, provided the trees are large enough. Thus $S(X,Z)$ is a class as desired.

□

The k-variety used in the proof of Theorem 3.3.4.4. (figure 3.3.4.3.) or an obvious variant of it with higher degree nodes and/or the one node that is not in perfect balance at some other place, is a regular variety for almost any class of height-balanced trees. Thus, stratification by means of such a variety will show that, theoretically, almost every type of height-balanced search trees can be "packed" or "almost perfectly balanced", without loosing the $O(\log n)$-maintainability of the class. Clearly, the maintenance algorithms for the classes of dense trees construed may be worse on the average than for the unconstrained classes, but this is the price to pay for density.

Degree-balanced trees

We will first consider B-trees (a generalization of 2-3 trees) as introduced by Bayer and McCreight [BayM] and later extended in several ways (see e.g. Knuth [Kn], Section 6.2.4.). Essentially, a B-TREE of order m is a tree which satisfies the following properties:

     (i) all leaves have equal depth,

     (ii) the root has a degree d, satisfying $2 \leq d \leq 2\left\lceil \dfrac{m}{2} \right\rceil - 1$,

     (iii) all remaining nodes have a degree d satisfying $\left\lceil \dfrac{m}{2} \right\rceil \leq d \leq m$.

(We ignore the details of how "keys" are stored. Note that property (ii) gives a slightly sharper bound on the degree of the root than is usually stated.) The following result shows that stratified trees and B-trees are intimately related. Let X be the class of B-trees of order m, Z the 1-variety of trees with a root of degree d with $\left\lceil \dfrac{m}{2} \right\rceil \leq d \leq m$. Z is a regular 1-variety for X and one easily verifies the following result:

Where ?

Theorem 3.3.4.5. With X and Z as defined, S(X,Z) is precisely the class of B-trees of order m.

From Theorem 3.3.4.1., the $O(\log n)$-maintainability of the class of B-trees is confirmed.

Interpreting nodes as tracks on a disk and m as the maximum number of records that fit on one track, B-trees are of use for practical file design in which nodes (tracks) are always filled at least half the maximum capacity, with the possible exception of the root. Knuth ([Kn] p.478) describes a variant type of B-trees, called B*-trees, in which all internal nodes except the root have a degree d satisfying $\left\lceil \frac{2m-1}{3} \right\rceil \leq d \leq m$. Thus, B*-trees guarantee a 67% minimum space utilization on every track (except for the root). Let X be the class of B*-trees of order m and Z the 1-variety of trees with a root of degree d satisfying $\left\lceil \frac{2m-1}{3} \right\rceil \leq d \leq m$. Z is a regular 1-variety for X and one easily verifies that $\alpha=2$ and that K (the degree bound at the root) must equal the following value:

$$K = \max\left\{ 2\left\lceil \frac{2m-1}{3} \right\rceil, \frac{\left\lceil \frac{2m-1}{3} \right\rceil - 1}{m - \left\lceil \frac{2m-1}{3} \right\rceil} \cdot \left\lceil \frac{2m-1}{3} \right\rceil \right\} - 1 =$$

$$= 2\left\lceil \frac{2m-1}{3} \right\rceil - 1 =$$

$$= 2\left\lfloor \frac{2m-1}{3} \right\rfloor + 1$$

(Compare [Kn], p. 478)

Theorem 3.3.4.6. With X and Z as defined, S(X,Z) is precisely the class of B*-trees of order m.

To obtain a statement about the maximum space utilization attainable in theory by B-trees, it is useful to distinguish the following class of trees:

Definition 3.3.4.7. Given 1, m with 1<1<m, a B-tree of order (1,m) is any tree which satisfies the following properties:

  (i) all leaves have equal depth,
  (ii) the root has a degree d satisfying $2 \leq d \leq \max\left\{2.1, \left\lceil \frac{1-1}{m-1} \right\rceil 1\right\} - 1$,
  (iii) all other nodes have a degree d satisfying $1 \leq d \leq m$.

The factual theory of B-trees culminates in the following theorem.

Theorem 3.3.4.8. The class of B-trees of order (1,m) is 2-proper and $O(\log n)$-maintainable, for every 1<1<m.

<u>Proof</u>

Let X be the class of B-trees of order (1,m) and Z the 1-variety of trees having a root of degree d with $1 \leq d \leq m$. Z is a regular 1-variety for X and it is easily seen that S(X,Z) is precisely the class X itself. X is clearly 2-proper. The theorem immediately follows from Theorem 3.3.4.1.

□

By choosing 1 close to m, an O(log n)-maintainable class of B-trees is obtained with a space utilization of nearly 100%. One might even take l=m-1, although this would force the root node to have a degree up to m^2-3m+1 and gives abominable constants in the O(log n) time bounds for the insertion and deletion routines.

1-2 TREES are trees in which all leaves have the same depth and each internal node has one or two sons. 1-2 Trees need not be balanced. To obtain classes of balanced 1-2 trees we have to put restrictions on the occurence of unary nodes. We will consider one example.

<u>Definition</u> 3.3.4.9. A 1-2 tree T is called a STANDARD SON TREE if and only if

       (i) the depth of T is even,

      (ii) the even levels of T contain no unary nodes.

Standard son trees where introduced by Olivié [Ol] because of their equivalence to symmetric binary B-trees (SBB-trees), introduced by Bayer [Bay] to obtain a suitable "binarization" of arbitrary B-trees.

Considering standard son trees more precisely, Let X be the class of 1-2 trees and Z be the 2-variety of standard son trees of depth 2 (see figure 3.3.4.4.). It is easily seen that Z is a regular 2-variety for X, with $l_Z=2$, $h_Z=4$, $\alpha=1$ and K=1.

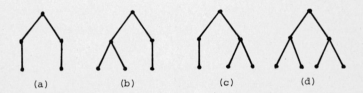

    (a)   (b)   (c)   (d)

figure 3.3.4.4.

<u>Theorem</u> 3.3.4.10. With X and Z as defined above, S(X,Z) is precisely the class of standard son trees.

From Theorem 3.3.4.1. one can immediately derive that the class of standard son trees is O(log n)-maintainable. (The resulting algorithms for performing insertions and deletions prove to be very similar to the ones described by Olivié [Ol].) In fact, the result indicates very clearly that standard son trees, hence SBB-trees, are B-trees of order (2,4) in disguise.

Other classes of balanced 1-2 trees (e.g. brother trees) also contain subclasses of stratified trees and density results can be obtained similar to those for AVL-trees.

For most other kinds of degree-balanced search trees, regular varieties can be found and hence O(log n)-maintainable subclasses can be identified. For example, stratified and hence, O(log n)-maintainable, subclasses of dense multiway search trees can be identified, although there is no O(log n) deletion algorithm known for dense multiway search trees in general ([CuOW]).

Path-balanced trees

Consider the class of trees Z in figure 3.3.4.5.

figure 3.3.4.5.

Z is a regular 2-variety for the class X of αBB-trees for α≤1/2 cause, when grafting a layer of Z-trees to a αBB-tree T, the length of the longest path for each node in T increases by 2 and the length of the shortest path increases by at least 1. Hence, S(X,Z) is an O(log n)-maintainable subclass of X. It should be noted that the class of trees we obtain is also a subclass of AVL-trees (see Proposition 3.3.4.3.). For α>1/2 we have to stratify with another class of trees. Choose a positive integer β, such that α ≤ (β-1)/β. Consider the class Z of binary trees of height β with shortest path ≥β-1, i.e., with leaves only on the lowest two levels. Z is a regular β-variety for the class X of αBB-trees. Hence, S(X,Z) is a O(log n)-maintainable subclass of X. X.

Weight-balanced trees

It has to be noted that no regular varieties have been found for classes of weight-balanced search trees and hence, the theory of stratification seems not to be applicable to such classes.

3.4. Balancing in augmented search trees.

In the preceding two sections we showed how balancing (local rebuilding) can be used for dynamizing search trees, yielding a dynamic solution for the member searching problem with

$$Q_S(n) = O(\log n),$$
$$I_S(n) = O(\log n),$$
$$D_S(n) = O(\log n),$$
$$M_S(n) = O(n).$$

As shown in Chapter 2, for a number of searching problems static data structures exist that use a search tree as underlying structure. In this search tree some extra information is associated with the nodes. Often, it is possible to maintain this associated information when local changes must be made in the tree as the result of an insertion or a deletion. In such cases balancing can be used for obtaining a dynamic solution to the problem. For example, consider the kth element/rank searching problem. The tree structure commonly used for this problem, as described in Section 2.2., consists of a leaf-search tree in which to each internal node is associated the number of points in its subtree. When performing some local rotation, the information that has to be associated to the affected nodes can easily be obtained from the information at their sons within $O(1)$ time. It follows that the amount of extra work needed when performing an update is bounded by the number of rotations, i.e., is $O(\log n)$ time.

Theorem 3.4.1. There exists a data structure S for solving the kth element/rank searching problem, such that

$$Q_S(n) = O(\log n),$$
$$I_S(n) = O(\log n),$$
$$D_S(n) = O(\log n),$$
$$M_S(n) = O(n).$$

A much more intriguing example is the super B-tree used for range searching (see Section 2.3.). A super B-tree is an augmented search tree but maintaining the associated information is much harder this time. A 1-dimensional super B-tree is a balanced leaf-search tree with the leaves linked in a doubly linked list. The linking can easily be maintained when inserting or deleting points. Hence, a 1-dimensional super B-tree can be maintained in $O(\log n)$ time per update using balancing. For a dynamic d-dimensional super B-tree ($d \geq 2$) a $BB[\alpha]$ leaf-search tree T is chosen in which to every internal node a d-1 dimensional super B-tree is associated (as described in Section 2.3.). To insert a point p in T, it has to be inserted in all structures associated to nodes on the search path towards p. Similar, to delete a point p, it has to be deleted from all structures associated to nodes on the search path towards p. In both cases, balance might be disturbed in the main $BB[\alpha]$-tree for some nodes on the search path.

When we perform single and/or double rotations to restore balance at these nodes,
we have to rebuild the associated structures at the nodes involved in the rotations.
This will take a lot of time when the structures are large. Lueker [Lu2] and Willard
[Wi1,Wi2] showed that by a proper choice of α the average time required for this rebuilding of associated structures can be kept low. They even succeeded in obtaining
low worst-case time bounds by spreading the work for rebuilding large structures over
a number of updates. In the meantime the old structures or the structures associated
to nearby descendants are used for query answering.

Theorem 3.4.2.([Lu2,Wi1,Wi2]) There exists a structure S for solving the d-dimensional
range searching/counting problem, such that

$$Q_S(n) = \begin{cases} O(\log^d n + k) & \text{for the searching problem,} \\ O(\log^d n) & \text{for the counting problem,} \end{cases}$$

$$P_S(n) = O(n \log^{d-1} n),$$
$$I_S(n) = O(\log^d n),$$
$$D_S(n) = O(\log^d n),$$
$$M_S(n) = O(n \log^{d-1} n).$$

In a similar way, one can get $O(\log^d n)$ update time bounds for the rectangle
intersection searching/counting problem (see Edelsbrunner [Ed2] and Edelsbrunner and
Maurer [EdM]).

On the other hand, for structures like quad-trees and k-d trees and structures
for solving e.g. the convex hull problem, local rebuilding does not seem to help in
obtaining dynamic solutions.

Bibliographical comments.

Overviews of balancing techniques for search trees can be found in e.g. Aho,
Hopcroft and Ullman [AhHU], Knuth [Kn], Olivié [Ol] and Reingold, Nievergelt and Deo
[ReND]. Section 3.3. is based on van Leeuwen and Overmars [vLO1]. A detailed descrip-
tion of balancing in super B-trees can be found in Willard [Wi1].

CHAPTER IV

PARTIAL REBUILDING

4.1. <u>Introduction</u>.

When the available data structures for some searching problem seem not to allow
for dynamization by means of the local rebuilding technique described in Chapter 3
(as e.g. quad-trees and k-d trees) or when the local changes needed for balancing are
very complex (as in e.g. super B-trees) another technique, named PARTIAL REBUILDING,
can be useful. Generally speaking, the idea of partial rebuilding is the following.
Assume that the (static) data structure for the searching problem in mind is a tree
structure (possible augmented by associating substructures to nodes) and that there
is some kind of balance criterion that each internal node should satisfy. The insertion or deletion of a point in the structure might cause some nodes, normally located
on the path towards the inserted or deleted point, to become "out of balance". As we
do not have a local rebuilding technique for rebalancing these nodes, we use a brute
force technique: we rebuild the complete subtree at the highest node that is "out of
balance" as a "perfectly balanced" subtree. This will sometimes take a lot of work,
especially when the root of the tree is out of balance. But one can often prove that
bigger subtrees have to be rebuilt less often than smaller ones and that the average
update time will remain low. Hence, the partial rebuilding technique, in general, will
yield only good average update time bounds. It is hard to give general conditions for
data structures that enable the use of partial rebuilding as a dynamization method.
Applications normally require (i) a lowerbound on the number of updates performed in
the subtree at some internal node β before it can go out of balance and (ii) an upperbound on the cost for rebuilding the subtree at a node that has gone out of balance
into some perfectly balanced tree. The analysis normally proceeds by charging the costs
for rebuilding a subtree to the updates that made it go out of balance and bounding
the total charge accumulated by every update that was performed on the tree. The chapter will show a number of examples to demonstrate how the technique can be used.

We will first apply the partial rebuilding technique to BB[α]-trees to make the
basic idea behind the method clear. Next we will follow Lueker [Lu1] in applying the
technique to super B-trees, yielding simpler (understandable and implementable) maintenance algorithms with the same update time bounds as the very complex methods that
use the local rebuilding technique, but with average rather than worst-case bounds.
In Sections 4.4. and 4.5. we will give the most important applications of the method,
namely the maintenance of structures similar to quad- and k-d trees.

4.2. BB[α]-trees.

In a BB[α]-tree (some α, $0<\alpha<\frac{1}{2}$) it is required that for each internal node β, the number of points below the leftson of β (denoted as $n_{lson(\beta)}$) divided by the total number of points below β (i.e., n_β) must lie between α and 1-α (see Section 3.2.2.). We will only consider leaf-search BB[α]-trees. We call a node β in perfect balance if $n_{lson(\beta)}$ and $n_{rson(\beta)}$ differ by at most 1. We call a tree perfectly balanced if each internal node is in perfect balance. Disregarding some lowest levels from consideration, a perfectly balanced tree is a BB[α]-tree for any $0<\alpha<\frac{1}{2}$.

Lemma 4.2.1. Given a node β in a BB[α]-tree that is in perfect balance. Let n_β be the number of points below β at the moment it gets out of balance. Then, there must have been $\Omega(n_\beta)$ updates in the subtree rooted at β.

Proof
Updates that are not performed in the subtree rooted at β clearly do not influence the balance at β. Let n_β', $n_{lson(\beta)}'$ and $n_{rson(\beta)}'$ denote the number of points below β, the leftson and the rightson of β, respectively, at the moment β is in perfect balance. Assume $n_{lson(\beta)}' \leq n_{rson(\beta)}'$. Then β will become out of balance the fastest when deletions are performed below lson(β) and insertions are performed below rson(β). Let there have been N_d deletions below lson(β) and N_i insertions below rson(β) before β goes out of balance. In this case $n_\beta = n_\beta'+N_i-N_d$ and $n_{lson(\beta)} = n_{lson(\beta)}'-N_d = \lfloor \frac{1}{2}n_\beta' \rfloor - N_d$. Since β is now out of balance, we have

$$\frac{n_{lson(\beta)}}{n_\beta} < \alpha$$

$$\Rightarrow \frac{\lfloor \frac{1}{2}n_\beta' \rfloor - N_d}{n_\beta} < \alpha$$

$$\Rightarrow \frac{1}{2}(n_\beta-N_i+N_d) - 1 - N_d < \alpha n_\beta$$

$$\Rightarrow -\frac{1}{2}N_i-\frac{1}{2}N_d < (\alpha-\frac{1}{2})n_\beta + 1$$

$$\Rightarrow N_i+N_d > 2(\frac{1}{2}-\alpha)n_\beta - 2$$

This is $\Omega(n_\beta)$ because $\alpha<\frac{1}{2}$.

□

Lemma 4.2.2. Given an ordered set of n points, a perfectly balanced binary tree of them can be built in $O(n)$ time.

Proof
This can be achieved by building the tree levelwise, starting at the leaves.

□

Lemmas 4.2.1. and 4.2.2. provide the tools we need to apply the partial rebuilding technique. Lemma 4.2.2. shows that subtrees can be rebuilt efficiently and Lemma 4.2.1. proves that after rebuilding the subtree at some node β, it takes a long time before another rebuilding operation at β is necessary.

Theorem 4.2.3. For each α, $0<\alpha<\frac{1}{2}$, one can maintain an initially empty BB$[\alpha]$-tree at the cost of $O(\log m)$ average time per update (where m denotes the maximum number of points that have been in the tree at some moment).

Proof

To insert or delete a point p in a BB$[\alpha]$-tree with n leaves we search with p in the tree to locate the position of p among the leaves, and perform the action. Next we walk back to the root of the tree and locate the highest node β that has become out of balance as a result of the update. To rebalance β we rebuild the complete subtree rooted at β as a perfectly balanced tree. Beside the rebuilding the work for an update is clearly bounded by $O(\log n)$. We will show that the amount of work for rebuilding is bounded by an average of $O(\log m)$ per update. As n≦m the bound will follow. The costs for rebuilding the subtree rooted at β are charged to the $\Omega(n_\beta)$ updates that have taken place since the latest rebuilding at β (due to Lemma 4.2.1.). As the rebuilding takes $O(n_\beta)$ time (Lemma 4.2.2.), each update is charged $O(1)$ time. Clearly, we might charge costs more than once to the same update. But we only charge the costs for rebuilding subtrees at nodes on the search path towards the updated point. Moreover we can charge costs to the same update at most once for every node on the path. It follows that to each update we charge at most $O(\log m)$ times $O(1)$ work for rebuilding. Hence, the total amount of time needed for rebuilding since the initialization of the BB$[\alpha]$-tree is bounded by $O(N \log m)$. So, the average rebuilding time is bounded by $O(\log m)$.

$\square$

Of course, BB$[\alpha]$-trees can even be maintained in $O(\log n)$ worst-case update time bounds using local rebuilding (see Section 3.2.2.). The application of partial rebuilding to BB$[\alpha]$-trees must be seen as an easy example to demonstrate the technique, rather than as a useful one. More interesting applications appear in the following sections.

4.3. Super B-trees.

In this section we follow Lueker [Lu1] in applying the partial rebuilding technique to super B-trees. To dynamize super B-trees by means of partial rebuilding, we use the same dynamic version as in Section 3.4., namely a BB$[\alpha]$ leaf-search tree T in which internal nodes are augmented with dynamic d-1 dimensional super B-trees. We call a super B-tree perfectly balanced if the main BB[α]-tree T is perfectly balanced and all associated super B-trees are perfectly balanced. The following analogs of Lemmas 4.2.1. and 4.2.2. can easily be shown.

Lemma 4.3.1. Given a node β in T that is in perfect balance. Let n_β be the number of points in T below β at the moment β gets out of balance. Then, there must have been $\Omega(n_\beta)$ updates in the subtree rooted at β.

Lemma 4.3.2. (see Theorem 2.3.3.) A perfectly balanced d-dimensional super B-tree of n points can be built in $O(n \log^{d-1} n)$ time.

To insert or delete a point p in the super B-tree, we search with p in T to locate its position among the leaves and insert or delete p, respectively, in all structures associated with the nodes on the search path. Next, we insert or delete p among the leaves of T and walk back to the root, meanwhile locating the highest internal node β that has become out of balance as a result of the update. To rebalance at β we rebuild the entire subtree rooted at β as a perfectly balanced super B-tree.

Theorem 4.3.3. Using the partial rebuilding technique, one can perform updates in an initially empty d-dimensional super B-tree at the cost of $O(\log^d m)$ average time per update.

Proof
    Let $F_d(n)$ denote the average time per update for a d-dimensional super B-tree containing n points while m is the maximum number of points that have been in the tree. The searching in T takes $O(\log n)$ time. The average amount of work for updating associated structures is clearly bounded by $O(\log m)F_{d-1}(n)$. As in the proof of Theorem 4.2.3. we can charge the costs for rebuilding at β to $\Omega(n_\beta)$ updates that have taken place since the latest rebuilding at β. It yields an average rebuilding time of $O(\log^d m)$ charged to every update. It follows that

$$F_d(n) = O(\log^d m) + O(\log m)F_{d-1}(n).$$

From Theorem 4.2.3. it follows that

$$F_1(n) = O(\log m).$$

This easily leads to $F_d(n) = O(\log^d m)$.

$\square$

We know from Section 3.4. that it is even possible to maintain super B-trees at the cost of $O(\log^d n)$ worst-case time using the methods of Lueker [Lu2] and Willard

[Wi1,Wi2]. But these methods are very complex. The use of partial rebuilding for dynamizing super B-trees yields a very easily understandable (and programmable) method
to achieve the same bounds on the average.

In a very similar way, the partial rebuilding technique can be used to obtain
dynamic segment-trees and dynamic structures for rectangle searching problems, which
rely on the same principles as super B-trees (Section 2.4.).

4.4. Quad-trees.

Quad-trees can apparently not be kept balanced by the technique of local rebuilding. The partial rebuilding technique on the other hand turns out to be very useful
for dynamizing quad-trees.

Quad-trees have two important draw-backs. Firstly, although in a d-dimensional
quad-tree each internal node has 2^d sons, the tree may have depth $\log_2 n$ rather than
$\log_{2d} n$, for example when all points lie on a diagonal line (see figure 4.4.1.).
Secondly, although it is possible to insert points in quad-trees (without rebalancing),

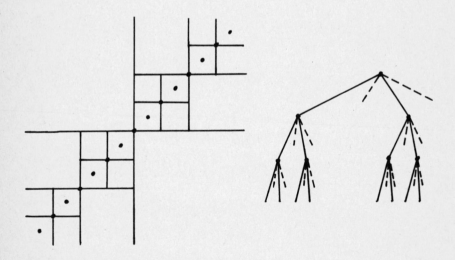

figure 4.4.1.

it is sometimes very hard to delete a point from the structure (even without rebalancing). For example, when we delete the root of the quad-tree we have to choose a new
splitting point as the new root. But each point in the set may split the set in a complete different way. Hence, large parts of the trees may have to be rebuilt. (See Samet

[Sam] for some results concerning deletions in quad-trees.)

To circumvent these difficulties we modify quad-trees into pseudo quad-trees, which are in fact the leaf-search variants of quad-trees. In Section 4.4.1. we define pseudo quad-trees and analyse their depth and constructability. In Section 4.4.2. we show how the partial rebuilding technique can be used for dynamizing pseudo quad-trees, yielding good average update time bounds. In the sequel we assume that no two points in the set have equal values in a same coordinate.

4.4.1. Pseudo quad-trees.

PSEUDO QUAD-TREES are very similar to ordinary quad-trees except that internal nodes that split the space (and therefore the set), no longer are points of the set. We use arbitrary points to split the space into quadrants, the quadrants into sub-quadrants and so on, until every subquadrant contains at most one point of the set. The points of the set thus occur as the leaves of the pseudo quad-tree. See figure 4.4.1.1. for an example, in which $p_1, \ldots, p_{12}$ are the points in the set and $h_1, \ldots, h_5$ are the chosen splitting points.

Because pseudo quad-trees are very similar to ordinary quad-trees, all kind of queries that can be answered using quad-trees, can be answered using pseudo quad-trees in essentially the same way. Hence, as far as queries are concerned, replacing quad-trees by pseudo quad-trees does not cause any difficulty.

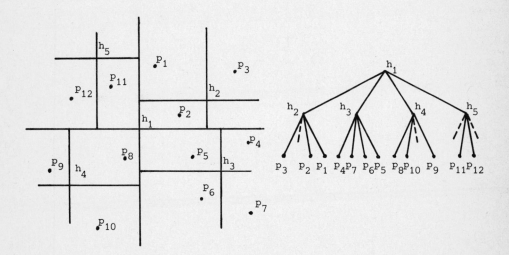

figure 4.4.1.1.

In addition to the fact in pseudo quad-trees both insertions and deletions can be processed efficiently, as will be shown in Section 4.4.2., it is also interesting to note that for a same set of points we can often build pseudo quad-trees that have a smaller depth than the corresponding quad-trees of the unmodified sort. (This is important because bounds on search and query time normally depend on the depth of the tree.) This results from the fact that in pseudo quad-trees we may choose any splitting point we like and hence that, at any stage of the construction, we can take the point that splits the set in the most "balanced" manner.

<u>Lemma</u> 4.4.1.1. Given a set of n points $p_1,\ldots,p_n$ in d-dimensional space, there exists a splitting point $h=(h_1,\ldots,h_d)$ such that each quadrant induced by h contains at most $\left\lceil \frac{1}{d+1} n \right\rceil$ points.

<u>Proof</u>

Choose h_1 such that $\left\lceil \frac{1}{d+1} n \right\rceil$ points of the set have x_1-coordinate smaller than h_1 and the other $\left\lfloor \frac{1}{d+1} n \right\rfloor$ points have x_1-coordinate bigger than h_1. Such a h_1 exists because of our assumption that no two points of the set have an equal value in a same coordinate. We have in fact constructed a hyperplane (of all points with x_1-coordinate equal to h_1) that separates the set in one part with $\left\lceil \frac{1}{d+1} n \right\rceil$ points and another part containing $\left\lfloor \frac{d}{d+1} n \right\rfloor$ points. In the two-dimensional case we get the situation displayed in figure 4.4.1.2.a. There are still d-1 coordinates of h left to determine. To find a proper value for h_2 we look at the $\left\lfloor \frac{d}{d+1} n \right\rfloor$ points in the set with x_1-coordinate bigger than h_1. The other part of the set is already small enough and it is not important how this part is split up by other hyperplanes. Choose h_2 such that $\left\lceil \frac{1}{d+1} n \right\rceil$ of

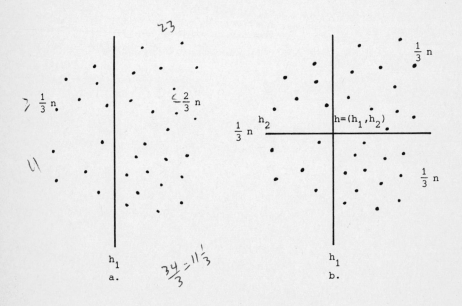

figure 4.4.1.2.

these $\left\lfloor \frac{d}{d+1} \ n \right\rfloor$ points have x_2-coordinate smaller than h_2 and the other $\leq \left\lfloor \frac{d-1}{d+1} \ n \right\rfloor$ points have x_2-coordinate bigger than h_2. Again, such a h_2 exists. We continue with the portion of $\leq \left\lfloor \frac{d-1}{d+1} \ n \right\rfloor$ points and choose the appropriate h_3 value in the same way, etc. By the time we have chosen the appropriate value of h_{d-1}, we are left with a subset of $\leq \left\lfloor \frac{2}{d+1} \ n \right\rfloor$ points. We can easily choose a h_d value that splits this remaining subset in two parts, one of size $\left\lceil \frac{1}{d+1} \ n \right\rceil$ points and the other of size $\leq \left\lfloor \frac{1}{d+1} \ n \right\rfloor$ points, to end the splitting process. So we have obtained a point $h=(h_1,\ldots,h_d)$ that splits the space into quadrants, each containing at most $\left\lceil \frac{1}{d+1} \ n \right\rceil$ points. See figure 4.4.1.2.b. for the two dimensional situation.

□

Corollary 4.4.1.2. Given a set of n points in d-dimensional space, there exists a pseudo quad-tree for the set with a depth of at most $\lceil \log_{d+1} n \rceil$.

Proof

According to Lemma 4.4.1.1. there exists a point h that divides the space into quadrants containing at most $\left\lceil \frac{1}{d+1} \ n \right\rceil$ points each. We use h as the root of the pseudo quad-tree and proceed in the same manner in every quadrant. Again by Lemma 4.4.1.1., in each quadrant there exists a point that splits the k points in that quadrant into parts containing at most $\left\lceil \frac{1}{d+1} \ k \right\rceil$ points each. These splitting points form the sons of h. Note that every subquadrant contains at most

$$\left\lceil \frac{1}{d+1} \left\lceil \frac{1}{d+1} \ n \right\rceil \right\rceil = \left\lceil \frac{1}{(d+1)^2} \ n \right\rceil$$

points of the set. Repeatedly applying Lemma 4.4.1.1. to the subquadrants, and using the obtained splitting points as internal nodes, gives the desired pseudo quad-tree. As the number of points in a subquadrant at the ith level is bounded by $\left\lceil \frac{1}{(d+1)^i} \ n \right\rceil$, the depth of the tree is bounded by $\lceil \log_{d+1} n \rceil$.

□

The result of Corollary 4.4.1.2. is optimal in the sense that there are configurations of points for which each pseudo quad-tree has depth at least $\lceil \log_{d+1} n \rceil$, as the following theorem shows.

Theorem 4.4.1.3. There exist sets of n points $p_1,\ldots,p_n$ in d-dimensional space, such that no pseudo quad-tree for such a set can have depth less than $\lceil \log_{d+1} n \rceil$.

Proof

Take points $p_i=(p_{i1},\ldots,p_{id})$ $(1\leq i\leq n)$ such that

$$\forall_{1\leq i\leq n}, \forall_{1\leq j\leq d} \quad p_{ij} < p_{i+1,j}.$$

Hence, p_i has to be smaller than p_{i+1} in all coordinates. (Note that in such a configuration no two points have an equal value in a same coordinate.) Let some pseudo quad-
tree for this set be given. The root h of this tree splits the set in 2^d quadrants.
We will show that only d+1 of these quadrants can possibly contain points of the set.
Walk through the set of points from p_1 to p_n. When we come into another quadrant we
must cross one of the hyper-planes induced by h. As all next points are larger in all
coordinates we can never cross this hyper-plane again. Hence, because h induces only
d hyper-planes, we can change quadrant only d times and hence there are at most d+1
quadrants filled. It follows that at least one of these quadrants contains $\geq \left\lceil \dfrac{1}{d+1} \, n \right\rceil$
points. The points in this quadrant have the same property as the original set of
points and therefore, by the same argument, there must be a subquadrant that contains
at least $\left\lceil \dfrac{1}{(d+1)^2} \, n \right\rceil$ points of the set. Repeating this argument shows that the pseudo
quad-tree must have a depth of at least $\lceil \log_{d+1} n \rceil$. See figure 4.4.1.3. for an example
in dimension 2.

□

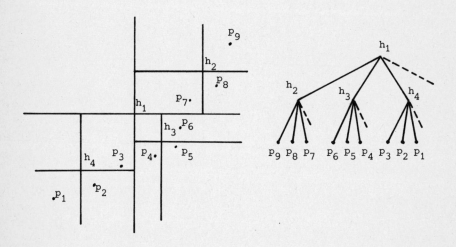

figure 4.4.1.3.

Merely knowing that a "nearly optimal" pseudo quad-tree exists is not enough;
we should also be able to build it efficiently.

Theorem 4.4.1.4. Given a set of n points in d-dimensional space, a pseudo quad-tree
of depth at most $\lceil \log_{d+1} n \rceil$ for this set can be built in $O(n \log n)$ time.

Proof

We will use the method of Lemma 4.4.1.1. and Corollary 4.4.1.2. Determination of the appropriate splitting point h in the proof of Lemma 4.4.1.1. consists of d times finding a ranked element of the set, with respect to some ordering, which takes $O(n)$ time due to results of Blum e.a. [Bl]. Splitting the set over the quadrants takes $O(n)$ as well. So, building the first level of the pseudo quad-tree takes $O(n)$ time. The splitting of a quadrant that contains k points takes $O(k)$ time by the same argument. The quadrants together contain n points, hence the total time needed for building the second level of the tree is bounded by $O(n)$ as well. The same argument holds for each level in the tree. Since the depth of the tree is bounded by $\lceil \log_{d+1} n \rceil$, according to Corollary 4.4.1.2., the bound of $O(n \log n)$ time for the entire construction follows.

□

It follows that (in general) pseudo quad-trees have lesser depth than the corresponding quad-trees and can be built just as efficiently. (Note that for each set of points a pseudo quad-tree can be built with depth at most 1 larger than the depth of the "best possible" quad-tree.)

4.4.2. Dynamic pseudo quad-trees.

The main reason for considering pseudo quad-trees is that they can be used in a dynamic environment. We will show in this section how the partial rebuilding technique can be used to insert and delete points in pseudo quad-trees in good average time bounds.

Inserting or deleting a point in a pseudo quad-tree is easy as long as we do not need to keep the tree balanced. To insert a point p the following actions must be performed:

Insertion method

(i) Search with p in the tree to locate the subquadrant p lies in.

(ii) If there is no point of the set present in this subquadrant, insert p here, i.e., add it as a leaf. If there already is some point p' of the set present, choose some point h that lies in between p and p' (for example a point on the line-segment $\overline{pp'}$) and use this point as a new splitting point. So we replace p' in the tree by h and add p and p' as the appropriate leaves to h.

To delete a point p the procedure is as follows:

Deletion method

   (i) Search for p in the tree.

  (ii) When p is found, delete the appropriate leaf. (When we do not find p, it does not belong to the set and we can stop.)

 (iii) If, as a result of the deletion of p, the father h of p has only one son p' left, replace h by p'.

Step (iii) is not strictly necessary. It is clear that insertions and deletions, performed in this way, both take O(depth of the tree) time. But there is no guarantee that the tree remains belanced, i.e., that the depth remains O(log n). For instance, when we insert all points at the left side of the tree, it might even get a depth of $\Omega(n)$.

To maintain the pseudo quad-tree in a balanced form we apply the technique of partial rebuilding. As a criterion of balance we use a kind of weight-balancing. Let δ be some fixed constant with $0<\delta<d$. For each node β in a d-dimensional pseudo quad-tree with n_β points of the set in its joint subtrees we demand that each subtree attached to β contains at most $\left\lceil \frac{1}{d+1-\delta} n_\beta \right\rceil$ points of the set. One easily verifies that such a pseudo quad-tree has a depth of at most $\left\lceil \log_{d+1-\delta} n \right\rceil + O(1)$. Hence, by choosing δ near 0, the depth bound approaches the optimal bound of $\left\lceil \log_{d+1} n \right\rceil$ shown in Theorem 4.4.1.4. We call a node β "in perfect balance" if each subtree attached to β contains at most $\left\lceil \frac{1}{d+1} n_\beta \right\rceil$ points of the set. We call a pseudo quad-tree "perfectly balanced" when all its internal nodes are in perfect balance. We will now prove the analogs of Lemmas 4.2.1. and 4.2.2.

Lemma 4.4.2.1. Given a node β in a d-dimensional pseudo quad-tree that is in perfect balance. Let n_β denote the number of points in the set in the subtree rooted at β at the moment β gets out of balance. Then, there must have been $\Omega(\delta n_\beta)$ updates in the subtree rooted at β.

Proof

Let n'_β denote the number of points in the set below β at the moment β was in perfect balance. Let there have been N_i insertions and N_d deletions in the subtree rooted at β (other updates do not influence balance at β). Hence, $n_\beta = n'_\beta + N_i - N_d$. At the moment β becomes out of balance, one subtree attached to β must have got size $> \left\lceil \frac{1}{d+1-\delta} n_\beta \right\rceil$. As the size of each subtree was $\leq \left\lceil \frac{1}{d+1} n'_\beta \right\rceil$ at the moment β was in perfect balance, no subtree can have become larger than $\left\lceil \frac{1}{d+1} n'_\beta \right\rceil + N_i$. It follows that

$$\left\lceil \frac{1}{d+1}\, n'_\beta \right\rceil + N_i > \left\lceil \frac{1}{d+1-\delta}\, n_\beta \right\rceil$$

$$\Rightarrow \left\lceil \frac{1}{d+1}(n_\beta - N_i + N_d) \right\rceil + N_i > \left\lceil \frac{1}{d+1-\delta}\, n_\beta \right\rceil$$

$$\Rightarrow \frac{1}{d+1}\, n_\beta + \frac{d}{d+1}\, N_i + \frac{1}{d+1}\, N_d + 1 > \frac{1}{d+1-\delta}\, n_\beta$$

$$\Rightarrow \frac{d}{d+1}\, N_i + \frac{1}{d+1}\, N_d > \left(\frac{1}{d+1-\delta} - \frac{1}{d+1}\right) n_\beta - 1$$

$$\Rightarrow N_i + N_d > \frac{\delta}{(d+1)(d+1-\delta)}\, n_\beta - 1$$

Because $0 < \delta < d$ the right hand side is $\Omega(\delta n_\beta)$.

$\square$

Lemma 4.4.2.2. A perfectly balanced pseudo quad-tree of n points can be built in $O(n \log n)$ time.

Proof

The method for building a pseudo quad-tree as described in the proof of Theorem 4.4.1.4. results in a perfectly balanced pseudo quad-tree. The bound follows.

$\square$

Lemmas 4.4.2.1. and 4.4.2.2. provide the tools needed to use the partial rebuilding technique for dynamizing pseudo quad-trees.

Theorem 4.4.2.3. For any fixed δ with $0 < \delta < d$, there is an algorithm to perform insertions and deletions in an initially empty pseudo quad-tree such that its depth is always bounded by $\lceil \log_{d+1-\delta} n \rceil + O(1)$ (where n is the current number of points in the set) and the average update time is bounded by $O(\frac{1}{\delta} \log^2 m)$ (where m is the maximal number of points that have once been in the set).

Proof

To insert or delete a point p we first perform the actions described above. This clearly takes $O(\log n) = O(\log m)$ time. Next we walk back from p to the root of the pseudo quad-tree to locate the highest node β at which the balance is disturbed and rebuild the subtree rooted at β as a perfectly balanced pseudo quad-tree. This takes $O(n_\beta \log n_\beta)$ time, due to Lemma 4.4.2.2. These costs we charge to the $\Omega(\delta\, n_\beta)$ updates that have taken place in the subtree rooted at β since its latest rebalancing. Hence, each update is charged $O(\frac{1}{\delta} \log n_\beta) = O(\frac{1}{\delta} \log m)$ work. Updates can only be charged to from nodes on the search path towards the updated point and at most once from each such node. Hence each update is charged at most $O(\lceil \log_{d+1-\delta} m \rceil) = O(\log m)$ times work. It follows that the total amount of work done for rebuilding during the first N updates is bounded by $O(N.\frac{1}{\delta}\log^2 m)$ and the average time needed for rebuilding is $O(\frac{1}{\delta}\log^2 m)$.

□

In practise, the expected amount of time needed for updates is likely to be much smaller than $O(\frac{1}{\delta}\log^2 m)$ because when subtrees of internal nodes expand and shrink equally fast there is no need for any rebalancing at all. (Using some additional techniques, demonstrated in Chapter 5, the time bound for deletions of Theorem 4.4.2.3. can even be lowered.)

Up to now we assumed that no two points in the set had an equal value in a same coordinate. This was necessary because otherwise it could be impossible to choose proper dividing points. (Lemma 4.4.1.1. makes essential use of this assumption.) It is possible to drop this restriction by modifying pseudo quad-trees into so-called EPQ-trees (Extended Pseudo Quad-trees), without affecting the efficiency of updates and query answering. Details can be found in Overmars and van Leeuwen [OvL3].

4.5. k-d trees.

k-d trees are similar to quad-trees in a number of respects. They are used for the same types of queries, they are also based on a division of the space in regions and they also can apparently not be dynamized using a local rebuilding technique. We will show that again the partial rebuilding technique will help in obtaining a dynamic version of the k-d tree with low average update time bounds.

We first modify k-d trees in a similar way as quad-trees were modified into pseudo quad-trees. A PSEUDO K-D TREE is a kind of leaf-search k-d tree in which we use arbitrary points of the space as internal nodes to split the space, rather than points of the set. See figure 4.5.1. for an example of a 2-dimensional pseudo k-d tree in which $p_1,\ldots,p_9$ are the points in the set and $h_1,\ldots,h_8$ are the chosen splitting points. Note that we do not really need all coordinates of a splitting point. We are only interested in the one coordinate of the point on which the set is split. We call a node β in a pseudo k-d tree in perfect balance when each subtree attached to it contains at most $\lceil \frac{1}{2} n_\beta \rceil$ points of the set. A pseudo k-d tree is called perfectly balanced when all internal nodes are in perfect balance. Clearly a perfectly balanced pseudo k-d tree has a depth of $\lceil \log n \rceil$. Assuming that no two points in the set have an equal value in a same coordinate, a perfectly balanced pseudo k-d tree can be built in $O(n \log n)$ time, essentially in the same way as ordinary k-d trees.

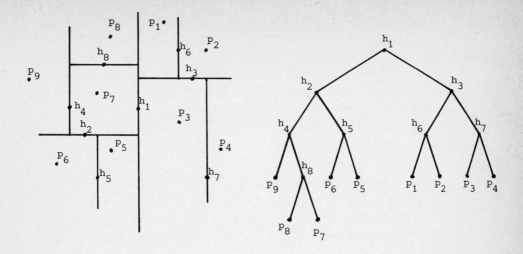

figure 4.5.1.

Willard [Wi5] already developed a dynamization of pseudo k-d trees (which he called k-d* trees), based on the decomposable nature of the problems they are used for, by building and maintaining a forest of pseudo k-d trees of different sizes (see also Overmars and van Leeuwen [OvL4]). This method of dynamizing pseudo k-d trees has the disadvantage that the query time tends to increase by a multiplicative factor of $O(\log n)$. Using partial rebuilding it is possible to maintain an undivided pseudo k-d tree dynamically in the same way as pseudo quad-trees.

Again we use a kind of weight-balancing. Let a constant δ be given with $0<\delta<1$. For each internal node β of a pseudo k-d tree we demand that each son contains at most $\left\lceil \frac{1}{2-\delta} n_\beta \right\rceil$ points. Such a pseudo k-d tree has depth at most $\lceil \log_{2-\delta} n \rceil + O(1)$.

Lemma 4.5.1. Given a node β in a pseudo k-d tree that is in perfect balance. Let n_β denote the number of points in the subtree rooted at β at the moment β gets out of balance. Then, there must have been $\Omega(\delta n_\beta)$ updates in the subtree rooted at β.

Proof

The proof is very similar to the proofs of Lemmas 4.2.1. and 4.4.2.1. and is left to the reader.

□

Lemma 4.5.2. A perfectly balanced pseudo k-d tree of n points can be built in $O(n \log n)$ time.

Theorem 4.5.3. For any fixed δ with $0<\delta<1$, there is an algorithm to perform insertions and deletions in an initially empty pseudo k-d tree such that its depth is always bounded by $\lceil \log_{2-\delta} n \rceil + O(1)$ and the average update time is bounded by $O(\frac{1}{\delta} \log^2 m)$.

Proof

Insertions and deletions are performed in the following way:

(i) Search for the appropriate leaf.

(ii) Perform the insertion or deletion (possibly by splitting a region or deleting some internal node).

(iii) Search for the highest internal node β along the search path that has become out of balance as a result of the update.

(iv) Rebuild the complete subtree rooted at β as a perfectly balanced pseudo k-d tree.

Beside the rebuilding the actions clearly take $O(\log n)$ time. In the same way as for pseudo quad-trees (Theorem 4.4.2.3.) the average time needed for rebuilding can be shown to be bounded by $O(\frac{1}{\delta} \log^2 m)$.

□

Again, in practise, the expected update time is likely to be much smaller than $O(\frac{1}{\delta} \log^2 m)$.

4.6. Concluding remarks.

In this chapter we have shown that for a number of structures for which a local rebuilding technique seems not applicable or quite complex, another dynamization technique, called partial rebuilding, can be used to obtain dynamic data structures with low average update time bound. The technique maintains balance in a tree structure by rebuilding the complete substructures at nodes that are out of balance in a "perfectly balanced" way. This sometimes takes a lot of time but when it takes a large number of updates before a subtree goes out of balance, the average update time bounds will remain low. This seems to be especially the case when a notion of weight-balance is used. Precise rules about when and how partial rebuilding can be used are hard to give and will have to be devised anew for every other type of structure where it appears to be applicable.

Bibliographical commments.

Section 4.3. on super B-trees was based on Lueker [Lu1]. The results on quad-trees and k-d trees are described in Overmars and van Leeuwen [OvL3].

CHAPTER V

GLOBAL REBUILDING

5.1. Introduction.

In a number of data structures one can easily perform updates (in particular deletions) as long as one is not concerned with restoring balance. For example, as shown in Chapter 4, one can perform insertions and deletions in pseudo quad-trees within $O(\log n)$ worst-case time when we do not rebalance. When such updates do not disturbe balance too drastically there is no need for rebalancing the structure after each single update. For example, in a pseudo quad-tree of n points one can perform $\frac{1}{2}n$ deletions while the query time remains of the same order of magnitude. (Insertions in pseudo quad-trees do disturb balance drastically.) In this case, we had better let the structure go out of balance somewhat during a number of updates, before cleaning it up, i.e., rebalancing it again. It will yield reasonable average update time bounds, while the bounds for query answering are not affected too seriously.

Updates that do disturb balance but do not disturb it too drastically will be called "weak", to distinguish them from normal updates (that do restore balance) that will sometimes be termed "strong" updates or "actual" updates.

Definition 5.1.1. Deletions and/or insertions are called WEAK if and only if there exist constants α and β, with $0<\alpha<1$ and $\beta>0$, such that the routines to carry them out on a new built (i.e., perfectly balanced) structure of n points guarantee that after $\leq \alpha n$ deletions and/or $\leq \beta n$ insertions, the query time, the amount of storage required, the weak deletion time and/or the weak insertion time on the resulting structure of m points are no more than a factor $k_{\alpha\beta}$ worse than the query time, the amount of storage required, the weak deletion and/or the weak insertion time, respectively, of a new built structure of m points, for some constant $k_{\alpha\beta}$ depending solely on α, β and the type of structure.

Hence, when a data structure S allows for weak deletions and weak insertions, one can perform αn such deletions and βn such insertions without the need for rebalancing because all bounds remain of the same order of magnitude.

<u>Notation</u>. Let S be a data structure containing n points on which no weak updates have been performed,

$$WD_S(n) = \text{the time required to perform a weak deletion on } S,$$
$$WI_S(n) = \text{the time required to perform a weak insertion on } S.$$

Clearly $WD_S(n) \leq D_S(n)$ and $WI_S(n) \leq I_S(n)$. We assume that both WD_S and WI_S are non-decreasing and smooth.

In Section 5.2. we will show how data structures that allow for weak updates can be transformed into fully dynamic data structures. We will first give a fairly simple method that yields good average update time bounds. Next we will describe a technique named "global rebuilding" to turn the averages into worst-case bounds. In Section 5.3. we will give a number of applications of the technique presented. It shows that especially the notion of weak deletion is a powerful tool in obtaining dynamic data structures. In Section 5.4. we offer some generalizations of the techniques.

5.2. <u>The dynamization result</u>.

In this section we will show how data structures that allow for weak updates can be transformed into fully dynamic data structures without essential loss in the efficiency of query answering and updates. In Subsection 5.2.1. we will give an easy (i.e., understandable and implementable) method that yields good average time bounds. In Subsection 5.2.2. we will describe a quite complex mechanism, called "global rebuilding", for turning the average update time bounds into worst-case bounds.

5.2.1. <u>Average time bounds</u>.

Given a data structure S that allows both for weak insertions and for weak deletions, let α, β and $k_{\alpha\beta}$ be as described in Definition 5.1.1. As stated in the introduction we do not need to do any rebalancing on S as long as the number of deletions and insertions after it was built from n points, is smaller than αn and βn, respectively. An obvious idea for keeping the structure in reasonable shape is to rebuild it completely in a perfectly balanced form after αn deletions or βn insertions have occurred since the latest rebuilding.

<u>Theorem</u> 5.2.1.1. Given a data structure S for some searching problem that allows for weak deletions and weak insertions, we can dynamize S into S' such that

$$Q_{S'}(n) = O(Q_S(n)),$$
$$D_{S'}^a(n) = O(WD_S(n) + P_S(n)/n),$$

$$I^a_{S'}(n) = O(WI_S(n) + P_S(n)/n),$$

$$M_{S'}(n) = O(M_S(n)).$$

Proof

S' is an S-structure (i.e., a structure of type S) on which we allow at most αn_0 weak deletions and βn_0 weak insertions after it was constructed of n_0 points. It follows immediately from definition 5.1.1. that $Q_{S'}(n) = O(Q_S(n))$ and $M_{S'}(n) = O(M_S(n))$. To perform an insertion on S' we perform a weak insertion on the S-structure. When the number of insertions becomes too big, i.e., larger than βn_0, we rebuild the complete S-structure. This rebuilding takes $P_S(n)$ time. But, as $n = n_0 - \alpha n_0 + \beta n_0 = (1+\beta-\alpha)n_0$ and βn_0 insertions have taken place since the latest rebuilding, it follows that the average rebuilding time per insertion is bounded by $O(P_S(n)/n)$. Hence, the average insertion time is bounded by $O(WI_S(n) + P_S(n)/n)$. Similarly, to perform a deletion on S', we perform a weak deletion on the underlying S-structure. When the number of deletions becomes larger than αn_0, we rebuild the entire structure. The average deletion time follows.

□

When the structure S allows for strong insertions and weak deletions, we can transform it in the same way into a structure S' such that

$$Q_{S'}(n) = O(Q_S(n)),$$

$$D^a_{S'}(n) = O(WD_S(n) + P_S(n)/n),$$

$$I_{S'}(n) = O(I_S(n)).$$

Similarly, when the structure allows for weak insertions and strong deletions, we get a structure S' with

$$Q_{S'}(n) = O(Q_S(n)),$$

$$D_{S'}(n) = O(D_S(n)),$$

$$I^a_{S'}(n) = O(WI_S(n) + P_S(n)/n).$$

5.2.2. Worst-case bounds.

In this subsection we will describe a technique, named GLOBAL REBUILDING, for turning the average time bounds of the previous subsection into worst-case bounds. In short, the idea behind the method is the following. At the moment the number of weak updates on the S-structure becomes large, we start building a new structure. As we do not want to build this structure all at once (like we did in the average case), we have to spread the work over a number of updates that follow. In the meantime we still perform these updates weakly on the old structure, such that it remains in use for query answering. By the time the new structure is ready we would like it to take over; but there is one problem here. One cannot, in general, perform updates on structures that are "under construction". Therefore we have to buffer updates that come in during the construction. After the construction is finished we start performing the buffered updates as weak updates on the new built structure. Only by the time the buffer is empty, the new structure can take over. We will see to it that this happens before the number of weak updates on the old structure becomes too large, and before the number of weak updates on the new structure becomes too large as well and we have to start building a new structure again. This will take care that there is always at most one structure under construction.

Theorem 5.2.2.1. Given a data structure S for some searching problem, that allows for weak deletions and for weak insertions, we can dynamize it into a structure S' such that

$$Q_{S'}(n) = O(Q_S(n)),$$
$$D_{S'}(n) = O(WD_S(n) + P_S(n)/n),$$
$$I_{S'}(n) = O(WI_S(n) + P_S(n)/n),$$
$$M_{S'}(n) = O(M_S(n)).$$

Proof

The structure S' consists of one S-structure MAIN on which we allow that αn_0 weak deletions and βn_0 weak insertions are performed since it was constructed from n_0 points. Queries are always performed on MAIN and hence, the query time is bounded by $O(k_{\alpha\beta} Q_S(n)) = O(Q_S(n))$.

Let MAIN be built from n_0 points. Let $\gamma = \min(\alpha,\beta)$. By the time the number of updates performed on MAIN becomes larger than $\frac{1}{2}\gamma n_0$, we start building a new S-structure NEW-MAIN of the points currently in the set. Let the size of NEW-MAIN be n_1. Clearly $(1-\frac{1}{2}\gamma)n_0 \leq n_1 \leq (1+\frac{1}{2}\gamma)n_0$. We will take care that NEW-MAIN can take over from MAIN within $\frac{1}{6}\gamma n_1$ updates. It follows that on MAIN never more than

$$\frac{1}{2}\gamma n_0 + \frac{1}{6}\gamma n_1 \leq \frac{1}{2}\gamma n_0 + \frac{1}{6}\gamma(1+\frac{1}{2}\gamma)n_0 = (\frac{2}{3}\gamma + \frac{1}{12}\gamma^2)n_0 < (\frac{2}{3} + \frac{1}{12})\gamma n_0 < \gamma n_0$$

weak updates are performed. The idea is to do with each next update $P_S(n_1)/\frac{1}{6}\gamma n_1$ work on the construction of NEW-MAIN. In this way, NEW-MAIN should be ready within $\frac{1}{6}\gamma n_1$ updates but, as pointed out in the introduction, we cannot perform updates on structures under construction. To this end, we add to the structure a buffer BUF in which we put all updates that need to be performed on NEW-MAIN when the construction is finished, in order of occurrence. Moreover, to guarantee that BUF is empty (and hence, NEW-MAIN can take over) within $\frac{1}{6}\gamma n_1$ updates, we speed up the construction of NEW-MAIN. To this end we do with each insertion

$$k_{\alpha\beta}WI_S(n_1 + \frac{1}{6}\gamma n_1) + P_S(n_1)/\frac{1}{6}\gamma n_1$$

work on the construction of NEW-MAIN and with each deletion we do

$$k_{\alpha\beta}WD_S(n_1 + \tfrac{1}{6}\gamma n_1) + P_S(n_1)/\tfrac{1}{6}\gamma n_1$$

work on the construction. Let the construction of NEW-MAIN be finished after N_i insertions and N_d deletions have taken place since the construction began. And let there be w time left with the latest update. Then clearly

$$(N_i+N_d)P_S(n_1)/\tfrac{1}{6}\gamma n_1 + N_i \cdot k_{\alpha\beta}WI_S(n_1 + \tfrac{1}{6}\gamma n_1) +$$
$$+ N_d \cdot k_{\alpha\beta}WD_S(n_1 + \tfrac{1}{6}\gamma n_1) - w = P_S(n_1)$$

, thus

$$N_i k_{\alpha\beta}WI_S(n_1 + \tfrac{1}{6}\gamma n_1) + N_d k_{\alpha\beta}WD_S(n_1 + \tfrac{1}{6}\gamma n_1) =$$
$$= P_S(n_1) + w - (N_i+N_d)P_S(n_1)/\tfrac{1}{6}\gamma n_1.$$

The left hand side of this expression is an upperbound on the amount of work needed to perform the N_i insertions and N_d deletions in BUF, because NEW-MAIN will never get a size larger than $n_1 + \tfrac{1}{6}\gamma n_1$ before it is turned into MAIN. Spending the w time left immediately on performing updates from BUF on NEW-MAIN, makes that the amount of time that is still needed to perform the buffered updates is bounded by $P_S(n_1) - (N_i+N_d)P_S(n_1)/\tfrac{1}{6}\gamma n_1$. (Note that clearly $N_i+N_d < \tfrac{1}{6}\gamma n_1$.) From this moment on we do with each next insertion (that is still performed on MAIN and put in BUF)

$$k_{\alpha\beta}WI_S(n_1 + \tfrac{1}{6}\gamma n_1) + P_S(n_1)/\tfrac{1}{6}\gamma n_1$$

work on performing updates from BUF on NEW-MAIN, and with each deletion

$$k_{\alpha\beta}WD_S(n_1 + \tfrac{1}{6}\gamma n_1) + P_S(n_1)/\tfrac{1}{6}\gamma n_1$$

work on performing updates from BUF. Hence, with each insertion the amount of work that still needs to be done increases by at most $k_{\alpha\beta}WI_S(n_1 + \tfrac{1}{6}\gamma n_1)$ because the insertion is put in BUF, and decreases by the same amount plus $P_S(n_1)/\tfrac{1}{6}\gamma n_1$. Similar for deletions. Hence with each next update the amount of work that needs to be done decreases with at least $P_S(n_1)/\tfrac{1}{6}\gamma n_1$. As the amount of work was $P_S(n_1)-(N_i+N_d)P_S(n_1)/\tfrac{1}{6}\gamma n_1$, it follows that the process overtakes itselfs after at most $\tfrac{1}{6}\gamma n_1 - (N_i+N_d)$ updates. It follows that NEW-MAIN can take over from the old MAIN within the desired $\tfrac{1}{6}\gamma n_1$ updates. One thing needs to be shown, namely, that NEW-MAIN does not call for a rebuilding before it is turned into MAIN. This follows from the fact that on NEW-MAIN, which was built from n_1 points, we only performed $\tfrac{1}{6}\gamma n_1$ weak updates while a reconstruction is only asked for after $\tfrac{1}{2}\gamma n_1$ updates.

With each insertion we do a total of at most

$$k_{\alpha\beta}WI_S(n) + k_{\alpha\beta}WI_S(n_1 + \tfrac{1}{6}\gamma n_1) + P_S(n_1)/\tfrac{1}{6}\gamma n_1$$

work. As $n_1 = \theta(n)$ and the functions are smooth, this is bounded by $O(WI_S(n) + P_S(n)/n)$. Similar the deletion time is bounded by $O(WD_S(n) + P_S(n)/n)$. The amount of storage required is clearly bounded by $O(M_S(n))$.

□

One easily verifies that when S allows for strong insertions we do not need to pay the $P_S(n)/n$ in the insertion time and that when S allows for strong deletions, we do not need to pay the $P_S(n)/n$ in the deletion time.

It should be noticed that the rebuilding (cleaning-up) of the structure is done in a brute force way. Instead of rebuilding the structure completely from scratch, we can sometimes use information from the old structure to speed up the construction (see e.g. the application to member searching as described in Section 5.3.1.).

5.3. Applications.

Especially the notion of weak deletions turns out to be very useful in the design of dynamic data structures for searching problems. The following lemma gives an important criterion for the "weakness" of deletions.

Lemma 5.3.1. Deletions that do not increase the future query, deletion and insertion time and the amount of storage required are weak.

Proof

Take an arbitrary α with $0<\alpha<1$. When we perform $\alpha'n \leq \alpha n$ deletions of the kind described and $\beta'n \leq \beta n$ (weak) insertions on a new-built structure of n points, the query time on the resulting structure is bounded by $k_\beta Q((1+\beta')n)$, where k_β is a constant depending on β, that comes in because insertion may be weak. The number of points currently in the set is $m = (1+\beta'-\alpha')n$. Observe that

$$k_\beta Q((1+\beta')n)$$
$$= k_\beta Q(\frac{1+\beta'}{1+\beta'-\alpha'}\, m)$$
$$\leq k_\beta Q(\frac{1+\beta}{1-\alpha}\, m)$$
$$\leq k_\beta k'_{\alpha\beta} Q(m)$$

for some constant $k'_{\alpha\beta}$ depending on α and β, because $\frac{1+\beta}{1-\alpha} > 0$ and Q is smooth. Hence, there is a constant $k''_{\alpha\beta}$ such that the query time is bounded by $k''_{\alpha\beta} Q(m)$. In the same way one can find such constant factors for bounding the deletion and insertion time and the amount of storage required.

□

5.3.1. Member searching.

All data structures for the member searching problem as described in Chapter 3 can be turned into structures that allow for weak deletions, by associating with each object in the structure a boolean tag that tells whether the object is really present. To perform a query on such a structure with a query object x we first search for x in the structure. If we do not find it, x is clearly not present. If we do find the object x, the associated boolean tells whether x is present or not. To insert a point p we search for p in the structure. When we find it, we turn the associated boolean into true. Otherwise, we insert the point using the normal insertion procedure (when available) and associate the value true with it. A weak deletion of a point p is performed by searching for p in the structure and turning the associated boolean into false. Such a deletion does not increase the future query, insertion and deletion time and hence, due to Lemma 5.3.1. it is a weak deletion. It follows that WD(n) = $O(Q(n))$.

Theorem 5.3.1.1. Given a half-dynamic structure S for solving the member searching problem, there exists a structure S' for member searching such that

$$Q_{S'}(n) = O(Q_S(n)),$$
$$I_{S'}(n) = O(I_S(n)),$$
$$D_{S'}(n) = O(Q_S(n)).$$

Proof

Applying Theorem 5.2.2.1. to the structure described above yields a deletion time of $O(Q_S(n) + P_S(n)/n)$. But, all structures for member searching, as described in Chapter 3, can be built in $O(n)$ time when the points are given in sorted order. When we have to rebuilt a structure we can obtain the points ordered, using the old structure. Hence the amount of work we have to do for rebuilding is $O(1)$ per deletion.

□

As an example, consider path-balanced trees (see Section 3.2.4.). No efficient deletion routines have been found for αBB-trees for most α, although $O(\log n)$ insertion routines do exist (see Olivié [O1]). Using the technique described above, one can perform deletion in αBB-trees in $O(\log n)$ time without affecting the bounds on query and insertion time in order of magnitude.

As a second example, consider AVL-trees. As described in Section 3.2.1. AVL-trees can be maintained by means of single and double rotations at the cost of $O(\log n)$ per update. One easily shows that insertions need at most one rotation. This is important when the structure is augmented by associating information to internal nodes. Often this associated information has to be recomputed when a rotation takes place. Unfortunately, deletions in AVL-trees can cause local rotations at many nodes along the path from the root to the deleted point. But performing weak deletions in AVL-trees does not cause any rotation at all. Hence, maintaining the structure in the way described above will, in a number of instances, lead to better deletion time bounds.

In a number of applications, one first visits a point of the set, before deciding whether it should be deleted. It follows that, when a deletion has to be performed, we already have a pointer to the point (in the structure) that has to be deleted. Data structures for member searching as described in Chapter 3 still need $O(\log n)$ time to perform the deletion. On the other hand, a weak deletion takes only $O(1)$ time in this case. As the cleaning up of the structure takes only $O(1)$ per deletion as well, we get the following result:

Theorem 5.3.1.2. There exist structures for the member searching problem with $O(\log n)$ query and insertion time, such that deletion take only $O(1)$ time when the position of the point that has to be deleted, is known.

5.3.2. Quad- and k-d trees.

It is possible to perform weak deletions in pseudo quad-trees by searching for the point that has to be deleted and removing the corresponding leaf. Such a deletion does not increase the depth of the pseudo quad-tree and, as the query time for most types of queries depends only on the depth of the pseudo quad-tree it does not increase the query time. Hence $WD(n) = O(\log n)$. But there is a problem. We cannot immediately apply Theorem 5.2.2.1. because this result assumed that the (weak) insertion time was a worst-case bound and we only have an average insertion time bound for pseudo quad-trees (see Section 4.4.). We needed this worst-case bound in the proof of Theorem 5.2.2.1. because we have to know in advance how much time the updates in BUF would take, to spend enough extra time on the construction of the new structure. One easily verifies that, when performing N_i insertions on a new built pseudo quad-tree of n points, the total amount of time needed will be bounded by $O(N_i \log^2(n+N_i))$. (Note that this is a stronger result than the one stated in Theorem 4.4.2.3.) It follows that when BUF contains N_i insertions, the time needed to perform them on NEW-MAIN is bounded by $N_i \cdot O(\log^2(n+N_i))$. Hence, doing with each insertion $O(\log^2(n+N_i)$ work on NEW-MAIN will guarantee that BUF is empty in time. This leads to the following result:

Theorem 5.3.2.1. Pseudo quad-trees can be maintained at the cost of $O(\log^2 n)$ average insertion time and $O(\log n)$ worst-case deletion time.

Note that the insertion time depends on n rather than m, the maximum number of points
that were once in the set.

The same result can be derived for pseudo k-d trees.

5.3.3. Super B-trees.

As described in Section 2.3. (3.4.) a one-dimensional super B-tree is a leaf-
search BB[α]-tree in which the leaves are linked in a list. To be able to perform
weak deletions in such a structure we link the leaves in a doubly linked list. To
perform a weak deletion of a point we search for the leaf where the point is stored,
remove it from the doubly linked list, delete the leaf and move its brother to the
position of the father in the tree. See figure 5.3.3.1. Note that we do not perform

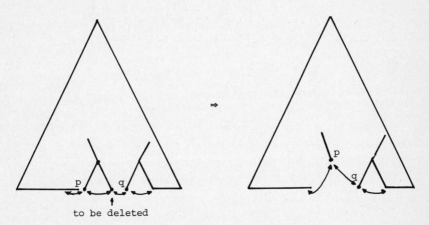

to be deleted

figure 5.3.3.1.

any rebalancing and that we do not update the balance information. It follows that
balance in the tree is maintained as if no weak deletions have been performed at all
and hence, that neither the query time nor the future update time increases by such
a deletion. Hence, the deletion is indeed a weak deletion. Clearly, the weak deletion
takes only O(1) time once we have located the leaf that has to be deleted. We will
use this property to obtain a better deletion time in d-dimensional super B-trees
(d≥2).

A two-dimensional super B-tree consists of a leaf search BB[α]-tree in which the
points are stored in sorted order with respect to their first coordinate and in which,
with each internal node β there is associated a BB[α]-tree that contains all points
below β ordered with respect to their second coordinate. To be able to perform weak
deletions efficiently we use the structure described above for the associated structures. Moreover we add to each point in the main structure a list of pointers to all

occurrences of the point in associated structures (see figure 5.3.3.2.).

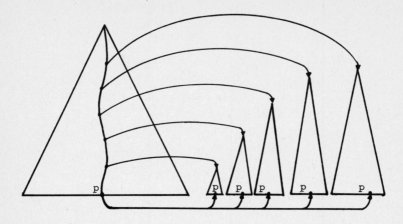

figure 5.3.3.2.

One easily verifies that maintaining these lists, while performing insertions, can be done without affecting the time bounds. To perform a weak deletion of a point p we search for p in the main structure, follow the list and perform a weak deletion of p in each of the associated structures that contain p and delete p from the main structure. This takes only $O(\log n)$ steps. Clearly, such a deletion is weak indeed. Because the building time of the structure is bounded by $O(n \log n)$ (the adaption of the result of e.g. Bentley [Be3] is easy) we can apply Theorem 5.2.2.1. and obtain a deletion time of $O(\log n)$ for two-dimensional super B-trees. The generalization to d-dimensional super B-trees is straightforward. This leads to the following result:

Theorem 5.3.3.1. There exists a structure S for d-dimensional range searching such that

$$Q_S(n) = O(\log^d n + k), \text{ where k is the number of answers,}$$
$$I_S(n) = O(\log^d n),$$
$$D_S(n) = O(\log^{d-1} n),$$
$$P_S(n) = O(n \log^{d-1} n),$$
$$M_S(n) = O(n \log^{d-1} n).$$

5.4. Conclusions and extensions.

In this chapter a general method was presented for turning weak updates, that let a structure go out of balance slowly, into strong updates that maintain a well balanced data structure continuously. It shows that, in order to dynamize a structure, we do not necessarily have to devise efficient update routines. Once we have a method for performing weak updates on the structure we can turn them into actual updates at the cost of only a minor loss in efficiency. The applications in Section 5.3. show that in particular the notion of weak deletion is a powerful one. The notion of weak insertion will be very useful in Chapter 7, in the study of decomposable searching problems.

The definition of weak updates can be extended in several ways. A first generalization allows that $\alpha(n)$ weak deletions and $\beta(n)$ weak insertions can be performed without increasing the time bounds and amount of storage required by more than a constant factor, for two functions $\alpha(n)$ and $\beta(n)$. The method given in the proof of Theorem 5.2.2.1. can easily be adapted to this more general definition, yielding

$$Q_{S'}(n) = O(Q_S(n)),$$
$$D_{S'}(n) = O(WD_S(n) + P_S(n)/\alpha(n)),$$
$$I_{S'}(n) = O(WI_S(n) + P_S(n)/\beta(n)),$$
$$M_{S'}(n) = O(M_S(n)).$$

The definition can be generalized even further by allowing that $\alpha(n)$ weak deletions and $\beta(n)$ weak insertions increase the bounds by at most a factor of $k(n)$ for some function $k(n)$. Again one can adapt Theorem 5.2.2.1. to yield

$$Q_{S'}(n) = O(k(n)Q_S(n)),$$
$$D_{S'}(n) = O(k(n)WD_S(n) + P_S(n)/\alpha(n)),$$
$$I_{S'}(n) = O(k(n)WI_S(n) + P_S(n)/\beta(n)),$$
$$M_{S'}(n) = O(k(n)M_S(n)).$$

Bibliographical comments.

Theorem 5.2.2.1. was first described in Overmars and van Leeuwen [OvL5], but only used for the dynamization of decomposable searching problems (see also van Leeuwen and Overmars [vLO2]). The contents of this chapter were based on Overmars [Ov4].

CHAPTER VI

ORDER DECOMPOSABLE SET PROBLEMS

6.1. Introduction.

In the previous three chapters we discussed dynamization techniques based on
properties of the (static) data structure known for the searching problem in mind.
In this chapter and the next one we will treat dynamization techniques based on properties of the searching problem itself. We will first concentrate on set problems and
show that for a wide class of such problems one general technique can be used for obtaining dynamic solutions. In Chapter 7 we will consider searching problems.

As mentioned before, static solutions to set problems in general consist of the
answers themselves. In such a case, the query time is $O(1)$ and the building time (P_S)
is the time required to compute the answer. Answers to set problems often consist of
configurations like for example a convex hull, a Voronoi diagram or a view. Hence,
they consist of more than a constant number of elements. In the dynamic case we like
to maintain such a configuration while points are inserted and deleted in the set.
This guarantees that the query time remains $O(1)$. This is of course not the only possibility. We could as well maintain some kind of decomposition of the answer and combine the parts when a query is performed (see Section 7.7.2. in the next Chapter).
Yet in this chapter we consider a way of dynamizing set problems such that after each
insertion or deletion the updated answer is again available.

For many set problems it is possible to derive the answer over the total set by
combining the answers over two, in some way separated, "halves" of the set. Set problems of this kind will be called "order decomposable". Let $C(n)$ be a smooth nondecreasing integer function.

Definition 6.1.1. A set problem PR is called $C(n)$-ORDER DECOMPOSABLE if and only if
there exists an ordering ORD and a function $\square$ such that for each set of points
$V=\{p_1,\ldots,p_n\}$, ordered according to ORD,

$$\forall_{1\leq i<n} \quad PR(\{p_1,\ldots,p_n\}) = \square(PR(\{p_1,\ldots,p_i\}) , PR(\{p_{i+1},\ldots,p_n\})),$$

where $\square$ takes at most $C(n)$ time to compute when V contains n points.

For example, as a result of Theorem 2.6.1., the convex hull problem in 2-dimensional space is an O(log n)-order decomposable set problem and, according to Theorem 2.6.3., the 3-dimensional version is an O(n)-order decomposable set problem. A set problem will be called order decomposable if it is C(n)-order decomposable for some C(n) that is appreciably smaller than the full building time for any known static solution to the problem, i.e., $C(n) = o(P_S(n))$ for any known static solution S. For a number of set problems we can meaningfully combine the answers over two separated halves of the set only when additional information about the points in the two halves is known. If this extra kind of "preconditioning" is C(n)-order decomposable with respect to the same ordering ORD as that used for the problem itself, then we can transform the problem to a C(n)-order decomposable set problem by including the preconditioning as part of the "answer". In such cases, □ will first combine the answers using the preconditioning and afterwards combine the preconditioning.

A well-known method for solving a number of static set problems is the divide-and-conquer technique (see e.g. Bentley and Shamos [BeSh1,BeSh3] and Bentley [Be4]). In Section 6.2. we will show that there is a strong relation between the notion of order decomposability of a set problem and the existence of a static solution based on the divide-and-conquer strategy. It will follow that for each order decomposable set problem an easy divide-and-conquer algorithm exists.

In Section 6.3. we describe a general method for dynamically maintaining the answers to order decomposable set problems while points are inserted and deleted in the set, with low worst-case update time bounds.

In Section 6.4. we give an extensive list of applications of the method to set problems that are described in Chapter 2, which shows the power of the dynamization method.

6.2. Static solution.

The divide-and-conquer technique, used for solving numerous set problems statically, asks for a merging routine that merges the answers over a number of (disjoint) subsets into the answer over the union of these subsets. The function □ in Definition 6.1.1. is such a merging routine. It follows that all order decomposable set problems can be solved using divide-and-conquer.

Theorem 6.2.1. Let PR be a C(n)-order decomposable set problem. Let ORD(n) be the time required to order n points according to the ordering ORD. There exists a divide-and-conquer solution S to PR such that

$$
P_S(n) = \begin{cases} O(n + ORD(n)) & \text{when } C(n)=O(n^\varepsilon) \text{ for some } 0<\varepsilon<1, \\ O(C(n) + ORD(n)) & \text{when } C(n)=\Omega(n^{1+\varepsilon}) \text{ for some } \varepsilon>0, \\ O(n + \log n.C(n) + ORD(n)) & \text{otherwise.} \end{cases}
$$

Proof

Let V be the set of points for which we want to solve PR. We first sort V accord-
ing to ORD, thus obtaining an ordered set $V'=\{a_1,\ldots,a_n\}$ ($a_i \leq a_j$ for $i<j$). To solve
PR we split V' in two halves, solve PR for the two halves, and merge the answers using
□. The algorithm is best described by the following recursive procedure.

procedure PR (ordered set V');
V' is an ordered subset of the total set of points.

> step 1: When V' consists of only one element then compute the answer directly
> and report this answer. Otherwise go to step 2.

> step 2: Let $V'=\{a_1,\ldots,a_u\}$. Let $h = \lfloor (1+u)/2 \rfloor$. Split V' in $V_1=\{a_1,\ldots,a_h\}$ and
> $V_2=\{a_{h+1},\ldots,a_u\}$.

> step 3: Report $\square(PR(V_1),PR(V_2))$.

end of PR;

Ordering the set V to obtain V' takes ORD(n) by definition. To obtain a bound
for the cost of the procedure PR note that, apart from the recursive calls, PR takes
O(C(n')) steps (n' the number of points in the set it is working on). Hence, the runtime of PR is bounded by a function F(n) that satisfies the following recurrence:

$$F(n) = F(\lfloor \tfrac{1}{2}n \rfloor) + F(\lceil \tfrac{1}{2}n \rceil) + O(C(n)).$$

One easily verifies that this leads to the bounds stated in the theorem.

□

Often $ORD(n) = \Theta(n \log n)$ but there are a number of order decomposable set problems
for which the set can be split in any way, i.e., for which we do not need any ordering ORD. In such cases one can take $ORD(n) = O(1)$. An example of such a problem is
the maximum problem (that asks for the largest element in a set). The problem is
O(1)-order decomposable and Theorem 6.2.1. immediately implies a solution in O(n) time.
(The O(n) bound can of course also be obtained in a direct way.)

6.3. Dynamic solution.

As Theorem 6.2.1. shows, there exist efficient algorithms to solve order decomposable set problems statically. But often one would like to maintain the answer to
an order decomposable set problem while points are inserted and/or deleted in the set.
In this section we will give a method of maintaining such answers efficiently. To
achieve this we keep track of how the divide-and-conquer algorithm splits the set and
how it merges the answers over subsets. To this end we exploit a BB[α]-tree T in which

the points currently in the set are stored at the leaves, ordered according to ORD.
(When ORD is vacuous we just choose a lexicographic ordering.) The root of the tree
corresponds to the total set. Its two sons correspond to the halves in which the set
is split by the divide-and-conquer algorithm. Their sons correspond to the next re-
cursion level of splitting of the algorithm, etc. At each internal node α of T we
would like to have the complete answer to the set problem for the corresponding subset, i.e., for the points in the subtree rooted at α. Such an answer associated with
a node α will from now on be called its PR structure (because answers normally are
complete configurations or structures) and will be denoted as PR_α. Let γ and δ be
the sons of α in T. It follows from the definition of C(n)-order decomposability that,
once PR_γ and PR_δ at γ and δ are available, the PR structure at α can be computed in
C(n') time (n' the number of points below α) by an application of $\square$ (see figure 6.3.1.).
But there is a problem. There is no guarantee in the definition of order decomposability that $\square$ leaves the PR structures it works on unchanged. In a number of applications

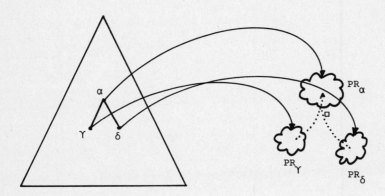

figure 6.3.1.

offered in Section 6.4. these PR structures are indeed largely destroyed. Copying
the PR structures before merging them may take much more than C(n') time. But, in
fact, there is no need to have the complete PR structure available at each internal
node in the tree. A full PR structure only has to be available at the root (this being
the answer over the whole set that must be maintained). All other structures are only
necessary to be able to update this root structure efficiently when insertions and
deletions occur. We will show that it is sufficient to maintain only partial information about the PR structures at the nodes below the root in order to update the root
structure.

When it is necessary to build PR_α at some internal node α out of the structures PR_γ and PR_δ at its sons γ and δ all actions that are performed to obtain PR_α are recorded at α and the leftover pieces of PR_γ and PR_δ are saved at γ and δ. This can be done in $O(C(n'))$ time. It follows that at some later moment PR_γ and PR_δ can be rebuilt from PR_α using the leftover pieces at γ and δ and unwinding the record of actions of α. This will take $O(C(n'))$ time. In most applications there are more efficient and, in particular, less storage demanding methods for reconstructing PR_γ and PR_δ from PR_α, but the method described above works in all cases. In the tree T only at the root we keep the complete PR structure of all points in the set. At each internal node α of T we keep the following fields; to facilitate the necessary splitting and building operations:

    (i) father(α) = a pointer to the father of α (if any),

    (ii) lson(α) = a pointer to the leftson of α,

    (iii) rson(α) = a pointer to the rightson of α,

    (iv) max(α) = the largest value (according to ORD) in the subtree of lson(α),

    (v) PR*(α) = the leftover piece of PR_α,

    (vi) INF(α) = the information needed to obtain $PR_{lson(\alpha)}$ and $PR_{rson(\alpha)}$ from PR_α (i.e., a record of actions).

PR*(α) and PR_α should not be confused. PR* is a field-identifier and PR_α denotes the answer over the set of points below α. Properties (i) to (iv) are needed to let T function as a search tree and properties (v) and (vi) supply the associated information. When α is the root: PR*(α)=PR_α. We will first describe the procedure DOWN to reconstruct the full PR_β structure at an arbitrary node β of T. DOWN also reconstructs the full PR_γ structure at each node γ bordering the search path towards β. These structures are needed to be able to return from β to the root of the tree, reassembling structures when we do so, to restore the structure associated to the root to its proper shape. Later β will be the father of some leaf that needs to be updated and the search will be guided by the usual decision criterion for search trees. We will not spell out this detail in the description of DOWN. DOWN works its way down the tree to β by disassembling the structure at the node visited and reassembling the structures at its sons.

procedure DOWN(node α,β);
α is the node just reached on the way towards β. PR*(α) currently contains the complete PR_α structure.

    step 1: If $\alpha=\beta$ then we are done. Otherwise go to step 2.

<u>step 2</u>: Build the structures PR_γ and PR_δ of the sons γ and δ of α using the leftover pieces in PR*(γ) and PR*(δ) and the record of action in INF(α), and store PR_γ and PR_δ in PR*(γ) and PR*(δ), respectively.

<u>step 3</u>: If β lies below lson(α) (or β=lson(α)) then call DOWN(lson(α),β). Otherwise call DOWN(rson(α),β).

<u>end</u> of DOWN;

The procedure is called as DOWN(root,β). Let the number of points currently in the set be n.

<u>Lemma</u> 6.3.1. DOWN reaches its goal after $O(C(n))$ steps when $C(n)=\Omega(n^\varepsilon)$ for some $\varepsilon>0$ and after $O(\log n.C(n))$ steps otherwise.

<u>Proof</u>

The expensive part of DOWN is step 2, the construction of PR_γ and PR_δ out of PR_α, INF(α) and the leftover pieces at γ and δ. When the subtree rooted at α contains n' points, this unwinding of INF(α) takes $O(C(n'))$ time. Because T was assumed to be a BB[α]-tree, at the ith recursive call of DOWN, the number of points below the node α is bounded by $(1-\alpha)^i.n$. So the total cost (except for the next recursive call) is bounded by $O(C((1-\alpha)^i n))$ because $C(n)$ is smooth. It follows that the total amount of time required for DOWN is bounded by

$$O(C(n) + C((1-\alpha)n) + C((1-\alpha)^2 n) + \ldots) =$$
$$= \sum_i (C((1-\alpha)^i n)).$$

As $0<1-\alpha<1$, it follows that the amount of time is bounded by $O(C(n))$ for $C(n)=\Omega(n^\varepsilon)$ and by $O(\log n.C(n))$ otherwise.

□

We will use the procedure DOWN to reach the father of a leaf that we want to update. After we have performed the insertion or deletion and made the necessary local changes (clearly bounded by $O(1)$ of work) we want to climb back to the root, meanwhile assembling updated answers along the search path. For this task we use the procedure UP. The assembling of structures can be done quite easily using (the merge operator) □ but there is one problem. Because we have updated the tree (by means of an insertion of a deletion) T may have gotten out of balance. Rebalancing in BB[α]-trees is done by means of single and double rotations (see Section 3.2.2.). It turns out to be possible to make the necessary changes in the associated PR-structures efficiently (see below). In the description of the procedure UP we delegate the task of rebalancing to a procedure BALANCE that will be clarified later.

<u>procedure</u> UP(<u>node</u> α);

α is the node most recently reached on the path towards the root of the tree. The PR* fields at the sons of α contain complete PR structures.

    <u>step 1</u>: Compute PR_α from $PR_{lson(\alpha)}$ and $PR_{rson(\alpha)}$ using □, meanwhile filling in the information in INF(α) and leaving the leftover pieces of $PR_{lson(\alpha)}$ and $PR_{rson(\alpha)}$ in PR*(lson(α)) and PR*(rson(α)), respectively. Store PR_α in PR*(α).

    <u>step 2</u>: If α is out of balance as a result of the update, call BALANCE(α).

    <u>step 3</u>: If α is the root of the tree then we are done. Otherwise call UP(father(α)).

<u>end</u> of UP;

The procedure is called as UP(father(β)) where β is the father of the updated leaf (assuming β is not the root of the tree).

<u>Lemma</u> 6.3.2. UP reaches its goal after O(C(n) + R) steps when $C(n)=\Omega(n^\varepsilon)$ (some ε>0) and after O(log n.C(n) + R) steps otherwise, where R is the total amount of time needed for performing the necessary rotations.

<u>Proof</u>

    The total cost for rebalancing is R by definition. Apart from rebalancing and the recursive call, the cost for one step of UP is bounded by O(C(n')), where n' is the number of points below the current node α. By the same argument as used in the proof of Lemma 6.3.1. this adds up to O(C(n)) when $C(n)=\Omega(n^\varepsilon)$ (some ε>0) and to O(log n.C(n)) otherwise.

                                                             □

To obtain a bound for R we have to look at the actions that are necessary to restore the associated PR structures after a local rotation is performed. We will only consider the case when a single rotation at α is needed, as double rotations can be handled in a similar way. Referring to figure 3.2.1.1., let the roots of the subtrees T_1, T_2 and T_3 be γ_1, γ_2 and γ_3, respectively. A single rotation at α is performed in the following way:

    (i) perform one iteration of DOWN at α to reconstruct the PR structures at its sons β and γ_3 (in figure 3.2.1.1.),

    (ii) perform one iteration of DOWN at β to reconstruct the PR structures at γ_1 and γ_2,

    (iii) perform the single rotation as displayed in figure 3.2.1.1.,

    (iv) perform one iteration of UP at the node that has now become α.

Had we noticed the need for rebalancing at the beginning of UP (i.e., interchanged step 1 and step 2) then (i) would not have been needed. This modification is left to the reader.

Lemma 6.3.3. $R = O(C(n))$ when $C(n) = \Omega(n^\varepsilon)$ (some $\varepsilon > 0$) and $R = O(\log n.C(n))$ otherwise.

Proof

A single rotation consists of (at most) two iterations of DOWN and one iteration of UP. A similar result holds for double rotations. Because at each node on the path towards the updated point there is at most once a need for a single or a double rotation, the bound follows from the bounds obtained for the procedures DOWN and UP.

□

Using the procedures DOWN and UP we are able to maintain the augmented $BB[\alpha]$-tree T, and hence the answer to an order decomposable set problem, efficiently.

Theorem 6.3.4. Given a $C(n)$-order decomposable set problem PR, there exists a dynamic data structure T with the following bounds on insertion and deletion time:

$$I_T(n) = \begin{cases} O(C(n)) & \text{when } C(n) = \Omega(n^\varepsilon) \text{ for some } \varepsilon > 0, \\ O(\log n.C(n)) & \text{otherwise,} \end{cases}$$

$$D_T(n) = \begin{cases} O(C(n)) & \text{when } C(n) = \Omega(n^\varepsilon) \text{ for some } \varepsilon > 0, \\ O(\log n.C(n)) & \text{otherwise.} \end{cases}$$

Proof

Keep the points ordered with respect to ORD, in a tree structure T as described. In T the required answer to the problem appears at the root. When we want to insert or delete a point p we use DOWN to reach the father β of the leaf where p needs to be inserted or deleted according to ORD. After performing the action and updating PR_β directly (i.e., rebuilding it), we climb back to the root using the procedure UP, meanwhile reassembling the updated answers along the path. UP also takes care of the rebalancing operations needed. When we have reached the root of T we have the updated answer over the total set. The time bounds follow from the bounds for DOWN, UP and BALANCE, shown in Lemmas 6.3.1., 6.3.2. and 6.3.3., respectively.

□

Two more things are worth considering, namely the time required to build T for some fixed set of points (i.e., P_T) and the amount of storage required to represent T (i.e., M_T). Let us consider the building time first.

The procedure PR as described in Section 6.2. to obtain static solutions for order decomposable set problems can easily be modified to deliver the complete tree T rather than the answer only. The recursive splitting of the set immediately gives us the BB[α]-tree. Saving the information of how answers are combined and leaving the leftover pieces at the appropriate nodes can be done without increasing the overall runtime in order of magnitude. Details are left to the interested reader.

Lemma 6.3.5. After the points in the set are ordered with respect to ORD, the structure T for a C(n)-order decomposable searching problem can be built in time bounded by

$$P_T(n) = \begin{cases} O(n) & \text{when } C(n)=O(n^\varepsilon), \text{ some } 0<\varepsilon<1, \\ O(C(n)) & \text{when } C(n)=\Omega(n^{1+\varepsilon}), \text{ some } \varepsilon>0, \\ O(n + \log n \cdot C(n)) & \text{otherwise.} \end{cases}$$

Proof

The result follows from Theorem 6.2.1. and the above discussion.

□

We can assume that the amount of time required to sort the set of points according to ORD is bounded by O(n log n).

It is clear that the amount of storage required is bounded by the amount of time needed for building T once the points are ordered, i.e.,

$$M_T(n) = \begin{cases} O(n) & \text{when } C(n)=O(n^\varepsilon) \text{ for some } 0<\varepsilon<1, \\ O(C(n)) & \text{when } C(n)=\Omega(n^{1+\varepsilon}) \text{ for some } \varepsilon>0, \\ O(n + \log n \cdot C(n)) & \text{otherwise.} \end{cases}$$

The first two bounds are optimal in the sense that we have to store all points, which takes $\Omega(n)$ storage, and that the answer over the total set might very well take C(n) storage. For C(n) at least linear, the third bound of O(n + log n·C(n)) can be lowered to O(n + log log n·C(n)) by slightly modifying the structure T, without affecting the update time bounds.

To this end we split the set of points V={$p_1,\ldots,p_n$}, ordered according to ORD, in subsets V_1={$p_1,\ldots,p_{\lceil n/\log n \rceil}$}, V_2={$p_{\lceil n/\log n \rceil+1},\ldots,p_{2\lceil n/\log n \rceil}$}, $\ldots$. Hence each V_i contains $\leq \lceil n/\log n \rceil$ points. Each V_i is structured as a balanced binary search tree T_i. Let the root of T_i be r_i. The nodes r_i we store in a augmented BB[α] leaf-search tree T as described above. Hence, with each r_i we have the leftover piece PR*(r_i) of all points in T_i.

An insertion of a point p is performed in the following way:

    (i) walk down the tree T using the procedure DOWN, to reach a root r_i,
    (ii) insert p in T_i,
    (iii) if the size of T_i has become $2\lceil n/\log n \rceil$ then split T_i in two equal halves, insert the extra root r_i' in T, build PR_{r_i} and $PR_{r_i'}$, and walk

back to the root using the procedure UP, starting at the new father of r_i and r_i',

(iv) otherwise, rebuild PR_{r_i} and walk back to the root using UP, starting at the father of r_i.

In this way the answer at the root is maintained correctly. (i) clearly takes at most $O(C(n))$ due to Lemma 6.3.1. and the fact that $C(n)$ is at least linear. (ii) takes $O(\log n)$. The construction of the structures PR_{r_i} and PR_r, takes

$$2.O(\log(\lceil n/\log n \rceil).C(\lceil n/\log n \rceil))) = O(C(n))$$

because $C(n)$ is at least linear and smooth. (This also holds for a number of other bounds on $C(n)$, e.g. $C(n) = \dfrac{n}{\log^\varepsilon n}$ for some $\varepsilon > 0$, but this is of no practical relevance.) As the splitting of T_i takes $O(\log n)$ and UP takes $O(C(n))$, step (iii) takes a total of $O(\log n)$ and UP takes $O(C(n))$ as well. It follows that the insertion time remains $O(C(n))$. As each T_i contains at least $\lceil n/\log n \rceil$ points, it follows that T is at most $O(\log \log n)$ levels deep. It is easy to show that the amount of storage required for leftover pieces of PR-structures and for INF-fields per level is bounded by $O(C(n))$. Hence, the total amount of storage required is bounded by $O(n + \log \log n.C(n))$.

A weak deletion of a point p is performed in the following way:

(i) walk down T using DOWN to reach a root r_i,

(ii) delete p from T_i,

(iii) rebuild PR_{r_i},

(iv) walk back to the root of T using UP, starting at the father of r_i.

This takes $O(C(n))$ time by the same arguments used for insertions. Turning the weak deletion into an actual deletion, using Theorem 5.2.2.1. does not change the time bound in order of magnitude. Hence, the structure described allows for insertions and deletions in $O(C(n))$ time.

Combining the result from Theorem 6.3.4. and Lemma 6.3.5., we get the following dynamization result for order decomposable set problems:

Theorem 6.3.6. Given a $C(n)$-order decomposable set problem PR, there exists a dynamic data structure T for PR such that

($Q_T(n) = O(1)$,)

$$P_T(n) = \begin{cases} O(n \log n) & \text{when } C(n) = O(n^\varepsilon) \text{ for some } 0 < \varepsilon < 1, \\ O(C(n)) & \text{when } C(n) = \Omega(n^{1+\varepsilon}) \text{ for some } \varepsilon > 0, \\ O(\log n.C(n) + n \log n) & \text{otherwise,} \end{cases}$$

$$I_T(n) = \begin{cases} O(C(n)) & \text{when } C(n) = \Omega(n^\varepsilon) \text{ for some } \varepsilon > 0, \\ O(\log n.C(n)) & \text{otherwise,} \end{cases}$$

$$D_T(n) = \begin{cases} O(C(n)) & \text{when } C(n) = \Omega(n^\varepsilon) \text{ for some } \varepsilon > 0, \\ O(\log n.C(n)) & \text{otherwise,} \end{cases}$$

$$M_T(n) = \begin{cases} O(n) & \text{when } C(n)=O(n^{\varepsilon}) \text{ for some } 0<\varepsilon<1, \\ O(C(n)) & \text{when } C(n)=\Omega(n^{1+\varepsilon}) \text{ for some } \varepsilon>0, \\ O(\log \log n.C(n)) & \text{when } C(n) \text{ is at least linear}, \\ O(n + \log n.C(n)) & \text{otherwise}. \end{cases}$$

6.4. Applications.

In this section we will discuss a number of set problems that are order decomposable and show how the results in the previous section can be used to immediately dynamize them in an efficient manner. For some of the problems no adequate dynamic solution was known before. For most of the applications it will yield the best currently known solution to the dynamic version.

6.4.1. Convex hulls.

A prime example of an order decomposable set problem is the convex hull problem in two- and three-dimensional space (see Section 2.6.). Due to Theorem 2.6.1. the two-dimensional convex hull problem is $O(\log n)$-order decomposable. Applying Theorem 6.3.6. yields the following result for convex hull maintenance:

Theorem 6.4.1.1. There exists a structure T for dynamically maintaining the convex hull of a two-dimensional point set at the cost of $O(\log^2 n)$ per update, while the structure uses only linear storage.

There are numerous problems that can be solved using convex hull determination as a tool (cf. Shamos [Sh2]). The algorithm we devised for dynamically maintaining a convex hull will enable us to tackle a few inherent dynamic problems.

In statistics considerable attention has been given to finding estimators which identify the centre of a population. For one-dimensional data it has given rise to the concept of an α-TRIMMED MEAN, obtained by taking the mean value of the points remaining after discarding the upper- and lower α-tiles of the set (see e.g. Huber [Hu]). Clearly the α-trimmed mean of a set of n points can be computed in $O(n)$ steps (using results of Blum e.a. [Bl]). In two dimensions a similar idea gave rise to the concept of PEELING a convex hull (Tukey [Tu]), again to remove some fixed percentage of outlying points from the set. Each time a point is removed, the convex hull must be updated accordingly. Applying Theorem 6.4.1.1. we can obtain the following result:

Theorem 6.4.1.2. One can peel a set of n points in the plane within $O(n \log^2 n)$ steps.

Proof

Building the structure T of Theorem 6.4.1.1. takes O(n log n). Removing a point takes O(log^2 n). As at most n points can be removed, the bound follows.

□

A closely related problem asks for all CONVEX LAYERS of a set. Starting with the convex hull as the first layer, the ith layer is defined as the convex hull of the set of points remaining after peeling all previous layers off. The statistical significance of the splitting of a set of points in its convex layers was recognized by Barnett [Bar], who defined the C-ORDER of a point as being the rank number of the convex layer it belongs to. Applying Theorem 6.4.1.1. one obtains:

Theorem 6.4.1.3. One can determine the joint convex layers of a set of n points in the plane in only O(n log^2 n) steps.

Another intriguing application of dynamic convex hull maintenance relates to the separability of sets of points in the plane. Two sets are said to be SEPARABLE if one can draw a straight line such that one set is entirely to its left, the other one entirely to its right. It is well-known that two sets are separable if and only if their convex-hulls are disjoint. As disjointness of two (properly represented) convex n-gons can be determined in O(log n) steps (Chazelle and Dobkin [ChD]), we obtain the following result:

Theorem 6.4.1.4. One can maintain two sets at the cost of O(log^2 n) per update such that separability can always be decided in O(log n) steps.

It is easy to represent the convex hull of a set of points in such a way that queries that ask whether a given point lies inside, on or outside the convex hull can be answered within O(log n) steps (see Theorem 2.6.5.). Using the results in this chapter, one easily shows:

Theorem 6.4.1.5. There exists a structure S for solving the two-dimensional convex hull searching problem such that

$$Q_S(n) = O(\log n),$$
$$I_S(n) = O(\log^2 n),$$
$$D_S(n) = O(\log^2 n),$$
$$M_S(n) = O(n).$$

The three-dimensional convex hull problem is O(n)-order decomposable due to Theorem 2.6.3. Hence we obtain:

Theorem 6.4.1.6. There exists a structure T for dynamically maintaining the convex hull of a three-dimensional point set at the cost of $O(n)$ per update, while the structure uses $O(n \log \log n)$ storage.

Concepts like peeling, convex layers and separability of sets can also be defined in three-dimensional space and similar results (with worse bounds) can be obtained by applying Theorem 6.4.1.6.

For three-dimensional convex hull searching one can obtain the following result:

Theorem 6.4.1.7. There exists a structure S for solving the three-dimensional convex hull searching problem such that

$$Q_S(n) = O(\log n),$$
$$I_S(n) = O(n),$$
$$I_S(n) = O(n),$$
$$M_S(n) = O(n \log \log n).$$

6.4.2. Common intersection of halfspaces.

Due to Theorem 2.7.1. the problem of computing the common intersection of a set of halfspaces in two dimensions is $O(\log n)$-order decomposable.

Theorem 6.4.2.1. There exists a structure T for dynamically maintaining the common intersection of a set of halfspaces in two dimensions at the cost of $O(\log^2 n)$ per update, while the structure uses only linear storage.

Again, there are a number of problems that can be solved using the computation of the common intersection of a set of planar halfspaces.

A LINEAR PROGRAM in n variables consists of a set of linear inequalities and a linear object function F, which must be minimized (or maximized) over the feasible region of points which satisfy all inequalities simultaneously. It is well-known that the feasable region is polyhedral and that (except in degenerated cases) F assumes its extreme values at the extreme points of the polyhedron. We observe that the feasible region is nothing but the common intersection of the set of halfspaces determined by the linear inequalities of the linear program. Hence, Theorem 6.4.2.1. shows:

Theorem 6.4.2.2. One can dynamically maintain the feasible region of a linear program in 2 variables at a cost of only $O(\log^2 n)$ steps for each inequality added or deleted, using only linear storage.

A second problem that can be solved using the common intersection of halfspaces is the kernel problem. One can compute the kernel of a polygon by determining the intersection of the halfspaces obtained by extending the edges of the polygon to infinity and considering the inside direction of each line as a halfspace.

Theorem 6.4.2.3. One can dynamically maintain the kernel of a simple polygon at a cost of only $O(\log^2 n)$ steps per transaction, assuming that transactions merely involve the insertion and/or deletion of some edges that keep the polygon simple.

The searching variant of the problem of finding the common intersection of a set of halfspaces in two-dimensional space can be solved as well using the techniques in this chapter. It yields a structure S such that
$$Q_S(n) = O(\log n),$$
$$I_S(n) = O(\log^2 n),$$
$$D_S(n) = O(\log^2 n),$$
$$M_S(n) = O(n).$$
Using a result of Brown [Br2] concerning the duality between convex hulls and common intersections of halfspaces, the problem of finding the intersection of a set of halfspaces in three dimensions is $O(n)$-order decomposable.

Theorem 6.4.2.4. There exists a structure T for dynamically maintaining the intersection of a set of halfspaces in three dimensions at the cost of $O(n)$ per update, using $O(n \log \log n)$ storage.

Related three-dimensional problems can be defined and treated in a similar way as in the two-dimensional case.

6.4.3. Maximal elements.

The maximal elements problem in two dimensions is order decomposable with $C(n) = O(\log n)$, due to Theorem 2.8.2. We immediately obtain:

Theorem 6.4.3.1. There exists a structure T for dynamically maintaining the maximal elements of a set of points in the plane at the cost of $O(\log^2 n)$ per update, using only linear storage.

One easily verifies that one can represent the maximal elements of a set in such a way that queries that ask whether a given point is maximal with respect to the set can be answered in $O(\log n)$ time. Hence the searching variant of the problem can be solved within a query time of $O(\log n)$, an update time of $O(\log^2 n)$ and $O(n)$ storage. (A direct solution to the maximal element searching problem, that does not maintain the set of maximal elements as such, yielding an update time of $O(\log n)$, was given by Lueker [Lu2].)

In the higher dimensional case one can use a trivial dynamization of the ECDF-counting problem to achieve $O(n)$ update time bounds for the maximal elements problem.

6.4.4. Union and intersection of segments on a line.

Due to Theorem 2.9.1. the problem of finding the union of a set of segments on a line is $O(\log n)$-order decomposable. Hence, we can apply Theorem 6.3.6. to dynamize the problem.

Theorem 6.4.4.1. There exists a structure T for dynamically maintaining the union of a set of segments on a line at the cost of $O(\log^2 n)$ per update, using linear storage.

The problem of maintaining the intersection of a set of segments on a line is even easier. Due to Theorem 2.9.3. the problem is $O(1)$-order decomposable.

Theorem 6.4.4.2. There exists a structure T for dynamically maintaining the intersection of a set of segments on a line at the cost of only $O(\log n)$ per update, using linear storage.

Searching variants can be treated similarly.

6.4.5. Voronoi diagrams.

One of the most interesting applications of the techniques presented in this chapter is the dynamization of Voronoi diagrams. Due to Theorem 2.5.1. the problem of computing the Voronoi diagram of a set of points in the plane is a $O(n)$-order decomposable set problem.

Theorem 6.4.5.1. There exists a structure T for dynamically maintaining the Voronoi diagram of a set of points in two-dimensional space at the cost of $O(n)$ per update, using $O(n \log \log n)$ storage.

Numerous problems can be solved using the Voronoi diagram (see Section 2.5.) and, applying Theorem 6.4.5.1., dynamic variants of these problems can now be solved efficiently as well.

A first application concerns the nearest neighbor searching problem. Theorem 2.5.3. shows that after each update, in another $O(n)$ steps we can represent the Voronoi diagram in such a way that nearest neighbor queries can be solved within $O(\log n)$ steps.

Theorem 6.4.5.2. There exists a dynamic structure S for solving the nearest neighbor searching problem, such that

$$Q_S(n) = O(\log n),$$
$$I_S(n) = O(n),$$
$$D_S(n) = O(n),$$
$$M_S(n) = O(n \log \log n).$$

Applying Theorem 2.5.5. one can solve the all closest points problem dynamically:

Theorem 6.4.5.3. One can dynamically maintain all closest pairs of points in a set of points in the plane at the cost of $O(n)$ per update.

The Voronoi diagram can also be used to obtain a minimum euclidean spanning tree (Theorem 2.5.6.).

Theorem 6.4.5.4. One can dynamically maintain a minimum euclidean spanning tree of a set of points at the cost of $O(n)$ per update.

By applying Theorem 2.5.7., we get:

Theorem 6.4.5.5. One can dynamically maintain a triangulation of a set of points in the plane at the cost of $O(n)$ per update.

A last application concerns the largest empty circle problem (Theorem 2.5.8.).

Theorem 6.4.5.6. One can dynamically maintain a largest empty circle with a centre within the convex hull of a set of points in the plane at the cost of $O(n)$ per update of the point set.

6.4.6. Views of line segments.

The problem of computing the view of a set of planar line segments in the plane from some fixed direction is $O(n)$-order decomposable, due to Theorem 2.10.1.

Theorem 6.4.6.1. There exists a structure T for dynamically maintaining the view from some fixed direction at the cost of $O(n)$ per update using $O(n \log \log n)$ storage.

Generalizations of the problem in which the set consists of simple objects rather than line segments and views are taken from points rather than from directions can be treated in a similar way (see Edelsbrunner, Overmars and Wood [EdOW]).

Bibliographical comments.

A first step in the direction of the general theory presented in this chapter, was made in Overmars and van Leeuwen [OvL2] (see also [OvL1]). The general framework was presented in Overmars [Ov2] from which also most of the examples are taken. A part of the theory was independently discovered by Gowda [Go] and Gowda and Kirkpatrick [GoK]. The method for decreasing the amount of storage required in Section 6.3. is a generalization of one of their observations.

CHAPTER VII

DECOMPOSABLE SEARCHING PROBLEMS

7.1. Introduction.

In the previous chapter we devised a general technique for obtaining dynamic
data structures for set problems that satisfy some decomposability constraint. In
this chapter we show how another (somewhat restricted) notion of decomposability can
be used for obtaining dynamic data structures from static structures for a class of
searching problems. The notion was introduced by Bentley [Be3]. He observed that one
does not need to keep all points of a set in one massive data structure as long as
it is possible to obtain the answer to a query over the total set out of the answers
to the same query over some partition of the set.

Definition 7.1.1. A searching problem PR is called DECOMPOSABLE if and only if for
any partition A∪B of the set V and any query object x, $PR(x,V) = \square(PR(x,A), PR(x,B))$
for some constant time computable operator $\square$.

For example, when we know whether x∈A and whether x∈B we can compute in $O(1)$ time
whether x ∈ V=A∪B using the or-function. Hence, the member searching problem is decomposable with $\square$=or. Another example is the nearest neighbor searching problem. Given
the point p in A nearest to x and the point p' in B nearest to x one clearly can compute the point in A∪B nearest to x in constant time as it is p or p'. Hence the nearest
neighbor searching problem is decomposable. Also the range searching problem is decomposable using $\square$=∪. (Note that, as A and B are disjoint, the answer sets over A and
B are disjoint and hence, the union operator takes only constant time to compute.)
Not all searching problems are decomposable. For instance, the convex hull searching
problem is not decomposable. Knowing whether a point x lies within the convex hull
of A and/or B does not tell us whether x lies within the convex hull of V.

For decomposable searching problems one need not store all points in one large
(static) data structure. Instead, the set can be maintained as a "dynamic system"
of disjoint subsets. Each subset is stored in a (static) data structure, called a
"block". Queries can be performed by querying the blocks separately and combining
the answers using the operator $\square$. The time required for combining the answers is
bounded by the number of blocks and is clearly overshadowed by the time required for
querying the blocks. Hence we can neglect it. Insertions are in general performed

by rebuilding some small blocks with the new point included. A deletion is performed
on the block the point belongs to (and in general will be weak). Observe that (i)
maintaining a large number of small blocks will lead to low update- and high query
times, while (ii) maintaining a small number of large blocks will lead to high update-
and low query times. Numerous methods have been proposed to decompose the set into
blocks and to maintain the partition when points are inserted or deleted, to try and
strike an "optimal" balance between the overhead required for processing updates and
queries. (See the bibliographical comments at the end of this chapter for a list of
the most important references.) There are two main methods for decomposing a set into
blocks: (i) the "equal block" method, that partitions the set into blocks of almost
the same size, and (ii) the "logarithmic" method, that partitions the set into blocks
of exponentially increasing sizes. The equal block method will be described in Section
7.2. It will yield in some sense optimal trade-offs between query- and deletion time,
but the insertion time can be rather bad. On the other hand, the logarithmic method,
as described in Sections 7.3. and 7.4. will yield optimal trade-offs between query-
and insertion time, while the deletion time can be rather bad. In Section 7.5. it
will be shown that both methods can be mixed to obtain a method with both optimal
insertion and deletion time bounds.

Some extensions of the methods are described as well. In Section 7.6. we show
that better deletion time bounds can be obtained for a restricted class of decomposable searching problems. In Section 7.7. we generalize the class of decomposable
searching problems to problems for which the "merging" of answers over subsets (by □)
takes more than $O(1)$ time.

Examples of the efficiency of the transforms will be given in all sections.

7.2. The equal block method.

The EQUAL BLOCK METHOD partitions the set V of n points in subsets $V_1,\ldots,V_i$
stored in (static) blocks $S_1,\ldots,S_i$ of almost equal size. This is only sensible when
i behaves as some function of n. For that purpose, let $f(n)$ be a smooth, nondecreasing integer function with $1 \leq f(n) \leq n$. We partition the set in blocks $S_1,\ldots,S_i$ such
that

(i) $f(\tfrac{1}{2}n) \leq i \leq f(2n)$, and

(ii) $\forall_{1 \leq j \leq i} \quad |S_j| \leq 2n/i$,

where $|S_j|$ denotes the number of points contained in S_j. Queries are answered by que-
rying each of the i blocks and composing the answers using □. An insertion is performed
by inserting the point in the smallest block. (As the blocks are statically structured,
this in general consists of rebuilding the complete block.) A deletion is performed
by deleting the point from the block it belongs to. (Again this in general consists

of rebuilding the complete block. But for some data structures good deletion methods exist while insertions cannot be performed efficiently. For example in quad-trees deletions take only $O(\log n)$ worst-case time while insertions take $O(\log^2 N)$ average time. See Section 5.3.2.) When constraints (i) or (ii) are violated after an update has taken place and V now has a total of n_0 points, the whole partition is built anew with $i=f(n_0)$ and $|S_j| = \lceil n_0/i \rceil$ for $j<i$ and $|S_i| = n_0-(i-1)\lceil n_0/i \rceil \leq \lceil n_0/i \rceil$. Note that this gives the blocks a considerable amount of leeway before one of the constraints will be violated again. Thus the work needed to reconfigure V will not have to be spent often. Assuming that the time required to build a static structure (a block) of n points is bounded by $P_S(n)$, the time required to reconfigure V is bounded by

$$i.P_S(n_0/i) = n_0.P_S(n_0/i)\big/n_0/i \leq \text{(because } P_S \text{ is at least linear)}$$
$$\leq n_0.P_S(n_0)/n_0 = P_S(n_0).$$

We will show that at least $\frac{1}{2}n_0$ updates must have taken place since the latest reconfiguration before another reconfiguration is needed, and hence, that the average time per update needed for performing reconfigurations is bounded by $O(P_S(n)/n)$.

Suppose V contained n_1 points the last time it was reconfigured. (Possibly $n_1=0$ when V was not reconfigured before.) As an insertion is always performed in the smallest block, it can never violate constraint (ii). Hence, there is only one case in which a reconfiguration is needed after an insertion.

Case I: $i<f(\frac{1}{2}n_0)$. As $i=f(n_1)$ we have $f(n_1)<f(\frac{1}{2}n_0) \Rightarrow n_1<\frac{1}{2}n_0$ (because f is non-decreas­ing) $\Rightarrow n_0>2n_1$. Thus at least $n_0-n_1>\frac{1}{2}n_0$ insertions must have taken place since the latest reconfiguration.

It follows that the average reconfiguration time per insertion is bounded by $2P_S(n)/n$. There are two cases in which a deletion can cause a constraint to be violated:

Case II: $i>f(2n_0)$. Hence $f(n_1)>f(2n_0) \Rightarrow n_1>2n_0 \Rightarrow n_0<\frac{1}{2}n_1$. Thus at least $\frac{1}{2}n_1>n_0$ deletions must have taken place after the latest reconfiguration.

Case III: $|S_j|>2n_0/i$, some j. Note that insertions always take place in the blocks of smallest size and that such blocks must have size $\leq n/i$ (n the current number of points in the set). It follows that a block can only violate the size constraint as the result of many deletions that take place in other blocks. Suppose V had n' points when the last insertion took place on S_j. (Take $n'=n_1$ if there were no insertions on S_j.) At that moment $|S_j|\leq n'/i$ and $|S_j|$ can only have shrunk since. Hence $2n_0/i<|S_j|\leq n'/i \Rightarrow$ $\Rightarrow 2n_0<n' \Rightarrow n_0<\frac{1}{2}n'$. Thus at least $\frac{1}{2}n'>n_0$ deletions must have taken place.

It follows that the average reconfiguration time per deletion is bounded by $P_S(n)/n$.

Theorem 7.2.1. Given a (static) data structure S for a decomposable searching problem PR and a smooth non-decreasing integer function f with $1 \leq f(n) \leq n$, there exists a structure S' for PR such that

$$Q_{S'}(n) = O(f(n) \cdot Q_S(n/f(n))),$$

$$I_{S'}^a(n) = O(\log n + P_S(n)/n + I_S(n/f(n))),$$

$$D_{S'}^a(n) = O(\log n + P_S(n)/n + D_S(n/f(n))),$$

$$M_{S'}(n) = O(f(n) \cdot M_S(n/f(n))).$$

Proof

To perform a query we need to query at most $f(2n)$ blocks, each of size at most $2n/f(\frac{1}{2}n)$. Because both f and Q_S are smooth and non-decreasing the amount of time is clearly bounded by $O(f(n) \cdot Q_S(n/f(n)))$. The amount of work needed to combine the answers is bounded by $O(f(n))$.

To perform an insertion we first have to locate the smallest block. This can be done in $O(\log f(n)) = O(\log n)$ steps. Next we insert the new point in a dictionary DICT in which we keep with each point the block it is in because we need this information when we want to delete a point. This also takes $O(\log n)$. Inserting the new point in the appropriate block takes at most $I_S(2n/f(\frac{1}{2}n))$ which is $O(I_S(n/f(n)))$ time. Performing reconfigurations adds an average of $O(P_S(n)/n)$ to the bound on the insertion time.

To perform a deletion we first locate the block the point is in using DICT and delete the point from DICT. This takes $O(\log n)$ time. Next we delete the point from the appropriate block, which takes at most $D_S(2n/f(\frac{1}{2}n)) = O(D_S(n/f(n)))$ time. Performing reconfigurations adds an average of $O(P_S(n)/n)$ to the bound.

$\square$

As S is a static structure, in general both $I_S(n)$ and $D_S(n)$ are $\theta(P_S(n))$.

Before giving examples of the efficiency of the method we will show that the averages for insertion and deletion time can be changed into worst-case bounds. We do not do this by working on the individual blocks, but by an application of the global rebuilding technique (Theorem 5.2.2.1.). Assume we perform αn deletions ($\alpha < 1$) and βn insertions on a structure that has just been reconfigured, in the same way as described above but without performing a reconfiguration when one of the constraints is violated which we thus no longer enforce strictly. One immediately verifies that the query time on the resulting structure of $m = (1+\beta-\alpha)n$ points is bounded by

$$f(n) \cdot Q_S((1+\beta)n/f(n)) \leq \text{ (because f is smooth)}$$

$$\leq k_{\alpha\beta} f(m) \cdot Q_S(\frac{1+\beta}{1+\beta-\alpha} m/k_{\alpha\beta} f(m)) \leq \text{ (because } Q_S \text{ is smooth)}$$

$$\leq k_{\alpha\beta} f(m) \cdot k'_{\alpha\beta} Q_S(m/f(m)) = k''_{\alpha\beta} f(m) \cdot Q_S(m/f(m)),$$

for suitable constants $k_{\alpha\beta}$, $k'_{\alpha\beta}$ and $k''_{\alpha\beta}$. Similar results can be obtained for the insertion and deletion time. It follows that updates without reconfigurations are weak. Hence we can apply Theorem 5.2.2.1. to obtain the following result:

Theorem 7.2.2. Given a (static) data structure S for a decomposable searching problem PR and a smooth, non-decreasing integer function f with $1 \leq f(n) \leq n$, there exists a structure S' for PR such that

$$Q_{S'}(n) = O(f(n) \cdot Q_S(n/f(n))),$$
$$I_{S'}(n) = O(\log n + P_S(n)/n + I_S(n/f(n))),$$
$$D_{S'}(n) = O(\log n + P_S(n)/n + D_S(n/f(n))),$$
$$M_{S'}(n) = O(f(n) \cdot M_S(n/f(n))).$$

Proof

From the above discussion it follows that $WI_{S'}(n) = O(\log n + I_S(n/f(n)))$ and $WD_{S'}(n) = O(\log n + D_S(n/f(n)))$. The bounds on query time and amount of storage required follow from Theorem 7.2.1. Applying Theorem 5.2.2.1. yields the result stated.

□

Applications.

a) Nearest neighbor searching.

As proven in Theorem 6.4.5.2., there exists a dynamic data structure S for the nearest neighbor searching problem such that

$$Q_S(n) = O(\log n),$$
$$I_S(n) = O(n),$$
$$D_S(n) = O(n).$$

Applying Theorem 7.2.2. with $f(n) = \lceil \sqrt{n}/\sqrt{\log n} \rceil$, we obtain the following result:

Theorem 7.2.3. There exists a structure S' for the nearest neighbor searching problem such that

$$Q_S(n) = O(\sqrt{n \log n}),$$
$$I_S(n) = O(\sqrt{n \log n}),$$
$$D_S(n) = O(\sqrt{n \log n}).$$

b) Common intersection of halfspaces.

Consider the searching variant of the 3-dimensional intersection of halfspaces problem. It asks whether a given point x lies within the common intersection of a set of 3-dimensional halfspaces. One immediately verifies that the problem is decomposable with $\square = \wedge$. From Theorem 6.4.2.4. it follows that there exists a structure S for the searching problem such that

$$Q_S(n) = O(\log n),$$
$$I_S(n) = O(n),$$
$$D_S(n) = O(n).$$

Applying Theorem 7.2.2. with $f(n) = \lceil \sqrt{n}/\sqrt{\log n} \rceil$, we obtain the following result:

Theorem 7.2.4. There exists a structure S' for determining whether a given point lies in the common intersection of a set of 3-dimensional halfspaces such that

$$Q_{S'}(n) = O(\sqrt{n \log n}),$$
$$I_{S'}(n) = O(\sqrt{n \log n}),$$
$$D_{S'}(n) = O(\sqrt{n \log n}).$$

7.3. The logarithmic method.

In this section we describe another way of dynamizing static data structures for decomposable searching problems based on a partition of the set of points into blocks of exponentially increasing sizes rather than equal sizes. In Subsection 7.3.1. we describe Bentley's [Be3] method that yields good average insertion time bounds. In Subsection 7.3.2. we turn the average bounds into worst-case bounds and in Subsection 7.3.3. we show how deletions can be performed as well.

7.3.1. Average bounds.

To transform a static data structure S for a decomposable searching problem PR into a dynamic data structure, yielding good average insertion time bounds, we split the set of points V into disjoint subsets $V_0, V_1, \ldots$, such that for each i $|V_i| = 2^i$ or V_i is empty. For example, when $n = |V| = 26$, V_1, V_3 and V_4 are filled. For each non-empty V_i we build a static structure S_i containing the 2^i points in V_i. So, in our example we have three blocks, S_1, S_3 and S_4. To insert a point in the configuration in our example we only have to build a block S_0 and we are done (see figure 7.3.1.1.). Performing a second insertion is less easy, because we already have a S_0. We have to discard S_0 and S_1 and build a S_2 out of the new point and the points from S_0 and S_1. In general, to insert a point p in the dynamic structure, we

    (i) locate the smallest i with $V_i = \emptyset$,
    (ii) discard $S_0, \ldots, S_{i-1}$,
    (iii) build S_i out of p and the points from $S_0, \ldots, S_{i-1}$.

It is clear that some insertions will take a lot of time (when i is big and we have to build a large structure) but, as after such an insertion all preceding S-structures are empty again, the average insertion time will remain low.

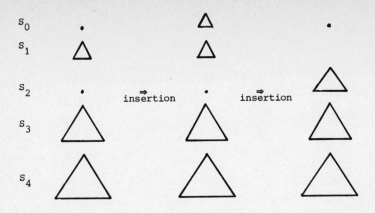

S_0 · △ ·

S_1 △ △

S_2 · insertion ⇒ · insertion ⇒ △

S_3 △ △ △

S_4 △ △ △

figure 7.3.1.1.

Theorem 7.3.1.1. Given a (static) data structure S for de decomposable searching problem PR, there exists a structure S' for PR such that

$$Q_{S'}(n) = \begin{cases} O(Q_S(n)) & \text{when } Q_S(n) = \Omega(n^\varepsilon), \text{ some } \varepsilon > 0, \\ O(\log n)Q_S(n) & \text{otherwise,} \end{cases}$$

$$I^a_{S'}(n) = \begin{cases} O(P_S(n)/n) & \text{when } P_S(n) = \Omega(n^{1+\varepsilon}), \text{ some } \varepsilon > 0, \\ O(\log n)P_S(n)/n & \text{otherwise,} \end{cases}$$

$$M_{S'}(n) = O(M_S(n)).$$

Proof

When the size of the set is n, the biggest i for which S_i is filled is $i = \lfloor \log n \rfloor$.
Hence the answer to a query over the total set can be derived in $O(\log n)$ time from
the answers to the query over each S_j, $0 \le j \le \lfloor \log n \rfloor$. A query over a single S_j takes
(at most) $Q_S(2^j)$ time. Hence, the total query time can be estimated as

$$Q_{S'}(n) \le \sum_{j=0}^{\lfloor \log n \rfloor} Q_S(2^j) + O(\log n).$$

This clearly leads to $Q_{S'}(n) = O(Q_S(n))$ when $Q_S(n) = \Omega(n^\varepsilon)$ for some $\varepsilon > 0$ and to
$Q_{S'}(n) = O(\log n)Q_S(n)$ otherwise.

To estimate the average insertion time, notice that when we build a block S_j,
all its points come from lower indexed blocks. Hence each point in the set has been
built at most once into each block S_j with $0 \le j \le \lfloor \log n \rfloor$. Dividing the costs for building a block S_j over the points it is built from makes for $P_S(2^j)/2^j$ per point. Hence
the total amount of time charged to an insertion is bounded by

$$\sum_{j=0}^{\lfloor \log n \rfloor} P_S(2^j)/2^j.$$

It follows that $I^a_{S'}(n) = O(P_S(n)/n)$ when $P_S(n) = \Omega(n^{1+\varepsilon})$ for some $\varepsilon > 0$ and that
$I^a_{S'}(n) = O(\log n)P_S(n)/n$ otherwise.

Because $M_S(n)$ is at least linear, the total amount of storage needed is bounded by

$$M_{S'}(n) \leq \sum_{j=0}^{\lfloor \log n \rfloor} M_S(2^j) \leq \left(\sum_{j=0}^{\lfloor \log n \rfloor} \frac{2^{\lfloor \log n \rfloor}}{2^{\lfloor \log n \rfloor - j}} \right) \cdot M_S(2^{\lfloor \log n \rfloor}) / 2^{\lfloor \log n \rfloor} \leq 2 M_S(n).$$

$\square$

One easily verifies that $P_{S'}(n) = O(P_S(n))$.

7.3.2. Worst-case bounds.

To achieve a worst-case bound on the insertion time, rather than an average bound, one cannot afford to do all constructions at once. Instead of building a new structure out of old structures at the moment this is needed, the work must be spread over a number of insertions to follow. Meanwhile the old structures remain in use for query answering.

To this end we have to modify the dynamic system of static data structures described in the previous subsection. Our new dynamic structure consists of bags BA_0, $BA_1, \ldots$. Each bag BA_i contains at most three blocks $S_i^u[1]$, $S_i^u[2]$ and $S_i^u[3]$ of size 2^i that are "in use" (i.e., available for query answering). Moreover each BA_i with $i>0$ contains at most one block S_i^c that is "under construction" and will become of size 2^i. To maintain the structure correctly, we have to guarantee that each point in the set is always in exactly one block in use, and that each bag will never get more than three blocks in use.

We keep the number of blocks in a bag BA_i from becoming too large in the following way. As soon as a second S_i^u becomes available in BA_i, we "take the two S_i^u's together" and start building S_{i+1}^c of 2^{i+1} points in BA_{i+1} out of them. (See figure 7.3.2.1.) The

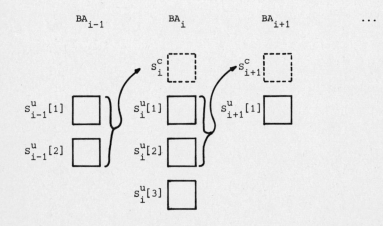

figure 7.3.2.1.

work is spread over the next 2^{i+1} insertions, each time doing $P_S(2^{i+1})/2^{i+1}$ steps of the construction. As long as the construction of s_{i+1}^c is not completed, $s_i^u[1]$ and $s_i^u[2]$ remain in use for query answering. After the 2^{i+1} insertions s_{i+1}^c will be ready and is made into a s_{i+1}^u "in use". The $s_i^u[1]$ and $s_i^u[2]$ are now no longer needed and are discarded. During the construction a third s_i^u may get into BA_i, but by the time a fourth would come in, the construction of s_{i+1}^c is completed and two s_i^u's are discarded and (hence) BA_i will have room again for storing the s_i^u. It becomes the second block in BA_i and hence we have to start constructing a s_{i+1}^c again. This is legitimate because the previous s_{i+1}^c was just finished (see the lemma's below).

We will now give a more formal description of the insertion procedure we use. For each bag BA_i we maintain the following information:

$s_i^u[1..3]$: the blocks in use of size 2^i,

s_i^c : the block under construction,

$work_i$: the number of steps we have done on building s_i^c.

The procedure INSERT takes care of all actions that need be performed when we want to insert a new point in the set.

procedure INSERT (point p);
p is the new point that has to be inserted.

    step 1: Repeat Steps 2-3 for all filled bags BA_i, starting at the highest indexed bag down to BA_1.

    step 2: If we are busy building s_i^c, do $P_S(2^i)/2^i$ work on its construction. $work_i := work_i+1$.

    step 3: If $work_i$ has become 2^i, s_i^c is finished and has to become in use. Hence, turn s_i^c in a s_i^u, empty s_i^c and discard $s_{i-1}^u[1]$ and $s_{i-1}^u[2]$. Shift $s_{i-1}^u[3]$ to $s_{i-1}^u[1]$ and set $work_i := 0$. If the new block is the second block in BA_i start constructing s_{i+1}^c out of the two blocks in BA_i.

    step 4: Build a s_0^u structure out of the new point p. If this is the second block in BA_0, start constructing s_1^c.

end of INSERT;

The following lemma's show the correctness of the insertion method presented.

Lemma 7.3.2.1. Every point p in the set is always contained in exactly one block in use.

Proof

When we insert p it is built in one s_0^u. p can only disappear when we throw the s_i^u it is part of away. But we do so only at the same moment we start using a larger block p is part of. p can never become part of more than one block in use because, when we start using a new block that contains p, the old block in use containing p is thrown away.

$\square$

Lemma 7.3.2.2. Each block in BA_i contains (or will contain) 2^i points.

Proof

Blocks in BA_0 are built from one point and blocks in BA_i are built out of the points in two blocks in BA_{i-1}. Hence, by induction, the result follows.

$\square$

Lemma 7.3.2.3. When $s_i^u[2]$ becomes present, s_{i+1}^c is empty.

Proof

When s_{i+1}^c is not empty, $s_i^u[1]$ and $s_i^u[2]$ are filled. Hence no new $s_i^u[2]$ can appear.

$\square$

Lemma 7.3.2.4. BA_i never contains more than three blocks in use.

Proof

At the moment BA_i gets a second block in use, we start building s_{i+1}^c. BA_i got a second block in use because s_i^c was turned into $s_i^u[2]$. Hence at this moment s_i^c is empty. It will take at least 2^i insertions before another s_i^c is completed and turned into $s_i^u[3]$. After another 2^i insertions yet another s_i^c may be ready and we would like to turn it into a block in use. But at this very moment (i.e., after 2^{i+1} insertions) s_{i+1}^c is also ready and is just made into a s_{i+1}^u while $s_i^u[1]$ and $s_i^u[2]$ are thrown away, because bags are treated in decreasing order. Hence, there is room again in BA_i.

$\square$

The following theorem shows the efficiency of the method described.

Theorem 7.3.2.5. Given a (static) data structure S for a decomposable searching problem PR, there exists a structure S' for PR such that

$$Q_{S'}(n) = \begin{cases} O(Q_S(n)) & \text{when } Q_S(n) = \Omega(n^\varepsilon), \text{ some } \varepsilon > 0, \\ O(\log n)Q_S(n) & \text{otherwise,} \end{cases}$$

$$I_{S'}(n) = \begin{cases} O(P_S(n)/n) & \text{when } P_S(n) = \Omega(n^{1+\varepsilon}), \text{ some } \varepsilon>0, \\ O(\log n)P_S(n)/n & \text{otherwise}, \end{cases}$$

$$M_{S'}(n) = O(M_S(n)).$$

<u>Proof</u>

We use the structure and insertion method described above. Let us consider the query time first. To query S' we have to query all filled blocks in use. One immediately verifies that $BA_{\lfloor \log n \rfloor +1}$ and all higher indexed bags do not contain a block in use. It follows that the query time can be estimated as

$$Q_{S'}(n) \leq 3 \cdot \sum_{i=0}^{\lfloor \log n \rfloor} Q_S(2^i) + O(\log n).$$

This clearly leads to $Q_{S'}(n) = O(Q_S(n))$ when $Q_S(n) = \Omega(n^{\varepsilon})$ for some $\varepsilon>0$ and to $Q_{S'}(n) = O(\log n)Q_S(n)$ otherwise.

To perform an insertion we have to do $P_S(2^i)/2^i$ work in every bag BA_i containing a block under construction. Clearly $BA_{\lfloor \log n \rfloor +1}$ and all higher indexed bags do not contain a block under construction. Hence, the insertion time is bounded by

$$I_{S'}(n) \leq \sum_{i=0}^{\lfloor \log n \rfloor} P_S(2^i)/2^i + O(\log n).$$

It follows that $I_{S'}(n) = O(P_S(n)/n)$ when $P_S(n) = \Omega(n^{1+\varepsilon})$ for some $\varepsilon>0$, and that $I_{S'}(n) = O(\log n)P_S(n)/n$ otherwise.

The amount of storage required is clearly bounded by

$$M_{S'}(n) \leq 4 \cdot \sum_{i=0}^{\lfloor \log n \rfloor} M_S(2^i) \leq 8 \cdot M_S(n),$$

which follows in the same way as in the proof of Theorem 7.3.1.1.

□

One immediately verifies that $P_{S'}(n) = O(P_S(n))$. It follows that the bounds of Theorem 7.3.1.1. are even valid as worst-case bounds.

7.3.3. <u>Supporting deletions</u>.

Assume our (static) data structure S supports (weak) deletions. We would like to be able to delete points in the transformed structure S' as well. In the structure yielding average insertion time bounds, as described in Subsection 7.3.1., deletions can be performed quite easily. To delete a point p, we first have to locate the block S_i the point is in. To this end we add to the structure a dictionary DICT in which we keep with each point currently in the set, the index of the block it is in. Updating and searching in DICT clearly takes only $O(\log n)$. When we have located the block p is in we just delete the point. This takes at most $D_S(n)$ time. In this way, the future query and update time do not increase. Hence, we have performed a weak deletion. It follows that $WD_{S'}(n) = O(\log n + D_S(n))$.

Theorem 7.3.3.1. Given a data structure S for a decomposable searching problem PR, there exists a structure S' for PR, such that

$$Q_{S'}(n) = \begin{cases} O(Q_S(n)) & \text{when } Q_S(n) = \Omega(n^\varepsilon), \text{ some } \varepsilon > 0, \\ O(\log n)Q_S(n) & \text{otherwise,} \end{cases}$$

$$I_{S'}^a(n) = \begin{cases} O(P_S(n)/n) & \text{when } P_S(n) = \Omega(n^{1+\varepsilon}), \text{ some } \varepsilon > 0, \\ O(\log n)P_S(n)/n & \text{otherwise,} \end{cases}$$

$$D_{S'}(n) = O(\log n + D_S(n) + P_S(n)/n),$$

$$M_{S'}(n) = O(M_S(n)).$$

Proof

This follows from Theorem 7.3.1.1., Theorem 5.2.2.1. and the above discussion.

□

In the structure described in Subsection 7.3.2. yielding worst-case insertion time bounds, weak deletions cannot be performed that easy. One can delete the point from the appropriate block in use but it is possible that we are also busy building the point into a block under construction. In general, one cannot delete points from blocks under construction. Hence, we have to buffer the deletion until the block is finished and perform the deletion afterwards. This can be done in a way, very similar to the method presented in the proof of Theorem 5.2.2.1. To each block under construction S_i^c we add a buffer BUF_i to store deletions that must be performed after the construction is finished. When we start building S_i^c, BUF_i is empty. With each insertion we do $P_S(2^i)/2^i$ work on the construction of S_i^c or, when S_i^c is finished and BUF_i is not yet empty, we do $P_S(2^i)/2^i$ work on performing buffered deletions. To guarantee that S_i^c is ready and BUF_i is empty after 2^i insertions, any time we put a deletion in BUF_i which should eventually be performed on S_i^c, we speed up the construction of S_i^c by doing $D_S(2^i)$ steps of work on the construction (or on performing deletions from BUF_i, when S_i^c is finished). Hence, performing a weak deletion of a point p in S' consists of

(i) locating the block in use S_i^u and possible block under construction S_{i+1}^c p is in, using a dictionary DICT,

(ii) updating DICT,

(iii) deleting p from the block in use,

(iv) putting p in BUF_{i+1},

(v) doing $D_S(2^{i+1})$ work on the construction of S_{i+1}^c.

This clearly maintains the dynamic structure S' correctly. (There is one problem. We assumed in the previous subsection that throwing structures away could be done in O(1) time. This is no longer the case, because we have to update DICT when we do so. To this end we include the time needed to update DICT in the building time $P_S(n)$. As this amount of time is bounded by O(n), $P_S(n)$ does not change in order of magnitude.) It follows that $WD_{S'}(n) = O(\log n + D_S(n))$.

<u>Theorem</u> 7.3.3.2. Given a data structure S for a decomposable searching problem PR, there exists a structure S' for PR such that

$$Q_{S'}(n) = \begin{cases} O(Q_S(n)) & \text{when } Q_S(n) = \Omega(n^\varepsilon), \text{ some } \varepsilon>0, \\ O(\log n)Q_S(n) & \text{otherwise,} \end{cases}$$

$$I_{S'}(n) = \begin{cases} O(P_S(n)/n) & \text{when } P_S(n) = \Omega(n^{1+\varepsilon}), \text{ some } \varepsilon>0, \\ O(\log n)P_S(n)/n & \text{otherwise,} \end{cases}$$

$$D_{S'}(n) = O(\log n + D_S(n) + P_S(n)/n),$$

$$M_{S'}(n) = O(M_S(n)).$$

<u>Proof</u>

This follows from Theorem 7.3.2.5., Theorem 5.2.2.1. and the above discussion.

□

7.3.4. <u>Applications</u>.

Let us consider some applications of the method described in this section.

a) Range searching.

The super B-tree, used to solve the d-dimensional range searching problems allows for (weak) deletions in time $D_S(n) = O(\log^{d-1} n)$. As $Q_S(n) = O(\log^d n)$ and $P_S(n) = O(n \log^{d-1} n)$, we can dynamize the structure, using Theorem 7.3.3.2., yielding a structure S' with

$$Q_{S'}(n) = O(\log^{d+1} n) \quad (\text{+ the number of reported answers}),$$
$$I_{S'}(n) = O(\log^d n),$$
$$D_{S'}(n) = O(\log^{d-1} n).$$

This is not the best possible result for range searching (compare Theorem 5.3.3.1.) but the method is much less complex and follows by applying a general technique.

b) Nearest neighbor searching.

By Theorem 6.4.5.2. there exists a structure S for solving the nearest neighbor searching problem yielding $Q_S(n) = O(\log n)$, $I_S(n) = O(n)$ and $D_S(n) = O(n)$. It is immediate to verify that $P_S(n) = O(n \log n)$. Applying Theorem 7.3.3.2., we obtain the following result:

<u>Theorem</u> 7.3.4.1. There exists a structure S' for the nearest neighbor searching problem such that

$$Q_{S'}(n) = O(\log^2 n),$$
$$I_{S'}(n) = O(\log^2 n),$$
$$D_{S'}(n) = O(n),$$
$$M_{S'}(n) = O(n \log \log n).$$

c) Common intersection of halfspaces.

Consider the searching problem that asks whether a given point lies in the common intersection of a set of three-dimensional halfspaces. For this problem a data structure S exists yielding $Q_S(n) = O(\log n)$, $P_S(n) = O(n \log n)$, $I_S(n) = D_S(n) = O(n)$. Applying Theorem 7.3.3.2. yields a structure S' with

$$Q_{S'}(n) = O(\log^2 n),$$
$$I_{S'}(n) = O(\log^2 n),$$
$$D_{S'}(n) = O(n),$$
$$M_{S'}(n) = O(n \log \log n).$$

7.4. A general, optimal insertion method.

In this section we will show how other - in fact, all optimal - trade-offs between query time and insertion time can be obtained using other ways of partitioning the set. Transformations from static to half-dynamic data structures, yielding average insertion time bounds, adhere to the following principles:

(i) A set V is represented by static data structures S_i for each subset V_i, $0 \leq i \leq r$ in some partition of V.

(ii) A query over V is performed by first querying the blocks S_i and afterwards combining the answers using the composition operator □.

(iii) An insertion of a new point p is processed by selecting some blocks S_{i_1}, ...,S_{i_s}, throwing these data structures away and constructing a new static data structure out of the points in $V_{i_1}, \ldots, V_{i_s}$ and the new point p.

The performance of a transformation is measured by two quantities: the query penalty factor qpf(n) and the update penalty factor upf(n). Let r_i be the number of blocks in the partition of the set V after the ith insertion and let m_i be the size of the subset for which a static block is built with the ith insertion (as described in (iii) above). Then

$$qpf(n) = \max\{r_i \; ; \; 1 \leq i \leq n\},$$
$$upf(n) = \sum_{i=1}^{n} m_i/n.$$

The names for quantities qpf(n) and upf(n) are justified by the observation that
qpf(n).Q_S(n) bounds the query time for the dynamic structure and that upf(n).P_S(n)/n
is a bound for the average insertion time, because the total time required for building structures during the first n insertions is bounded by

$$\sum_{i=1}^{n} P_S(m_i) = \sum_{i=1}^{n} m_i P_S(m_i)/m_i \leq$$

$$\leq \sum_{i=1}^{n} m_i P_S(n)/n =$$

$$= upf(n).P_S(n).$$

The pair (qpf(n), upf(n)) is called the characteristic of the transformation.

Lowerbounds on the efficiency of transformations were shown by Saxe and Bentley
[SaB] and Mehlhorn [Me]. Mehlhorn [Me] proved the following relation between the query
penalty factor and the update penalty factor:

Theorem 7.4.1.([Me]) There exists a constant c>0 such that for any transformation
with characteristic (qpf(n), upf(n)):

$$upf(n) \leq \begin{cases} c.\log n/\log(qpf(n)/\log n) & \text{when } qpf(n) > 2\log n, \\ c.qpf(n).n^{1/qpf(n)} & \text{when } qpf(n) \leq 2\log n. \end{cases}$$

In this section we will give general transformation schemes that will obtain the bounds
stated in Theorem 7.4.1. (up to some constant factor). It shows that the bounds in
Theorem 7.4.1. are sharp. In Subsection 7.4.1. we will show how these bounds can be
obtained with average insertion times. In Subsection 7.4.2. we show how the average
bound can be turned into a worst-case bound. In Subsection 7.4.3. we consider the problem of performing deletions as well.

We will assume that both qpf(n) and upf(n) are smooth.

7.4.1. Average bounds.

We will describe two general methods of dynamization: method A and B. Method A
will be used for transformations with low query penalty factor and high update penalty
factor and method B will be used for transformations with high query penalty factor
and low update penalty factor. We will describe method A first. Let g(n) be a smooth,
nondecreasing integer function with 0 < g(n) = O(log n). Let

$$b = \left\lceil n^{1/g(n)} \right\rceil.$$

Let $n = \sum_{j \geq 0} a_j.b^j$, where $0 \leq a_j < b$, $a_j \in \mathbb{N}$. Although b depends on n we will fix its value
over the range of a certain number of insertions that increment n.

Method A.

The structure consists of blocks S_j, $j \geq 0$, such that $|S_j| = a_j.b^j$. (Clearly, we
do not actually store empty blocks.) A block S_j is called completely filled if it

contains $(b-1)b^j$ points. A weak insertion is carried out in the following way:

    (i) locate the smallest block S_j that is not completely filled, i.e., $a_j < b-1$,

    (ii) discard all blocks $S_0, \ldots, S_{j-1}$ (which must be completely filled by the choice of j),

    (iii) build a new structure S_j of $(a_j+1)b^j$ points out of the points in $S_0, \ldots, S_{j-1}$, the new point and the points that are already in S_j. (Note that $|S_0|+|S_1|+\ldots+|S_{j-1}|+1 = 1 + \sum_{i=0}^{j-1}(b-1)b^i = b^j$, which shows that this step is correct.)

Such an insertion is weak because we do not adjust the value of b, which is a function of the number of points in the set. We will show below that this does not influence the query time too drastically, i.e., that it is indeed a weak insertion.

    To estimate the query penalty factor we will prove a bound on the number of non-empty blocks at the moment the structure contains n points (and no weak insertions have been performed on it). A block S_j can only be non-empty when

$$|S_j| \leq n$$
$$\Rightarrow b^j \leq n$$
$$\Rightarrow j \leq \log_b n$$
$$\Rightarrow j \leq \frac{\log n}{\log\lceil n^{1/g(n)}\rceil}$$
$$\Rightarrow j \leq \frac{\log n}{\log(n^{1/g(n)})}$$
$$\Rightarrow j \leq \frac{\log n}{(1/g(n)) \cdot \log n}$$
$$\Rightarrow j \leq g(n)$$

Hence, the number of blocks is bounded by $g(n)+1$. As $g(n)$ is nondecreasing it follows that $qpf(n) = O(g(n))$.

    Before estimating the insertion time we will show that insertions performed in the way described above are indeed weak. We choose to perform a clean-up of the structure after n_0 insertions have occurred, where n_0 is the size of the structure at the latest reconstruction (i.e., we choose β in Definition 5.1.1. to be 1). Let $\beta' n_0$ ($\beta' < 1$) insertions have been performed since the latest clean-up. b is still equal to $\lceil n_0^{1/g(n_0)} \rceil$. Hence a block S_j can be non-empty if

$$j \leq \frac{\log(1+\beta)n_0}{\log(n_0^{1/g(n_0)})}$$
$$\Rightarrow j \leq g(n_0)\frac{\log(1+\beta)n_0}{\log n_0}$$
$$\Rightarrow j \leq c \cdot g(n_0) \text{ for some constant c.}$$

As $g(n)$ is nondecreasing the number of structures is bounded by $c \cdot g(n)+1$, where n is the current number of points in the set ($n=(1+\beta)n_0$). Hence, the query time is increased by no more than a constant factor.

Let the weak update penalty factor $wupf(n) = \sum_{i=1}^{n} m_i/n$ where m_i is the size of the block built after the ith weak update when the building of the block is not the result of a clean-up. To estimate the weak insertion time we first consider the sum of the sizes of blocks built in between two successive clean-ups. Let n_0 be the size of the set at the first of these two clean-ups and, hence, $2n_0$ be the size at the second clean-up (as we did choose $\beta=1$). During this period of time $b = \lceil n_0^{1/g(n_0)} \rceil$. Note that each point is built at most b times into each of the blocks S_j and that each block will have size at most $2n_0$. As the number of blocks is bounded by $c.g(n_0)+1$ as shown above, the total size of blocks built is bounded by

$$\lceil n_0^{1/g(n_0)} \rceil . (c.g(n_0)+1).2n_0 \leq c'.n_0^{1/g(n_0)}.g(n_0).n_0$$

for some constant c'. It follows that

$$wupf(n) \leq \sum_{i=0}^{\lfloor \log n \rfloor} (c'.(2^i)^{1/g(2^i)}.g(2^i).2^i)/n$$

$$= O(n^{1/g(n)}.g(n))$$

using the fact that $n^{1/g(n)} = 2^{\log n/g(n)}$ is nondecreasing (as $g(n) = O(\log n)$).

Theorem 7.4.1.1. For each smooth, nondecreasing query penalty factor $qpf(n) = O(\log n)$, there exists a transformation with characteristic $(\theta(qpf(n)), upf(n))$, where

$$upf(n) = O(qpf(n).n^{1/qpf(n)}).$$

Proof

Follows from the above discussion, taking $qpf(n)$ for $g(n)$ and noting that applying Theorem 5.2.1.1. adds only $O(1)$ to the weak update penalty factor, i.e., $upf(n) = O(wupf(n))$.

□

The following table shows some possible choices for $qpf(n)$ and the resulting $upf(n)$.

	qpf(n)	upf(n)
a	$O(\log n)$	$O(\log n)$
b	$O(c)$, c constant	$O(c.\sqrt[c]{n})$
c	$O(\frac{\log n}{\log \log n})$	$O(\frac{\log^2 n}{\log \log n})$
d	$O(\sqrt{\log n})$	$O(2^{\sqrt{\log n}} \sqrt{\log n})$

We will now describe method B. Let $g'(n)$ be a smooth, nondecreasing integer function with $0 < g'(n) = O(\log n)$. Let $b = \left\lceil n^{1/g'(n)} \right\rceil$ and let $n = \sum_{j \geq 0} a_j b^j$, where $0 \leq a_j < b$, $a_j \in \mathbb{N}$.

Method B.

The structure consists of blocks $S_{j,i}$, $j \geq 0$, $1 \leq i < b$, such that $S_{j,i}$ contains b^j points when $i \leq a_j$ and $S_{j,i}$ is empty otherwise. The structure is very similar to the structure of method A, except that a block S_j of size $a_j b^j$ is now split into a_j blocks of size b^j. A weak insertion is carried out in the following way:

(i) locate the smallest j such that $S_{j,b-1}$ is empty. Let $i = a_j + 1$ ($< b$),

(ii) discard all blocks $S_{k,l}$, $0 \leq k < j$, $1 \leq l < b$,

(iii) build $S_{j,i}$ out of the points in these blocks and the new point. (This is possible as the discarded blocks contain $\sum_{i=0}^{j-1} (b-1)b^i = b^j - 1$ points.)

Again, insertions are weak because we do not adjust b.

In the same way as for method A one can show that the largest j for which $S_{j,1}$ might be filled is bounded by $j \leq g'(n)$. It follows that the number of blocks is bounded by $b \cdot (g'(n)+1) = \left\lceil n^{1/g'(n)} \right\rceil \cdot g'(n)+1)$. It follows that $qpf(n) = O(g'(n)n^{1/g'(n)})$.

We again assume that a clean-up is done after n_0 insertions, where n_0 is the size of the set at the latest clean-up. One easily verifies that insertions performed in the way described above are indeed weak and that a block $S_{j,i}$ is filled only for $j \leq c \cdot g'(n_0)$ for some constant c, where n_0 is the size of the set at the latest clean-up. To estimate the weak update penalty factor we again consider the period between two successive clean-ups. Let n_0 denote the size of the set at the first clean-up. Note that for each $j \leq g'(n_0)$ each point is built at most once in a block $S_{j,i}$ for some $i < b$. It follows that the total size of blocks built is bounded by

$$(c \cdot g'(n_0)+1) \cdot 2n_0 \leq c' \cdot g'(n_0) \cdot n_0$$

for some constant c'. It follows that

$$wupf(n) \leq \sum_{i=0}^{\lfloor \log n \rfloor} (c' \cdot g'(2^i) \cdot 2^i)/n = O(g'(n))$$

Theorem 7.4.1.2. For each smooth, nondecreasing update penalty factor $upf(n) = O(\log n)$, there exists a transformation with characteristic $(qpf(n), \theta(upf(n)))$, where

$$qpf(n) = O(upf(n) \cdot n^{1/upf(n)}).$$

Proof

Follows from the above discussion, taking $upf(n)$ for $g'(n)$ and applying Theorem 5.2.1.1.

□

Note the duality between Theorem 7.4.1.1. and Theorem 7.4.1.2. The following table shows some possible trade-offs between query and update penalty factor that can be obtained.

	$qpf(n)$	$upf(n)$
a	$O(\log n)$	$O(\log n)$
b	$O(c.\sqrt[c]{n})$, c constant	$O(c)$
c	$O(\dfrac{\log^2 n}{\log \log n})$	$O(\dfrac{\log n}{\log \log n})$
d	$O(2^{\sqrt{\log n}} \sqrt{\log n})$	$O(\sqrt{\log n})$

We would like to express the update penalty factor in terms of the query penalty factor rather than the other way round. Let

$$g(n) = O(upf(n).n^{1/upf(n)})$$

$$\Rightarrow g(n) \leq c.\log n.n^{1/upf(n)}$$

$$\Rightarrow \frac{g(n)}{c.\log n} \leq 2^{\frac{\log n}{upf(n)}}$$

$$\Rightarrow \log(\frac{g(n)}{c.\log(n)}) \leq \frac{\log n}{upf(n)}$$

$$\Rightarrow upf(n) \leq c' \log n/\log(g(n)/\log n)$$

Combining this result with Theorem 7.4.1.1. we obtain:

Theorem 7.4.1.3. Let $g(n)$ be a smooth, nondecreasing integer function with $0<g(n)\leq n$. Given a static data structure S for a decomposable searching problem PR, there exists a structure S' for solving PR such that

$$Q_{S'}(n) = O(g(n))Q_S(n),$$

$$I^a_{S'}(n) = \begin{cases} O(\log(n)/\log(g(n)/\log n))P_S(n)/n & \text{when } g(n) = \Omega(\log n), \\ O(g(n).n^{1/g(n)})P_S(n)/n & \text{when } g(n) = O(\log n), \end{cases}$$

$$M_{S'}(n) = O(M_S(n)).$$

Proof

The query time and average insertion time follow from Theorem 7.4.1.1., Theorem 7.4.1.2. and the above discussion. The bound on the amount of storage required follows from the fact that $M_S(n)$ is assumed to be at least linear.

□

Theorem 7.4.1.3. shows that the lowerbounds given in Theorem 7.4.1. can indeed be obtained (up to some constant factor).

Before giving some applications of the method we will demonstrate how the averages can be turned into worst-case bounds.

7.4.2. Worst-case bounds.

The method we will use for turning the average insertion time bound into a worst-case bound is very similar to the method described in Section 7.3.2. We will only briefly describe the method. Details are left to the interested reader.

We will consider method A first. Each block S_j is replaced by a bag BA_j containing three blocks $S_j^u[1]$, $S_j^u[2]$ and $S_j^u[3]$ that are "in use", i.e., queries can be performed on them, and one block S_j^c that is "under construction". $S_j^u[1]$ and $S_j^u[3]$ can have size $a_j \cdot b^j$ for some $0 \le a_j < b$ and $S_j^u[2]$ can have size 0 or b^j. S_j^c will be used for constructing a block that will replace $S_j^u[1]$, $S_j^u[2]$ or $S_j^u[3]$ when it is ready. $S_j^u[2]$ will not be filled until $S_j^u[1]$ contains $(b-1)b^j$ points and $S_j^u[3]$ will not be filled until both $S_j^u[1]$ and $S_j^u[2]$ are completely filled. At the moment both $S_j^u[1]$ and $S_j^u[2]$ become fully filled, we start constructing S_{j+1}^c in the following way:

(i) when $S_{j+1}^u[1]$ is not completely filled we construct a new $S_{j+1}^u[1]$, i.e., S_{j+1}^c is built from the points in $S_j^u[1]$, $S_j^u[2]$ and the points in $S_{j+1}^u[1]$,

(ii) when $S_{j+1}^u[1]$ is completely filled and $S_{j+1}^u[2]$ is empty we construct a new $S_{j+1}^u[2]$ out of the points in $S_j^u[1]$ and $S_j^u[2]$,

(iii) when $S_{j+1}^u[2]$ is filled as well and $S_{j+1}^u[3]$ is not completely filled we construct a new $S_{j+1}^u[3]$,

(iv) when all three structures are completely filled we build a new structure of b^{j+1} points out of $S_j^u[1]$ and $S_j^u[2]$ that will take over from $S_{j+1}^u[1]$ when it is ready ($S_{j+1}^u[1]$ will be discarded by then).

(Note that $|S_j^u[1]| + |S_j^u[2]| = (b-1)b^j + b^j = b^{j+1}$, which shows that the constructions are correct.) Let the size of S_{j+1}^c become n'. With each forthcoming insertion we do $b \cdot P_S(n')/b^{j+2}$ work on the construction. As $n' \le b^{j+2}$ this is bounded by $b \cdot P_S(n)/n$. Hence, S_{i+1}^c will be ready after b^{j+1} insertions. In the meantime BA_j may have got a completely filled $S_j^u[3]$ and at the same moment S_j^c may be ready containing a structure of b^j points. But at this very moment we can discard $S_j^u[1]$ and $S_j^u[2]$, and make $S_j^u[1] := S_j^u[3]$ and $S_j^u[2] := S_j^c$. In the same way as in Section 7.3.2. one can show that the construction indeed proceeds in the proper way. It follows that with each weak insertion we have to do at most $b \cdot P_S(n)/n$ work in each bag, i.e., a total of $O(g(n) \cdot n^{1/g(n)} \cdot P_S(n)/n$ work. As each block is replaced by a bag containing at most three blocks in use, the query time does not change in order of magnitude.

In method B, we replace each row of blocks $S_{j,1}, \ldots, S_{j,b-1}$ by a bag BA_j containing blocks $S_{j,1}^u[1], \ldots, S_{j,b-1}^u[1]$, $S_j^u[2]$, $S_{j,1}^u[3], \ldots, S_{j,b-1}^u[3]$ that are in use and a block S_j^c that is under construction, each containing b^j or 0 points. Blocks will

be filled in the order in which they are listed. When all blocks $s^u_{j,1}[1],\ldots,s^u_{j,b-1}[1]$
and $s^u_j[2]$ are filled we start constructing s^c_{j+1} out of them, doing with each insertion $P_S(b^{j+1})/b^{j+1}$ work on the construction. When it is ready we replace the first empty
block in BA_{j+1} by s^c_{j+1}. During the construction all blocks $s^u_{j,1}[3],\ldots,s^u_{j,b-1}[3]$ might
have become filled and at the moment s^c_{j+1} is ready, s^c_j might be ready as well. But at
this moment $s^u_{j,1}[1],\ldots,s^u_{j,b-1}[1]$ and $s^u_j[2]$ can be discarded, the $s^u_{j,i}[3]$ blocks can
be shifted to the $s^u_{j,i}[1]$ blocks and the new s^c_j can be stored in $s^u_j[2]$. As the number
of bags is bounded by $O(g'(n))$, with each weak insertion we have to do at most $O(g'(n))$
times $P_S(n)/n$ work. Hence, the weak insertion time is bounded by $O(g'(n))P_S(n)/n$. As
each row of $b-1$ blocks is replaced by at most $2b-1$ blocks in use, the query time remains of the same order of magnitude.

Applying global rebuilding, we obtain:

Theorem 7.4.2.1. Let $g(n)$ be a smooth, nondecreasing integer function with $0<g(n)\leqq n$.
Given a data structure S for a decomposable searching problem PR, there exists a structure S' for solving PR dynamically such that

$$Q_{S'}(n) = O(g(n))Q_S(n),$$

$$I_{S'}(n) = \begin{cases} O(\log n/\log(g(n)/\log n))P_S(n)/n & \text{when } g(n) = \Omega(\log n), \\ O(g(n)n^{1/g(n)})P_S(n)/n & \text{otherwise,} \end{cases}$$

$$M_{S'}(n) = O(M_S(n)).$$

7.4.3. Supporting deletions.

To be able to support deletions in the structure described in the previous subsection, we add a dictionary DICT in which we keep for each point in the set a pointer
to the blocks in use or under construction in which the point is present (or will become present). This will add a term of $O(\log n)$ to the insertion time because with each
insertion we have to update DICT. Keeping with each point in the set a pointer to its
location in DICT, it can be updated in no extra time when blocks are rebuilt. To delete
a point weakly we search for it in DICT and delete it from the block in use it is in.
To be able to delete points from blocks under construction, we add to each such block
a buffer BUF in the same way as described in Section 7.3.3. To delete the point we put
it in BUF and do $D_S(n')$ work on the construction of the block under construction, where
n' is the size the block will get. Next we delete the point from DICT. This maintains
the structure in the same way as described in Section 7.3.3. It follows that the weak
deletion time is bounded by $O(\log n + D_S(n))$.

Theorem 7.4.3.1. Let $g(n)$ be a smooth, nondecreasing integer function with $0<g(n)\leqq n$.
Given a (static) data structure S for a decomposable searching problem PR, there exists
a structure S' for solving PR dynamically such that

$$Q_{S'}(n) = O(g(n))Q_{S}(n),$$

$$I_{S'}(n) = \begin{cases} O(\log n/\log(g(n)/\log n))P_{S}(n)/n + O(\log n) & \text{when } g(n) = \Omega(\log n), \\ O(g(n)n^{1/g(n)})P_{S}(n)/n & \text{otherwise,} \end{cases}$$

$$D_{S'}(n) = O(\log n + D_{S}(n) + P_{S}(n)/n),$$

$$M_{S'}(n) = O(M_{S}(n)).$$

Proof

The result follows from Theorem 7.4.2.1. and the above discussion.

□

7.4.4. Applications.

Let us consider some applications of the general method described in this section.

a) Range searching.

Applying Theorem 7.4.3.1. to the super B-tree with e.g. $g(n)=c$ for some $c>1$, $c\in \mathbb{N}$, we obtain a structure S for solving the range searching problem such that

$$Q_{S}(n) = O(c \log^{d} n) \quad (+ \text{ the number of answers}),$$
$$I_{S}(n) = O(\sqrt[c]{n} \log^{d-1} n),$$
$$D_{S}(n) = O(\log^{d-1} n),$$
$$M_{S}(n) = O(n \log^{d-1} n).$$

Applying Theorem 7.4.3.1. to the super B-tree choosing $g(n)=\sqrt[c]{n}$ for some $c>1$, $c\in \mathbb{N}$, we obtain a dynamic structure S for solving the range searching problem such that

$$Q_{S}(n) = O(\sqrt[c]{n} \log^{d} n) \quad (+ \text{ the number of answers}),$$
$$I_{S}(n) = O(c \log^{d-1} n),$$
$$D_{S}(n) = O(\log^{d-1} n),$$
$$M_{S}(n) = O(n \log^{d-1} n).$$

b) Nearest neighbor searching.

Applying Theorem 7.4.3.1. to the result of Theorem 6.4.5.2. and choosing $g(n)=c$, $c>1$, $c\in \mathbb{N}$, we obtain the following result:

Theorem 7.4.4.1. For each $c\in \mathbb{N}$, $c>1$, there exists a structure S for solving the nearest neighbor searching problem such that

$$Q_{S}(n) = O(c \log n),$$
$$I_{S}(n) = O(\sqrt[c]{n} \log n),$$
$$D_{S}(n) = O(n),$$
$$M_{S}(n) = O(n \log \log n).$$

7.5. Mixed method.

The equal block method for dynamizing decomposable searching problems, described in Section 7.2., yields an optimal trade-off between query- and deletion time, but the insertion time is quite bad. On the other hand, the logarithmic method, described in Sections 7.3. and 7.4. yields an optimal trade-off between query- and insertion time, but for this method the deletion time is rather bad. In this section we will show how the two methods can be combined into one method with both an optimal trade-off between query- and insertion time and between query- and deletion time.

Since both the equal block method and the logarithmic method use an "arbitrary" data structure S with known characteristics as a start, we can apply e.g. the logarithmic method on the structure resulting from the equal block method. This leads to the following result:

Theorem 7.5.1. Let $f(n)$ and $g(n)$ be two smooth, nondecreasing integer functions with $0 < f(n) \leq n$ and $0 < g(n) \leq n$. Given a (static) data structure S for a decomposable searching problem PR, there exists a data structure S' for solving PR dynamically such that

$$Q_{S'}(n) = O(f(n).g(n))Q_S(n/f(n)),$$

$$I_{S'}(n) = \begin{cases} O(\log n/\log(g(n)/\log n))P_S(n)/n + O(\log n) & \text{when } g(n) = \Omega(\log n), \\ O(g(n).n^{1/g(n)})P_S(n)/n & \text{when } g(n) = O(\log n), \end{cases}$$

$$D_{S'}(n) = O(D_S(n/f(n)) + \log n + P_S(n)/n),$$

$$M_{S'}(n) = O(f(n)M_S(n/f(n))).$$

Proof

Apply Theorem 7.4.3.1. to the result described in Theorem 7.2.2.

□

This method has the best insertion and deletion times of both methods, but the penalty factor in query time has become $f(n).g(n)$. A different technique for combining the two methods will reduce $qpf(n)$ to $f(n)+g(n)$. We will give a general result first.

Theorem 7.5.2. Let $f(n)$ and $g(n)$ be two smooth, nondecreasing integer functions with $0 < f(n) \leq n$ and $0 < g(n) \leq n$. Given a (dynamic) structure S_1 composed of $O(g(n))$ S-blocks structured for a decomposable searching problem PR, there is a structure S_2 for solving PR such that

$$Q_{S_2}(n) = O(f(n)+g(n))Q_S(n/f(n)),$$
$$I_{S_2}(n) = O(I_{S_1}(n) + \log n + P_S(n)/n),$$
$$D_{S_2}(n) = O(D_S(n/f(n)) + \log n + P_S(n)/n),$$
$$M_{S_2}(n) = \min(O(f(n)+g(n))M_S(n/f(n)), O(M_S(n))).$$

Proof

Split each S-block in S_1 of size $> n/f(n)$ into subblocks (again structured "like S") of size $n/f(n)$. This leads to a structure consisting of at most $f(n)+g(n)$ (sub)-blocks of size $\leq n/f(n)$. The bound on the query time follows. The bound on the amount of storage required follows also, noting that each point in the set is in one S-structure and that $M_S(n)$ is at least linear. A weak deletion is performed by a deletion of the point on the block it is in. This takes $O(\log n)$ time for finding the block, using a dictionary DICT, plus $O(D_S(n/f(n)))$ for performing the actual deletion. Such a deletion is weak for we do not adjust the number of blocks and the sizes of the blocks. Hence, $WD_{S_2}(n) = O(\log n + D_S(n/f(n)))$. The deletion time follows, using global rebuilding. Insertions are carried out as for S_1 except that new constructed blocks of size $> n/f(n)$ are immediately split into subblocks of size $n/f(n)$. Such an insertion is weak because we do not adjust $f(n)$. It follows that $WI_{S_2}(n) = O(\log n + I_{S_1}(n))$ because the building of blocks for a partition of a set is cheaper than the building of one for the total set. (The $O(\log n)$ term comes in for updating DICT.) The insertion time follows.

$\square$

Using for S_1 the structure resulting from the logarithmic method (Theorem 7.4.3.1.) we obtain the result we were after.

Theorem 7.5.3. Let $f(n)$ and $g(n)$ be two smooth, nondecreasing integer functions with $0<f(n)\leq n$ and $0<g(n)\leq n$. Given a (static) data structure S for a decomposable searching problem PR, there exists a structure S' for solving PR dynamically such that

$$Q_{S'}(n) = O\{f(n)+g(n)\}Q_S(n/f(n)),$$

$$I_{S'}(n) = \begin{cases} O(\log n/\log(g(n)/\log n))P_S(n)/n + O(\log n) & \text{when } g(n) = \Omega(\log n), \\ O(g(n).n^{1/g(n)})P_S(n)/n & \text{otherwise,} \end{cases}$$

$$D_{S'}(n) = O(D_S(n/f(n)) + \log n + P_S(n)/n),$$

$$M_{S'}(n) = \min(O(f(n)+g(n))M_S(n/(n)), O(M_S(n))).$$

It combines the best results and optimal worst-case bounds in one single method.

Applications.

a) Nearest neighbor searching.

Applying Theorem 7.5.3. with $f(n) = g(n) = \lceil \sqrt{n}/\sqrt{\log n} \rceil$ to the structure for nearest neighbor searching described in Theorem 6.4.5.2. one obtains the following, nowadays best known, solution:

Theorem 7.5.4. There exists a structure S' for solving the nearest neighbor searching problem such that

$$Q_{S'}(n) = O(\sqrt{n \log n}),$$
$$I_{S'}(n) = O(\log n),$$
$$D_{S'}(n) = O(\sqrt{n \log n}),$$
$$M_{S'}(n) = O(n \log \log n).$$

b) Common intersection of halfspaces.

Applying Theorem 7.5.3. to the problem of determining whether a point x lies in the common intersection of a set of 3-dimensional halfspaces and choosing $f(n) = g(n) = \lceil \sqrt{n}/\sqrt{\log n} \rceil$, we obtain a dynamic structure with

$$Q_{S'}(n) = O(\sqrt{n \log n}),$$
$$I_{S'}(n) = O(\log n),$$
$$D_{S'}(n) = O(\sqrt{n \log n}),$$
$$M_{S'}(n) = O(n \log \log n).$$

Compare Theorem 7.2.4.

7.6. Decomposable counting problems.

By restricting the class of decomposable searching problems further, we can obtain a class of problems with even better perspectives for the deletion time bound than the ones shown in the preceding sections.

Definition 7.6.1. A decomposable searching problem PR is called a DECOMPOSABLE COUNTING PROBLEM if and only if for each subset A of the set V and any query object x,

$$PR(x, V \backslash A) = \tilde{\Delta}(PR(x,V), PR(x,A))$$

for some constant time computable operator Δ.

While decomposable searching problems are problems for which one can "add" answers, decomposable counting problems also allow for "subtracting" answers. Most counting variants of decomposable searching problems are decomposable counting problems. For example, the range counting problem is a decomposable counting problem because the number of points of $V \backslash A$ that lie in a range x is equal to the number of points of V in x minus the number of points of A in x. Clearly not all decomposable searching problems are decomposable counting problems. When the point p in V nearest to x and the point p' in A nearest to x are given, it can be impossible to decide which point in $V \backslash A$ is nearest to x (when p=p'). Hence, the nearest neighbor searching problem is no decomposable counting problem.

For decomposable counting problems there is no need to perform deletions immediately at the moment they occur. We can buffer them by inserting them in a separate, so-called GHOST-structure. All insertions are performed on the MAIN-structure. Queries are performed by querying both structures and subtracting the answer over GHOST from the answer over MAIN, using the operator Δ. There is only one problem. We have to take care that the GHOST structure does not become too large. To this end we use the global rebuilding technique described in Chapter 5.

Theorem 7.6.2. Let S be a half-dynamic data structure for a decomposable counting problem PR. There exists a fully dynamic data structure S' for PR such that

$$Q_{S'}(n) = O(Q_S(n)),$$
$$I_{S'}(n) = O(I_S(n)),$$
$$D_{S'}(n) = O(I_S(n) + P_S(n)/n),$$
$$M_{S'}(n) = O(M_S(n)).$$

Proof

The structure S' consists of two S-structures, MAIN and GHOST. Initially (i.e., when the structure is built for some set of points) GHOST is empty. Insertions are performed on MAIN. Deletions are performed by inserting the points in GHOST. Such deletions are weak because, when S' initially contained n_0 points (i.e., $|MAIN| = n_0$) and αn_0 deletions ($\alpha < 1$) and n_1 insertions have been performed on it, the query time has become $O(Q_S(n_0+n_1) + Q_S(\alpha n_0)) = O(Q_S(n_0+n_1)) = O(Q_S((1-\alpha)n_0+n_1))$ which is the query time on a new built structure of the $(1-\alpha)n_0+n_1$ points that are in S' at this moment. Hence, $WD_{S'}(n) = I_S(n)$ and hence, $D_{S'}(n) = O(I_S(n) + P_S(n)/n)$.

□

Using for S the structure described in Section 7.3.2. (Theorem 7.3.2.5.) we obtain the following result:

Theorem 7.6.3. Given a (static) data structure S for a decomposable counting problem PR, there exists a dynamic structure S' for solving PR such that

$$Q_{S'}(n) = \begin{cases} O(Q_S(n)) & \text{when } Q_S(n) = \Omega(n^\varepsilon) \text{ for some } \varepsilon > 0, \\ O(\log n)Q_S(n) & \text{otherwise,} \end{cases}$$

$$I_{S'}(n) = \begin{cases} O(P_S(n)/n) & \text{when } P_S(n) = \Omega(n^{1+\varepsilon}) \text{ for some } \varepsilon > 0, \\ O(\log n)P_S(n)/n & \text{otherwise,} \end{cases}$$

$$D_{S'}(n) = \begin{cases} O(P_S(n)/n) & \text{when } P_S(n) = \Omega(n^{1+\varepsilon}) \text{ for some } \varepsilon > 0, \\ O(\log n)P_S(n)/n & \text{otherwise,} \end{cases}$$

$$M_{S'}(n) = O(M_S(n)).$$

Applications.

a) Range counting.

According to Theorem 2.3.3. a static solution to the range counting problem exists with $Q_S(n) = O(\log^d n)$, $P_S(n) = O(n \log^{d-1} n)$ and $M_S(n) = O(n \log^{d-1} n)$. Applying Theorem 7.6.3. we obtain a dynamic structure S' with

$$Q_{S'}(n) = O(\log^{d+1} n),$$
$$I_{S'}(n) = O(\log^d n),$$
$$D_{S'}(n) = O(\log^d n),$$
$$M_{S'}(n) = O(n \log^{d-1} n).$$

This comes close to the best result presently known (see Section 3.4.) and the method is quite general.

b) Rectangle intersection counting.

Applying Theorem 7.6.3. to the structure in Theorem 2.4.3., we obtain a structure S' for dynamic rectangle intersection counting such that

$$Q_{S'}(n) = O(\log^{d+1} n),$$
$$I_{S'}(n) = O(\log^d n),$$
$$D_{S'}(n) = O(\log^d n),$$
$$M_{S'}(n) = O(n \log^{d-1} n).$$

Again, this is not the best possible result but it follows in a simple way.

It is, of course, also possible to use the more general dynamization techniques described in Section 7.4. for dynamizing decomposable counting problems. The details are left to the interested reader.

7.7. C(n)-decomposability.

In this section we give a generalization of the notion of decomposability. In Definition 7.1.1., □ was constrained to be computable in O(1) time. We will show how this restriction can be dropped, to allow for a treatment of more problems in an integral way.

7.7.1. Definition and method.

C(n)-decomposable searching problems are searching problems for which the composition operator □ takes C(n) time to compute.

<u>Definition</u> 7.7.1.1. A searching problem PR is called $C(n)$-DECOMPOSABLE if and only if for any partition $A \cup B$ of the set V and any query object x,

$$PR(x,V) = \square(PR(x,A), PR(x,B)),$$

where $\square$ takes $C(n)$ time to compute when V contains n points.

Clearly, the decomposable searching problems are $O(1)$-decomposable. There are a number of searching (set) problems that are $C(n)$-decomposable for some $C(n) \neq O(1)$. For example, the three-dimensional convex hull (set) problem is $O(n)$-decomposable, as shown by Bentley and Shamos [BeSh2].

All dynamization results described in this chapter can be generalized for $C(n)$-decomposable searching problems. We will only consider the generalization of Theorem 7.3.3.2.

<u>Theorem</u> 7.7.1.2. Given a (static) data structure S for a $C(n)$-decomposable searching problem PR, there exists a structure S' for solving PR dynamically such that

$$Q_{S'}(n) = \begin{cases} O(Q_S(n) + C(n)) & \text{when } Q_S(n) + C(n) = \Omega(n^\varepsilon), \text{ some } \varepsilon > 0, \\ O(\log n) \cdot (Q_S(n) + C(n)) & \text{otherwise,} \end{cases}$$

$$I_{S'}(n) = \begin{cases} O(P_S(n)/n) & \text{when } P_S(n) = \Omega(n^{1+\varepsilon}), \text{ some } \varepsilon > 0, \\ O(\log n) P_S(n)/n & \text{otherwise,} \end{cases}$$

$$D_{S'}(n) = O(\log n + D_S(n) + P_S(n)/n),$$

$$M_{S'}(n) = O(M_S(n)).$$

<u>Proof</u>

The bounds on insertion and deletion time and on the amount of storage required follow immediately from Theorem 7.3.3.2. To perform a query we start at the smallest block and proceed towards the largest block. It follows that when we come at a block of size n', the number of points in preceding blocks is $O(n')$. Hence, the time required for querying the block and combining the answer with the answer over the preceding blocks takes $O(Q_S(n') + C(n'))$ time. This adds up to $O(Q_S(n) + C(n))$ when $Q_S(n) + C(n) = \Omega(n^\varepsilon)$ for some $\varepsilon > 0$ and to $O(\log n) \cdot (Q_S(n) + C(n))$ otherwise in the same way as in the proof of the query time for Theorem 7.3.3.2. (see Theorem 7.3.2.5.).

$\square$

7.7.2. <u>$C(n)$-decomposable set problems</u>.

The theory of $C(n)$-decomposability is especially applicable to set problems. Clearly $C(n)$-decomposable set problems are $C(n)$-order decomposable (see Chapter 6). It are precisely those $C(n)$-order decomposable set problems for which ORD is vacuous.

Combining Theorem 7.7.1.2. and Theorem 6.3.6. we obtain the following result:

<u>Theorem</u> 7.7.2.1. Given a C(n)-decomposable set problem PR, we can dynamize it such that

$$
Q_S(n) = \begin{cases} O(C(n)) & \text{when } C(n) = \Omega(n^\varepsilon), \text{ some } \varepsilon > 0, \\ O(\log n)C(n) & \text{otherwise,} \end{cases}
$$

$$
I_S(n) = \begin{cases} O(\log^2 n) & \text{when } C(n) = O(n^\varepsilon), \\ O(C(n)/n) & \text{when } C(n) = \Omega(n^{1+\varepsilon}), \text{ some } \varepsilon > 0, \\ O(\log^2 n.C(n)/n) + O(\log^2 n) & \text{otherwise,} \end{cases}
$$

$$
D_S(n) = \begin{cases} O(C(n)) & \text{when } C(n) = \Omega(n^\varepsilon), \text{ some } \varepsilon > 0, \\ O(\log n.C(n)) & \text{otherwise,} \end{cases}
$$

$$
M_S(n) = \begin{cases} O(n) & \text{when } C(n) = O(n^\varepsilon), \text{ some } 0 < \varepsilon < 1, \\ O(C(n)) & \text{when } C(n) = \Omega(n^{1+\varepsilon}), \text{ some } \varepsilon > 0, \\ O(\log \log n.C(n)) & \text{when } C(n) \text{ is at least linear,} \\ O(n + \log n.C(n)) & \text{otherwise.} \end{cases}
$$

So, at the cost of an increase in query time, the insertion time is decreased considerably.

As an example, consider the three-dimensional convex hull problem. The problem is O(n)-decomposable. Hence, we can solve it dynamically within

$$
Q_S(n) = O(n),
$$
$$
I_S(n) = O(\log^2 n),
$$
$$
D_S(n) = O(n),
$$
$$
M_S(n) = O(n \log \log n).
$$

7.8. <u>Concluding remarks</u>.

We have shown how the notion of decomposability of searching problems can be used for obtaining dynamic solution from static solutions yielding efficient query and update time bounds. Two different techniques have been considered, the "equal block" method and the "logarithmic" method. Both methods were combined into one general method that can be tuned to obtain all dynamization methods for decomposable searching problems in general, with optimal trade-off between query and insertion time and between query and deletion time. Some special cases and generalizations of decomposable searching problems were considered as well. Not all results available nowadays have been mentioned. In Overmars and van Leeuwen [OvL4] a class of so-called "MD-searching problems" is described. These problems are decomposable and their static solutions allow for

some kind of merging scheme. For this class of problems better insertion time bounds
can be achieved. Edelsbrunner [Ed5] studies trade-offs by tuning transformation methods
and determines the in some sense "best" tunings for some problems.

The notion of decomposability is not only useful in obtaining dynamic data structures. By splitting a large static data structure into smaller structures it is possible to reduce the amount of storage required at the cost of an increase in query time
(when $M_S(n) = \Omega(n^{1+\varepsilon})$ for some $\varepsilon > 0$). In Overmars [Ov7] decomposability is used to obtain static solutions for searching problems. Moreover, decomposability is used to
add range restrictions to searching problems (see Lueker [Lu2] and Saxe [Sax]).

Bibliographical comments.

The study of decomposable searching problems was initiated by Bentley [Be3]. He
gave the first version of the logarithmic method described in Section 7.3. These results were extended by Saxe and Bentley [SaxB] (see also Bentley and Saxe [BeSa]) who
gave some more general methods and by Overmars and van Leeuwen [OvL4,OvL6] who showed
how to perform deletions. In Mehlhorn and Overmars [MeO] the general framework presented in Section 7.4. was given, but only average time bounds were obtained. Overmars
and van Leeuwen [OvL7] succeeded in turning the averages into worst-case bounds. The
equal block method was developed by Maurer and Ottmann [MaO], van Leeuwen and Wood
[vLW] and van Leeuwen and Maurer [vLM]. The simple version described in Section 7.2.
is based on van Leeuwen and Overmars [vLO2]. The general result in Section 7.5. combining the two methods was given in Overmars and van Leeuwen [OvL5]. The notion of
decomposable counting problem was introduced in Bentley and Saxe [BeSa]. The notion
of C(n)-decomposability was defined in Overmars [Ov6].

CHAPTER VIII

BATCHED DYNAMIZATION

8.1. <u>Introduction</u>.

In this chapter and the next we will consider two special kinds of dynamic data structures: structures for "batched dynamic" problems and structures for "searching in the past". Before describing batched dynamic data structures we will first consider "batched static" solutions. The BATCHED STATIC version of a searching problem PR is the following: given a set of points V and a set of n_q query objects $x_1,\ldots,$ x_{n_q}, perform these queries on V, i.e., compute $PR(x_i,V)$ for all x_i, $1 \leq i \leq n_q$. Hence, we are not interested in the processing of every individual query but only in the overall runtime for answering the set of queries. We are not bound to a specific order of the queries nor is there a need to perform them one after the other. Clearly, the batched static version of a searching problem can be solved using a static data structure for the problem, but in a number of cases one can do better.

The BATCHED DYNAMIC version of a searching problem PR is the following: given a sequence of insertions, deletions and queries, report all answers to the queries when the sequence of actions is performed (in the given order) on an initially empty set. We are again only interested in the overall runtime. There is no need for actually performing the updates and queries in the given order, as long as it is made certain that queries are performed over the proper sets of points. Clearly, a dynamic structure can be used for solving the problem, but often one can do better. Batched static and batched dynamic versions of searching problems often occur in an off-line (i.e., batched) environment. A number of (static) set problems can be formulated in terms of batched dynamic searching problems. For example, the set problem that asks for all intersecting pairs in a set of rectangles can be solved by the batched dynamic version of the rectangle intersection searching problem. Just consider it as the problem to perform the following sequence of updates and queries: query with rectangle r_i and next insert r_i, for all rectangles r_i in the set.

In this chapter we will describe a number of techniques that can be used for obtaining batched (static or dynamic) solutions to searching problems. The methods will be particularly useful for decomposable searching problems.

In Section 8.2. we will show that for a number of problems the batched static version can be solved in a more efficient way than by using a known static data structure for the problem. Next it will be shown that static data structures for decomposable searching problems with a large discrepancy between the bounds for query- and building time can be changed into static structures in which these bounds are better balanced and which (hence) have better perspectives for use in a batched environment.

In Section 8.3. we consider batched dynamic solutions for decomposable searching problems. A general method will be given for turning static solutions to decomposable searching problems into batched dynamic solutions.

In Section 8.4. we show how a technique, called "streaming", can be used for reducing the space requirements for batched versions of searching problems. It shows, for example, that the batched dynamic version of the range searching problem can be solved in $O(n \log^d n)$ time using only $O(n)$ storage, when n is the length of the sequence of updates and queries.

Section 8.5. shows how for a number of searching problems better results can be obtained by changing the set objects into query objects and the query objects into set objects and solving a kind of reversed searching problem.

Throughout this chapter we will use the following notations:

    (i) in the batched static case:

        n = the number of points in the set,

        n_q = the number of queries,

        $P^s(n)$ = the amount of time required for solving the batched static version of a searching problem (with n_q implicitely understood),

        $M^s(n)$ = the amount of storage required for solving the batched static version of a searching problem,

    (ii) in the batched dynamic case:

        m = the maximum number of points that ever are in the set at some moment,

        N = the number of updates,

        n_q = the number of queries,

        $P^d(n)$ = the amount of time required for solving the batched dynamic version of a searching problem,

        $M^d(n)$ = the amount of storage required for solving the batched dynamic version of a searching problem,

P^s, M^s, P^d and M^d are assumed to be smooth and at least linear.

8.2. Batched static solutions.

Given a data structure S for a searching problem PR, one can solve the batched static version of PR by first building a S-structure of all points in the set and, next, performing all queries on the structure. This leads to a solution for the batched static version of PR with

$$P^S(n) = O(P_S(n) + n_q \cdot Q_S(n)),$$
$$M^S(n) = O(M_S(n)).$$

But, for a number of problems one can do better. Consider for example the two-dimensional rectangle containment searching problem (see Section 2.4.). The best known static data structure S for this problem yields a query time of $O(\log^3 n)$, while $P_S(n) = O(n \log^3 n)$ and $M_S(n) = O(n \log^3 n)$ (see Theorem 2.4.4.). Use of this data structure for solving the batched static version of the rectangle containment searching problem would yield

$$P^S(n) = O(n \log^3 n + n_q \log^3 n) \quad (\text{+ the total number of reported answers}),$$
$$M^S(n) = O(n \log^3 n).$$

Lee and Preparata [LeP1] have shown that the problem that asks for all pairs of rectangles (r_1, r_2) in a set V such that r_1 is contained in r_2, can be solved within time $O(n \log^2 n)$ (+ the number of reported pairs) using $O(n)$ space. Their solution can easily be adapted to solving the problem of reporting all pairs (r_1, r_2) of rectangles such that r_1 is contained in r_2 where r_1 is in a set V_1 and r_2 is in V_2. Choosing V_1 to be the set of rectangles and V_2 to be the set of query rectangles, this method solves the batched static version of the two-dimensional rectangle containment searching problem within

$$P^S(n) = O((n+n_q)\log^2(n+n_q)) \quad (\text{+ the number of reported answers}),$$
$$M^S(n) = O(n+n_q).$$

When a static data structure is used for solving the batched static version of a searching problem, it is important that the query time and preprocessing time of the structure are "in balance", i.e., that $P_S(n) \approx n_q Q_S(n)$. For a number of static data structures $P_S(n)$ is very large compared with $Q_S(n)$ and as n_q is often $\theta(n)$, we had better look for solutions with better trade-offs, i.e., with a lower preprocessing time and a higher query time. For decomposable searching problems this can be done by means of a general transformation, as we will show.

For decomposable searching problems the answer over the total set can be computed in $O(n)$ time from the answers over the individual elements. Computing the answer over one element takes constant time. It follows that the batched static version of a decomposable searching problem can always be computed in

$$P^S(n) = O(n_q \cdot n),$$
$$M^S(n) = O(n).$$

In this way we have reduced the building time to $O(n)$ (just to store the points in the set), with an increase of the query time to $O(n)$. To obtain other trade-offs between query time and preprocessing time of a static data structure for a decomposable searching problem we split the set of points into a number of equally sized subsets and build

a static data structure for each of the subsets. To perform a query all subsets are
queried separately and the answers are combined.

Theorem 8.2.1. Given a static data structure S for a decomposable searching problem
PR and some integer function f(n) with $1 \leq f(n) \leq n$, there exists a static data structure S' for solving PR such that

$$Q_{S'}(n) = O(f(n) \cdot Q_S(n/f(n))),$$
$$P_{S'}(n) = O(f(n) \cdot P_S(n/f(n))),$$
$$M_{S'}(n) = O(f(n) \cdot M_S(n/f(n))).$$

Proof
    Split the set into f(n) subsets of size at most $\lceil n/f(n) \rceil$ and build a S-structure
for each subset.

□

Using this new static data structure S' for solving the batched static version of
PR, we obtain the following result:

Corollary 8.2.2. Given a static data structure S for a decomposable searching problem
PR and an integer function f(n) with $1 \leq f(n) \leq n$, the batched static version of PR can
be solved such that

$$P^S(n) = O(f(n) \cdot P_S(n/f(n)) + n_q \cdot f(n) \cdot Q_S(n/f(n))),$$
$$M^S(n) = O(f(n) \cdot M_S(n/f(n))).$$

Let us consider some applications. We will assume that $n = \theta(n_q)$.

Applications.

a) Fixed radius nearest neighbor searching.
    The FIXED RADIUS NEAREST NEIGHBOR SEARCHING problem asks for all elements of a
set of points in the plane that lie within some fixed distance ε from a query point.
It is the special instance of the circular range searching problem in which all query
circles must have the same radius. Bentley and Maurer [BeM2] describe a static structure S for solving the problem such that

$$Q_S(n) = O(\log n) \quad \text{(+ the number of reported answers)},$$
$$P_S(n) = O(n^3),$$
$$M_S(n) = O(n^3).$$

(Preparata [Pr] states $O(n^2 \log n)$ bounds on the preprocessing time and amount of
storage required but his bounds are not quite correct, as he does not count storage

and time needed for storing partial answers.) The problem is clearly decomposable.
Hence, we can apply Theorem 8.2.1. and, choosing $f(n) = \left\lceil n^{2/3}/\log^{1/3} n \right\rceil$, obtain a data
structure S' such that

$$Q_{S'}(n) = O(n^{2/3} \log^{2/3} n) \quad (\text{+ the number of answers}),$$

$$P_{S'}(n) = O(n^{5/3} \log^{2/3} n),$$

$$M_{S'}(n) = O(n^{5/3} \log^{2/3} n).$$

Using this structure for solving the batched static version of the problem, we obtain
the following result:

Theorem 8.2.3. The batched static version of the fixed radius nearest neighbor searching problem can be solved such that

$$P^S(n) = O(n^{5/3} \log^{2/3} n) \quad (\text{+ the total number of answers}),$$

$$M^S(n) = O(n^{5/3} \log^{2/3} n).$$

b) Half-planar range counting.

The HALF-PLANAR RANGE COUNTING problem asks for the number of elements of a set
of points in the plane that lie above or below a given query line. The problem can
be solved using a slightly modified version of a structure presented in Edelsbrunner,
Kirkpatrick and Maurer [EdKM], yielding

$$Q_S(n) = O(\log n),$$

$$P_S(n) = O(n^2 \log n),$$

$$M_S(n) = O(n^2).$$

One easily verifies that the problem is decomposable. Applying Theorem 8.2.1. with
$f(n) = \lceil \sqrt{n} \rceil$, we obtain a static structure S' for the problem with

$$Q_{S'}(n) = O(\sqrt{n} \log n),$$

$$P_{S'}(n) = O(n \sqrt{n} \log n),$$

$$M_{S'}(n) = O(n \sqrt{n}).$$

Theorem 8.2.4. The batched static version of the half-planar range counting problem
can be solved such that

$$P^S(n) = O(n \sqrt{n} \log n),$$

$$M^S(n) = O(n \sqrt{n}).$$

Theorem 8.2.1. and Corollary 8.2.2. are applicable to numerous other searching problems
as well, like e.g. the polygon retrieval problem and the polygon intersection searching
problem. For each of these problems, the batched static version can be solved in time
$O(n^2)$.

8.3. <u>A general batched dynamic solution</u>.

Once we have a fully dynamic data structure S for a searching problem PR, the batched dynamic version of PR can be solved by performing the sequence of insertions, deletions and queries on an initially empty S-structure. This clearly leads to a solution of the problem such that

$$P^d(n) = O(n_q \cdot Q_S(m) + N_i \cdot I_S(m) + N_d \cdot D_S(m)),$$
$$M^d(n) = O(M_S(m)),$$

where N_i and N_d denote the number of insertions and deletions, respectively $(N_i + N_d = N)$.

Let us from now on assume that PR is a decomposable searching problem and that only a static data structure S is available for solving PR. We will show that in this case an efficient solution to the batched dynamic version of PR exists. We will solve the batched dynamic version of PR by transforming it to the addition of inverse range restrictions to PR, i.e., the composition of PR and the inverse range searching problem. Next we will show how the structure S for PR can be transformed into a structure that solves the composed problem.

To transform the batched dynamic version of PR we number the actions in the transaction sequence from 1 to $N+n_q$. So we get a row of actions $act_1, \ldots, act_{N+n_q}$ where each act_i is either an insertion, a deletion or a query. For an action act_i we say that i is the moment at which the action is performed. For each point p that ever belongs to the set there is a moment mi_p at which the point is inserted and possibly a moment md_p at which p is deleted. When p is not deleted we choose $md_p = N+n_q+1$. When a point is reinserted later we treat it as a separate point. (We assume that when a point gets inserted it is not present and that when it has to be deleted it is present.) Hence, with each point p we can associate an interval $[mi_p : md_p]$ during which p was present. We call this interval the "existence interval" of p. As a running example consider the following sequence of actions (where $INS(p_i)$ denotes the insertion of p_i, $DEL(p_i)$ denotes the deletion of p_i and $QRY(x_i)$ denotes a query with object x_i):

$$act_1 = INS(p_1) \qquad act_7 = INS(p_4)$$
$$act_2 = INS(p_2) \qquad act_8 = DEL(p_1)$$
$$act_3 = INS(p_3) \qquad act_9 = QRY(x_3)$$
$$act_4 = QRY(x_1) \qquad act_{10} = INS(p_5)$$
$$act_5 = DEL(p_2) \qquad act_{11} = QRY(x_4)$$
$$act_6 = QRY(x_2)$$

Figure 8.3.1. shows the existence intervals of the points $p_1, \ldots, p_5$. When we have to perform a query at some time moment i, we must perform it on those points that are in the set at moment i, i.e., on the points whose existence interval contains i. For example, the query with x_3, i.e., action act_9, has to be performed on the points p_3 and p_4. Hence, to perform a query we first perform an inverse range query with

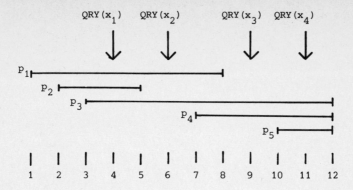

figure 8.3.1.

the moment of the query on the existence intervals of the points to locate the points
that are present and next perform the query on these points. Note that we only need
a static data structure for solving the problem. We will show now how to transform
the structure S for PR into a static data structure S' to solve the addition of inverse range restrictions. To this end we store all existence intervals of the points
in the set in a segment tree (see Section 2.4.). With each internal node we do not
store the segments but the points to which these existence intervals belong. These
points we build into a S-structure. Hence, with each internal node α we have associated a S-structure S_α of all points whose existence interval does contain the interval below α but does not contain the interval below the father of α. See figure 8.3.2.

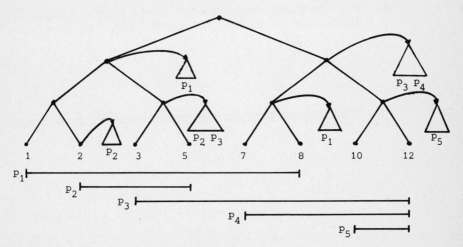

figure 8.3.2.

for the structure we get for our running example. To perform a query at moment i, we search with i down the segment tree. The structures S_α associated to nodes α on the search path precisely contain the points that are present at moment i. To obtain the answer to the query we query these structures and combine the answers using the composition operator $\square$ (PR was assumed to be decomposable).

Theorem 8.3.1. Given a static data structure S for solving a decomposable searching problem PR, the batched dynamic version of PR can be solved such that

$$P^d(n) = O(n_q . \log N . Q_S(m) + \log N . P_S(N)),$$
$$M^d(n) = O(\log N . M_S(N)).$$

Proof

Let us analyse the space requirements first. One easily verifies that at each level of the tree, each point occurs at most twice. As the number of points is bounded by N, it follows that the total amount of storage needed per level is bounded by $O(M_S(N))$ (because M_S is assumed to be at least linear). As the depth of the segment tree is bounded by $O(\log N)$ the bound on the amount of storage follows.

The amount of time required for solving the batched dynamic version of PR can be divided into two parts: the amount of time required for constructing the structure, and the amount of time required for performing the queries. Computing the existence intervals of the points can be done in time $O(n_q + N \log N)$. The construction of the segment tree takes $O(N \log N)$ and the amount of time needed for constructing the associated S-structures can be estimated by $O(P_S(N))$ per level, by the same arguments as used for estimating the amount of storage required. As each associated structure contains at most m points, the time needed per query is bounded by $O(\log N) . Q_S(m)$ and hence, the total time needed for performing queries is bounded by $O(n_q . \log N . Q_S(m))$. The bound on P^d follows.

$$\square$$

One easily verifies that

$$P^d(n) = O(n_q . Q_S(N) + \log N . P_S(N)) \quad \text{when } Q_S(n) = \Omega(n^\varepsilon), \text{ some } \varepsilon > 0,$$

that

$$P^d(n) = O(n_q . \log N . Q_S(m) + P_S(N)) \quad \text{when } P_S(n) = \Omega(n^{1+\varepsilon}), \text{ some } \varepsilon > 0,$$

and that

$$M^d(n) = O(M_S(N)) \quad \text{when } M_S(n) = \Omega(n^{1+\varepsilon}), \text{ some } \varepsilon > 0.$$

Let us consider some applications. We assume that $n = \theta(n_q) = \theta(m) = \theta(N)$.

Applications.

a) Nearest neighbor searching.

The best dynamic data structure known for nearest neighbor searching yields $Q_S(n) = O(\sqrt{n \log n})$, $I_S(n) = O(\log n)$ and $D_S(n) = O(\sqrt{n \log n})$, using $O(n \log \log n)$ storage (see Theorem 7.5.4.). Using this structure for solving the batched dynamic version of the nearest neighbor searching problem, we obtain

$$P^d(n) = O(n \sqrt{n \log n}),$$
$$M^d(n) = O(n \log \log n).$$

On the other hand, the best static solution to the nearest neighbor searching problem has $Q_S(n) = O(\log n)$, $P_S(n) = O(n \log n)$ and $M_S(n) = O(n)$. Applying Theorem 8.3.1. we obtain a batched dynamic solution with

$$P^d(n) = O(n \log^2 n),$$
$$M^d(n) = O(n \log n).$$

b) Fixed radius nearest neighbor searching.

As shown in Section 8.2. a static data structure exists with

$$Q_S(n) = O(n^{\frac{2}{3}} \log^{\frac{2}{3}} n) \quad (+ \text{ the number of answers}),$$
$$P_S(n) = O(n^{\frac{5}{3}} \log^{\frac{2}{3}} n),$$
$$M_S(n) = O(n^{\frac{5}{3}} \log^{\frac{2}{3}} n).$$

Applying Theorem 8.3.1. we obtain the following result:

Theorem 8.3.2. The batched dynamic version of the fixed radius nearest neighbor searching problem can be solved such that

$$P^d(n) = O(n^{\frac{5}{3}} \log^{\frac{2}{3}} n) \quad (+ \text{ the total number of answers}),$$
$$M^d(n) = O(n^{\frac{5}{3}} \log^{\frac{2}{3}} n).$$

Hence, we obtain exactly the same bounds for the problem as for the batched static version (compare Theorem 8.2.3.).

c) Half-planar range counting.

As shown in Section 8.2. a static structure for the problem exists with $Q_S(n) = O(\sqrt{n} \log n)$, $P_S(n) = O(n \sqrt{n} \log n)$ and $M_S(n) = O(n \sqrt{n})$. Applying Theorem 8.3.1. we obtain:

Theorem 8.3.3. The batched dynamic version of the half-planar range counting problem can be solved such that

$$P^d(n) = O(n \sqrt{n} \log n),$$
$$M^d(n) = O(n \sqrt{n}).$$

8.4. Streaming.

In this section we will describe a method, called "streaming", for reducing the amount of space required for solving batched (static or dynamic) versions of searching problems. The idea of STREAMING is the following. Rather than performing queries one after another on the data structure, we perform them simultaneously. As the data structure is traversed only once we do not need to build the complete structure beforehand but only need the part of the structure at which we are busy performing the queries. We will first consider batched static solutions to decomposable searching problems.

In Section 8.2. a simple technique was described to "balance" the query time and building time of data structures for decomposable searching problems, by splitting the set of points in $f(n)$ subsets and building a structure for each of them. When we want to use such a structure in a batched static environment, there is no need for constructing all $f(n)$ structures beforehand. We can proceed in the following way: for all i from 1 to $f(n)$; build the ith structure, perform all queries on it, combine the answers with the answers over all preceding structures and discard the ith structure. There is only one problem, we have to store partial answers (i.e., answers over a part of the set). Let the answer to a query over a set of n points take $A(n)$ storage. ($A(n)$ is assumed to be nondecreasing.)

Theorem 8.4.1. Given a data structure S for a decomposable searching problem PR and an integer function $f(n)$ with $1 \leq f(n) \leq n$, the batched static version of PR can be solved such that

$$P^S(n) = O(f(n).P_S(n/f(n) + n_q.f(n).Q_S(n/f(n))),$$
$$M^S(n) = O(n + M_S(n/f(n)) + n_q.A(n)).$$

For a number of problems there is no need for storing partial answers. For example in the range searching problem we can immediately report answers found. In such case one can take $A(n)=1$.

Let us consider some applications, again assuming that $n=\theta(n_q)$.

Applications.

a) Fixed radius nearest neighbor searching.

Choosing $f(n) = \left\lceil n^{\frac{2}{3}}/\log^{\frac{1}{3}} n \right\rceil$ in Theorem 8.4.1. (using the structure in [BeM2]), we obtain a solution to the batched static version of the fixed radius nearest neighbor searching problem with

$$P^S(n) = O(n^{\frac{5}{3}} \log^{\frac{2}{3}} n) \quad (+ \text{ the total number of answers}),$$

$$M^S(n) = O(n \log n).$$

Compare Theorem 8.2.3.

b) Half-planar range counting.

Applying Theorem 8.4.1. to the structure for half-planar range counting presented in Section 8.2. with $f(n) = \lceil \sqrt{n} \rceil$, yields a batched static solution with

$$P^S(n) = O(n \sqrt{n} \log n),$$
$$M^S(n) = O(n).$$

Compare Theorem 8.2.4.

Streaming can also be used in other types of data structures. We will demonstrate this by applying the method to super B-trees to obtain a batched static solution to the range searching problem using only linear storage. We will first consider the 2-dimensional case. The idea is to construct the super B-tree level after level. When a level is constructed we immediately perform all partial queries on that level. We subsequently construct the next lower level out of this level (while discarding the former) and proceed. To be able to do this efficiently we order all points in the point set V_s with respect to their x_2-coordinate. All query ranges we order with respect to the left endpoint in the x_2-coordinate (i.e., $([x_{i_1}:y_{i_1}],[x_{i_2}:y_{i_2}]) \leq$ $\leq ([x_{j_1}:y_{j_1}],[x_{j_2}:y_{j_2}])$ when $x_{i_2} \leq x_{j_2}$) and put them in a set V_q. This takes $O(n \log n + n_q \log n_q)$ time. The remainder of the algorithm to solve the batched static version of the range searching problem is best described by the following recursive procedure:

procedure RANGE (point set V_s, range set V_q);
V_s contains a part of the point set (with respect to the first coordinate) ordered
  with respect to the second coordinate and V_q contains ranges that possibly contain
  points of V_s that were not reported before. In other words, refering to the range
  query procedure described in Section 2.3., V_s contains the points below a node α
  in the super B-tree and V_q contains those queries one of whose search paths comes
  through α. #

step 1: Determine the median of the x_1-values of the points in V_s and split V_s
in two subsets $V_s[1]$ of the points with x_1-value smaller than the median
and $V_s[2]$ of points with x_1-value larger than the median, both ordered
with respect to their x_2-values.

step 2: Split V_q in subsets:

$V_q[1]$: ranges that (partially) lie left of the median but do not contain all points in $V_s[1]$ with respect to the first coordinate,

$V_q^c[1]$: ranges that contain all points in $V_s[1]$ with respect to the first coordinate,

$V_q[2]$:
$\left.\begin{array}{l} \\ \\ \end{array}\right\}$ Similar to $V_q[1]$ and $V_q^c[1]$ but with $V_s[2]$ instead of $V_s[1]$.
$V_q^c[2]$:

step 3: Perform the queries in $V_q^c[1]$ on the points in $V_s[1]$ and the queries in $V_q^c[2]$ on the points in $V_s[2]$.

step 4: Call recursively

RANGE$(V_s[1], V_q[1])$;

RANGE$(V_s[2], V_q[2])$.

end of RANGE;

To estimate the amount of time required for RANGE, we make the following observations:

Observation 1: At each moment, a range is in at most two V_q sets and one V_q^c set. A point is always in at most one V_s set.

Observation 2: The splitting of V_s (step 1) can be done in time $O(|V_s|)$ and the splitting of V_q (step 2) can be done in time $O(|V_q|)$.

Observation 3: The level of nesting of the recursive calls is bounded by $O(\log n)$.

Lemma 8.4.2. Step 3 can be performed in $O(n')$ time (+ the number of reported answers), where $n' = |V_s| + |V_q^c[1]| + |V_q^c[2]|$.

Proof

We will only consider the actions necessary to perform the queries in $V_q^c[1]$ on $V_s[1]$. Both $V_s[1]$ and $V_q^c[1]$ are ordered with respect to the x_2-coordinate. We will perform the query during one simultaneous walk along both sets. Let the first range in $V_q^c[1]$ be $([x_{11}:y_{11}],[x_{12}:y_{12}])$. We walk along $V_s[1]$ until we find the first point p_i with x_2-coordinate $\geq x_{12}$. Next we report all points until we find a point with x_2-coordinate $> y_{12}$. In this way we find all points that lie in the range. Next we take the second range and perform the same actions, starting at p_i (preceding points can never lie in the range). This clearly takes time $O(|V_s[1]| + |V_q^c[1]|)$ + the number of answers.

□

It follows from Observations 2 and 3 and Lemma 8.4.2. that the total amount of time needed is bounded by $O((n+n_q)\log n)$ (+ the number of reported answers). From Observation 1 it follows that the amount of storage required is bounded by $O(n+n_q)$.

To solve the batched static version of the d-dimensional range searching problem we use exactly the same procedure, except that we replace step 3 by

step 3: Solve the batched static version of the d-1 dimensional range searching problem with as point set the points in $V_s[1]$ ($V_s[2]$), restricted to the last d-1 coordinates, and as query set the ranges in $V_q^c[1]$ ($V_q^c[2]$), restricted to the last d-1 coordinates.

This easily leads to the following result:

Theorem 8.4.3. The batched static version of the d-dimensional range searching problem can be solved such that

$$P^s(n) = O((n+n_q)\log^{d-1} n + n_q \log n_q) \quad (\text{+ the total number of answers}),$$
$$M^s(n) = O(n+n_q).$$

Similar results can be obtained for the rectangle intersection searching problem.

The idea of streaming can also be applied to the structure for solving the batched dynamic version of decomposable searching problems, given in Section 8.3. (Theorem 8.3.1.). We again build the structure level by level. Assume a batched static solution to a decomposable searching problem PR is known. Let V_s denote the set of points and let with each point its existence interval be given. We order the points in V_s by the begin point of their existence intervals. Let V_q be the set of query objects and let with each query object the moment at which it is performed be given. We order V_q with respect to those moments. Computing the existence intervals and constructing the sets V_s and V_q can be done in time $O(n_q + N \log N)$. As we will perform the queries simultaneously we have to store partial answers (although this may not be necessary for all decomposable searching problems). For this task we use an array ANSW that stores for each query object the answer over the part of the set examined up to now. Each time we compute the answer to a query over a part of the set, we combine it with the corresponding answer in ANSW using the composition operator □. The batched dynamic solution to PR is best described by the following recursive procedure:

<u>procedure</u> BATCHDYN (<u>point set</u> V_s, <u>query set</u> V_q);

\# Refering to the structure described in Section 8.3., V_s contains all points whose existence interval lies partially below some node α but does not cover the whole interval below α and V_q contains those query objects, whose moment lies below α. \#

    <u>step 1</u>: Split V_q in two equal sized subsets $V_q[1]$ and $V_q[2]$ such that all queries in $V_q[1]$ precede the queries in $V_q[2]$.

    <u>step 2</u>: Split V_s in subsets:

        $V_s[1]$: points whose existence interval partially contains the time moments in $V_q[1]$ but does not contain all of them,

        $V_s^c[1]$: points whose existence interval contains all time moments in $V_q[1]$,

        $\left. \begin{array}{l} V_s[2]: \\[1em] V_s^c[2]: \end{array} \right\}$ Similar to $V_s[1]$ and $V_s^c[1]$ but with $V_q[2]$ instead of $V_q[1]$.

        Note that a point can enter in more than one subset.

    <u>step 3</u>: Solve the batched static version of PR with $V_s^c[1]$ ($V_s^c[2]$) as point set and $V_q[1]$ ($V_q[2]$) as query set, combining the answers with the corresponding answers in ANSW.

    <u>step 4</u>: Call recursively:

        BATCHDYN($V_s[1],V_q[1]$);

        BATCHDYN($V_s[2],V_q[2]$).

<u>end</u> of BATCHDYN;

Clearly step 1 takes $O(|V_q|)$ time, step 2 takes $O(|V_s|)$ time and step 3 takes $O(P^s(n'))$ time where $n' = |V_s^c[1]| + |V_s^c[2]|$. As the depth of the recursion is bounded by $O(\log n_q)$, this makes a total of $O(\log n_q.P^s(N) + n_q \log n_q)$ time plus $O(N \log N)$ for computing the existence intervals. Beside the amount of storage required for ANSW, the algorithm takes $O(M^s(N) + n_q + N)$ storage.

<u>Theorem</u> 8.4.4. Given a batched static solution to a decomposable searching problem PR, the batched dynamic version of PR can be solved such that

$$P^d(n) = O(\log n_q.P^s(N) + n_q \log n_q + N \log N),$$
$$M^d(n) = O(n_q.A(m) + M^s(N)),$$

where $A(m)$ denotes the amount of space required for storing the answer over a set of m points.

Assuming that $n=\theta(n_q)=\theta(N)=\theta(m)$, the theorem shows that

$$P^d(n) = O(\log n \cdot P^s(n)),$$
$$M^d(n) = O(M^s(n) + n \cdot A(n)).$$

One easily verifies that $P^d(n) = O(P^s(n))$ when $P^s(n) = \Omega(n^{1+\varepsilon})$ for some $\varepsilon > 0$.

Let us consider some applications.

Applications.

a) Range searching.

Applying Theorem 8.4.4. to the batched static solution of the range searching problem in Theorem 8.4.3., we obtain the following result:

Theorem 8.4.5. The batched dynamic version of the d-dimensional range searching problem can be solved such that

$$P^d(n) = O(n \log^d n) \quad (+ \text{ the total number of answers}),$$
$$M^d(n) = O(n).$$

A similar result can be obtained for the rectangle intersection searching problem.

b) Nearest neighbor searching.

Applying Theorem 8.4.4. to the static data structure known for nearest neighbor searching (Section 2.5.) we obtain:

Theorem 8.4.6. The batched dynamic version of the nearest neighbor searching problem can be solved such that

$$P^d(n) = O(n \log^2 n),$$
$$M^d(n) = O(n).$$

8.5. Reversing searching problems.

For a number of searching problems one can obtain efficient batched static or dynamic solutions by viewing the query objects as set objects and vice versa. We will demonstrate the idea by applying it to the triangular range searching problem. The TRIANGULAR RANGE SEARCHING problem is the following: given a set of points in the plane, report all points that lie within a given query triangle. Some data structures are known for the problem. Willard [Wi4] describes a structure with $Q_s(n) = O(n^{\log_6 4})$, $P_s(n) = O(n^2)$ and $M_s(n) = O(n \log n)$. Edelsbrunner, Kirkpatrick and Maurer [EdKM] solve the problem in $Q_s(n) = O(\log n)$, $P_s(n) = O(n^7)$ and $M_s(n) = O(n^7)$. Hence, both structures are quite inappropriate for solving the batched static version of the problem,

even when we apply Theorem 8.4.1. But to solve the batched static version we might as
well ask for each point in the set in which query triangles it lies. Hence we can solve
the problem by considering the following searching problem: given a set of triangles
in the plane and a query point x, which triangles of the set contain x. One can easily
give a data structure for this problem with $Q_S(n) = O(\log n)$, $P_S(n) = O(n^3)$ and
$M_S(n) = O(n^3)$, based on a data structure for point location in a planar subdivision
due to Kirkpatrick [Ki2]. Applying Theorem 8.4.1. with $f(n) = \left\lceil n^{\frac{2}{3}}/\log^{\frac{1}{3}} n \right\rceil$, we obtain
tain a batched static solution to the problem with

$$P^S(n) = O(n^{\frac{5}{3}} \log^{\frac{2}{3}} n),$$
$$M^S(n) = O(n \log n),$$

assuming that $n = \theta(n_q)$. It follows that we can solve the batched static version of
the triangular range searching problem within these bounds. Applying Theorem 8.4.4.
we obtain the following result:

Theorem 8.5.1. The batched dynamic version of the triangular range searching problem
can be solved such that

$$P^d(n) = O(n^{\frac{5}{3}} \log^{\frac{2}{3}} n) \quad (+ \text{ the number of reported answers}),$$
$$M^d(n) = O(n \log n).$$

It is hard to give a general definition of problems that can be "reversed" (i.e.,
in which query and set objects can be interchanged). One class of problems that can
be reversed is the class of so-called "set independent" searching problems.

Definition 8.5.2. A searching problem PR is called SET INDEPENDENT if and only if there
exist some function $f(p)$ that maps points into answers and a relation $R(p,x)$ between
points and query objects such that for every set of points V

$$PR(x,V) = \{f(p) \mid p \in V \wedge R(p,x)\}.$$

Hence, the answer to such a searching problem consists of a set of answers $f(p)$ for
those points $p \in V$ that satisfy the relation $R(p,x)$. Whether $f(p)$ is reported or not
is independent of the other elements of the set. Clearly, a set independent problem
is decomposable. Some examples of set independent problems are the range searching
problem, the rectangle intersection searching problem, the fixed radius nearest
neighbor searching problem and the triangular range searching problem defined above.

Theorem 8.5.3. A set independent searching problem PR is reversible.

Proof

The answer to the batched static version of PR consists of a number of pairs $(x, f(p))$, where x is one of the query objects and $p \in V$ and $R(p,x)$. We can compute the pairs by solving for each $p \in V$ the searching problem $PR'(p, V_q)$ where V_q is the set of query objects, and

$$PR'(p, V_q) = \{x \in V' \mid R(p,x)\}.$$

                                               □

The interchange of set and query objects does not give better results for all set independent searching problem. An example for which we do get better results is the circular range searching problem (see Section 2.11.). The reversed problem asks for those circles in a set that contain a given query point. Using the planar point location algorithm of Preparata [Pr] this problem can be solved statically within $Q_S(n) = O(\log n)$, $P_S(n) = O(n^3)$ and $M_S(n) = O(n^3)$. Applying Theorem 8.4.1. with $f(n) = \left\lceil n^{\frac{2}{3}}/\log^{\frac{1}{3}} n \right\rceil$ we can solve the batched static version of this problem, and hence, the batched static version of the circular range searching problem within

$$P^S(n) = O(n^{\frac{5}{3}} \log^{\frac{2}{3}} n),$$
$$M^S(n) = O(n \log n)$$

(assuming that $n = \theta(n_q)$). Applying Theorem 8.4.4. we obtain the following result:

Theorem 8.5.4. The batched dynamic version of the circular range searching problem can be solved such that

$$P^d(n) = O(n^{\frac{5}{3}} \log^{\frac{2}{3}} n) \quad (+ \text{ the number of reported answers}),$$
$$M^d(n) = O(n \log n).$$

8.6. Concluding remarks.

We have given a number of techniques for turning static solutions to searching problems into batched static or batched dynamic solutions. The techniques are especially applicable to decomposable searching problems. It shows in particular that batched versions of searching problems can normally be solved using relatively little space.

The technique can be improved in a number of ways. For example, when the number of query objects, set objects and updates are not of the same order of magnitude, the structures can be tuned to obtain better time bounds. (See [EdO2] for some details.)

Bibliographical comments.

This chapter was based on Edelsbrunner and Overmars [EdO2].

CHAPTER IX

SEARCHING IN THE PAST

9.1. Introduction.

In this chapter we will consider yet another way of dynamizing searching problems. When we have a dynamically changing set of objects stored in a dynamic data structure, it is sometimes important to be able to answer queries over the set of objects as it was at some moment in the past. For example, given a database containing a company's personnel administration, it might be important to be able to ask questions like: how many people had a salary $\geq x$ one year ago. Most known data structures are unable to give this kind of information because they overwrite and eliminate old information about objects that are deleted. To answer this kind of so-called in-the-past queries, we require that the data structure can remember relevant information concerning its own history.

Definition 9.1.1. Let S be a dynamic data structure for a searching problem. Define $\{t_i\}_{i \geq 0}$ by:

t_0 = the moment of time at which we initiated the empty structure S,

t_i = the moment of time just before the ith update is performed on S ($i \geq 1$).

N will always denote the number of the next update to consider, that will be performed at (i.e., just after) time moment t_N. In fact, without loss of generality, we will view t_N as being "now". In an ordinary dynamic data structure one can perform updates at t_N and queries over the situation at t_N. To solve a searching problem PR "IN THE PAST" (also called the in-the-past version of PR) we need a data structure S' that allows for updates at time t_N and queries over the situation at any specified moment t in the past (i.e., with $t \leq t_N$). If $t_i < t \leq t_{i+1}$, then performing a query at moment t means performing the query over the point set as it was after the ith update.

A first structure for answering queries in the past was given by Dobkin and Munro [DoM]. They gave a structure for performing in-the-past queries for the kth element searching problem and the rank searching problem (see Section 2.2.). Their structure is static in the sense that all updates, together with the moments at which they are performed, are given beforehand and hence, once the structure is built no updates can be performed anymore. The structure can be built in O(N log N) time, uses O(N log N) storage and has a query time of $O(\log^2 N)$. Dobkin and Munro [DoM] use their structure for solving certain polyhedra problems.

We will concentrate on the online version of in-the-past searching problems, in which the updates are not known beforehand. Hence our structures have to be dynamic. In Section 9.2. we show that member searching in the past can be solved within $O(\log N)$ query and update time bounds, using only linear space. In Section 9.3. we consider the online in-the-past version of the kth element/rank searching problem. We will devise a structure for it with a query time of $O(\log N)$ and an update time of $O(\log N)$, using $O(N \log N)$ storage. In this way we improve the bounds of the static structure of Dobkin and Munro [DoM]. We also show that, using this structure, the in-the-past version of the range counting problem can be solved efficiently.

In Sections 9.4. - 9.5. we focus on general methods for turning dynamic and static data structures for searching problems into structures for solving the corresponding in-the-past searching problems. In Section 9.4. we give a ("brute force") transformation, applicable to all searching problems for which a dynamic data structure is known. The method yields reasonable, but not extremely efficient, structures for the in-the-past problems. In Sections 9.5. and 9.6. we concentrate on decomposable searching problems. First we devise a transformation that turns static data structures for searching problems into half-dynamic data structures (only supporting insertions) for the corresponding in-the-past problems. Next we give a transformation that maps dynamic data structures for decomposable searching problems into fully dynamic in-the-past structures. In Section 9.7. we give some extensions and conclusions.

Throughout this chapter we will use the notations $Q_S(N)$, $I_S(N)$, $D_S(N)$, $P_S(N)$ and $M_S(N)$ to denote the query, insertion, deletion, preprocessing time and amount of storage required for an in-the-past structure S on which N updates have been performed since it was initiated (empty).

9.2. Member searching.

The in-the-past version of the member searching problem is the following: given a dynamic set of object V, an object x and a moment t in the past, we want to know whether $x \in V$ at moment t. To be able to answer such queries we have to store all objects that have once been in the set. We will allow that objects that are deleted can be reinserted at some later moment, but we assume that when we want to insert a point it is not present and that when we want to delete a point it is present. (It can always be checked whether or not these conditions are satisfied by first performing a query with the point at moment t_N.) Let us look at some point p that has been, or possibly is, in the set. At t_0 (the moment we initiated the structure) p surely was not present, but at some first moment t_{i_1} p was inserted. It is possible that at some later moment t_{i_2} $(i_2 > i_1)$ p was deleted. Maybe it was reinserted again at t_{i_3}, deleted again at t_{i_4} etc. Hence, we get a number of non-overlapping intervals of time $[t_{i_1}:t_{i_2}], [t_{i_3}:t_{i_4}], \ldots$

with the last one possibly open (hence up to t_N) at which p was present in the set.
See figure 9.2.1.; a 1 denotes that p is present, a 0 that it is not present. These
observations lead to a fairly simple data structure for member searching in the past.

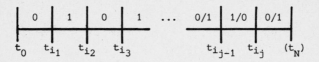

figure 9.2.1.

As a main structure we use a balanced binary leaf-search tree T (for example an AVL-
tree) in which we store all points that have once been in the set. With each point p
in T we associate a structure T_p that represents the intervals of time at which p was
present. Because these intervals are non-overlapping, we can use for T_p a balanced
binary search tree in which we store t_0, t_{i_1}, t_{i_2}, ... With each t_{i_j} we mark whether
x was present in the set after moment t_{i_j} or not. Hence, we get the structure of the
type as displayed in figure 9.2.2. To perform a query with object x at moment t, we
first search for x in T. If we do not find x, we know that x has never been present

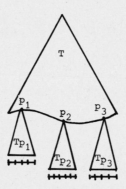

figure 9.2.2.

in the set and, hence, surely not at moment t. Otherwise, we find a structure T_x that
holds the intervals at which x was present. We search in T_x for the largest $t_i < t$. The
information stored with t_i tells us whether x was present at moment t or not.

To insert a point p in the structure, we first search for p in t. If we do not
find p, it has never been present before, and we have to insert it in T. Next, we associate with it a structure T_p, containing t_0 and t_N (i.e., the moment of insertion),

noting that p is present after t_N. Otherwise, if we do find p in T, we insert t_N in T_p, noting that p is present after t_N. When we want to delete a point p we first search for p in T (it must be present). Next, we insert t_N in T_p, noting that p is no longer present after t_N.

Theorem 9.2.1. There exists a structure T for member searching in the past such that

$$Q_T(N) = O(\log N),$$
$$I_T(N) = O(\log N),$$
$$D_T(N) = O(\log N),$$
$$M_T(N) = O(N).$$

Proof

The main structure T contains at most N points and all associated structures T_p together contain O(N) moments of time. Hence, a query consists of two member queries on balanced structures of at most N points, and thus takes at most O(log N) time. Because an insertion consists of a search on T and an insertion in T or in a T_p, and a deletion consists also of a search on T and an insertion in a T_p, the update time is clearly bounded by O(log N). T clearly takes O(N) storage and the associated structures together also need O(N) storage.

□

9.3. k^{th} element/rank searching.

We will describe one data structure for solving both the kth element searching problem and the rank searching problem in the past. The structure we use consists of a BB[α]-tree (see Section 3.2.2.) augmented in a way similar to the structure for range searching described by Willard [Wi3]. In this BB[α]-tree we keep all points that have once been in the set in the appropriate order at the leaves. At each internal node β of the tree T we would like to have some information about the number of the points in the subtree, rooted at β, that were present at different moments in the past. To this end, we associate with each internal node β a list L_β that contains all moments of time t_{ij} at which a point in the subtree, rooted at β, got inserted or deleted. With each such moment t_{ij} we give the number of the points below β that were present after t_{ij} (i.e., between t_{ij} and t_{ij+1}). With β, we keep two pointers first(β) and last(β) pointing to the first and the last moment in L_β, respectively (see figure 9.3.1.). To be able to search fast through the associated lists, we link them internally. To this end we add to a record in L_β with time moment t_{ij} a pointer lson to the last moment of time before or equal to t_{ij} in $L_{lson(\beta)}$ (the list associated with the leftson of β) and a pointer rson to the last moment of time before or equal

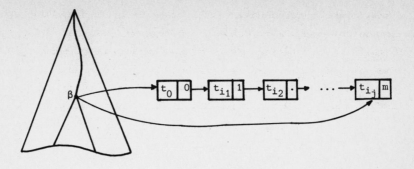

figure 9.3.1.

to t_{i_j} in $L_{rson(\beta)}$. Hence, each record in a list L_β contains the following fields (see figure 9.3.2.).

        time: the moment of time t_{i_j},

        numb: the number of the points in the subtree below β that were present

             after t_{i_j},

        lson: the pointer to $L_{lson(\beta)}$ as described above,

        rson: the pointer to $L_{rson(\beta)}$ as described above,

        next: a pointer to the next record in the list L_β.

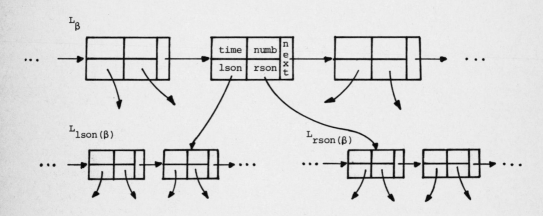

figure 9.3.2.

To be able to search in the list L_{root} associated with the root of T, that contains all moments of time t_i at which an update was performed on the tree, we build a balanced binary search tree T_{root} on top of L_{root}.

We will first show how queries can be performed on the structure described. To perform a kth element query at time t we first search in T_{root} for the last $t_i < t$. In this way we reach a record rec in L_{root}. The actions we have to perform from this moment on are best described by the following recursive procedure FINDK that steadily works its way down the tree T with one pointer in the main structure to find the appropriate k^{th} element and another pointer in the associated lists to guide the search.

procedure FINDK (node β, record rec, integer k);
the point we are searching for is the kth element of the points below β at time t.
  rec is the record in $L_β$ that contains the last moment t_{ij} before t at which some
  point below β got inserted or deleted (or $t_{ij} = t_0$). #

    step 1: If β is a leaf, k=1 and numb of rec = 1 (i.e., the point in β was present
          at moment t) then report the point contained in β.
          If β is a leaf but k≠1 or numb of rec = 0 then report that the point we
          searched for did not exist at moment t (i.e., the set contained too few
          elements at moment t).

    step 2: If β is not a leaf, then let l be numb of lson of rec (i.e., the number
          of points present below lson(β) at moment t). If l≥k then the point we
          search for is the kth element (at moment t) below lson(β). Hence, call
                    FINDK(lson(β), lson of rec, k);
          Otherwise, the point we search for is the $(k-1)^{th}$ element (at moment t)
          below rson(β) and thus call
                    FINDK(rson(β), rson of rec, k-1);

end of FINDK;

We call the procedure as FINDK(root, rec, k);

Lemma 9.3.1. A kth element query in the past takes O(log N) time.

Proof

    As both T and T_{root} are balanced search trees containing N objects their depth is bounded by O(log N). Hence, the search for the appropriate moment $t_i < t$ in T_{root} takes O(log N). Aside from the recursive call, FINDK takes O(1) time. Hence, the amount of time needed by FINDK is bounded by the depth of T, hence, by O(log N).

                                              □

    To perform a rank query with some object x at time moment t in the past we again search with one pointer through T and with a second pointer through the associated lists, but this time the pointer in T guides the search towards the position of x among the leaves while the pointer in the lists is used to compute the answer. Again we start searching with t in T_{root} to locate the last t_i in L_{root} with $t_i < t$. In this way we find a record rec in L_{root}. The remaining steps are best described by the following recursive procedure FINDR.

procedure FINDR (point x, node β, record rec, integer k),
x is the query object of which we want to know the rank at time moment t, β is the
  node we most recently reached on our search in T towards x, rec is the record in $L_β$
  containing the last moment <t at which a point below β got inserted or deleted and
  k gives the number of points we already found to be smaller than x at moment t. #

  step 1: If β is a leaf, β contains x and numb of rec = 1 (i.e., x was present
          at moment t) then report k+1.
          If β is a leaf but β does not contain x or numb of rec = 0 then x was
          not present at moment t and thus report k.

  step 2: If β is not a leaf and x lies below lson(β) then call
                    FINDR(x, lson(β), lson of rec, k);
          otherwise, when x lies below rson(β), all points below lson(β) are smaller
          than x. Hence, call
                    FINDR(x, rson(β), rson of rec, k + numb of lson of rec);
end of FINDR;

We call the procedure as FINDR(x, root, rec, 0);

Lemma 9.3.2. A rank query in the past takes O(log N) time.

Proof
     The arguments are exactly the same as in the proof of Lemma 9.3.1.

                                                                        □

Hence, the structure described enables us to perform both k^{th} element and rank queries in the past, efficiently. It remains to be shown that updates can be performed efficiently as well.
     We will assume that a point is inserted only once and possibly deleted at some later moment. (This restriction is not essential as we can consider a reinserted point as a "different" point.) We will first consider insertions. Note that an insertion is always performed at t_N. So in all lists $L_β$ associated with nodes β on the search path towards the newly inserted point, we have to add a record containing t_N. As t_N is bigger than any moment of time in the lists sofar, it has to be added at the right side of the lists. This can be done easily, following the pointers last(β). Filling in the

fields of the new record is easy (see the procedure INSERT described below). There is only one problem. Because the inserted point p has never been present before, we have to add a new leaf to the tree. This may cause the tree to go out of balance. The task of rebalancing we delegate to a procedure BALANCE that will be described later. The procedure INSERT described below works its way down the tree towards the place the new point needs to be inserted, meanwhile updating the lists associated with the nodes on the search path. After it reaches the leaf it calls for the procedure BALANCE that works its way back to the root, meanwhile making the appropriate rebalancings.

procedure INSERT(point p, node β);
p is the point that has to be inserted (at time moment t_N) and β is the node we
  most recently reached on our way down the tree towards the place where p must be
  inserted. #

    step 1: Construct a new record rec with

$$\text{time of rec} := t_N;$$
$$\text{numb of rec} := \text{numb of last}(β) + 1;$$

          and put it in the list $L_β$ by performing

$$\text{next of last}(β) := \text{rec};$$
$$\text{last}(β) := \text{rec};$$

    step 2: If β is not the root of the tree, then fill in the lson and rson fields
          of the new record added to the list of the father of β, in the following
          way

$$\text{lson of last}(\text{father}(β)) := \text{last}(\text{lson}(\text{father}(β)));$$
$$\text{rson of last}(\text{father}(β)) := \text{last}(\text{rson}(\text{father}(β)));$$

    step 3: If β is a leaf then build two nodes, one containing the point in β and
          the other containing p. Construct the lists that have to be associated
          with the two nodes (each list containing at most three records) and add
          the two nodes as sons to β, leaving β with an intermediate value to guide
          the search. Fill in the lson and rson fields of the records in $L_β$. Call
          BALANCE.

    step 4: If β is not a leaf and p must come below lson(β) then call

$$\text{INSERT}(p, \text{lson}(β));$$

          else, if p must come below rson(β) then call

$$\text{INSERT}(p, \text{rson}(β));$$

end of INSERT;

We call the procedure as INSERT(p, root);. Afterwards we insert t_N in T_{root} with a pointer to the last record in L_{root}. In this way the structure is maintained correctly, provided that we have an algorithm for BALANCE.

To keep the structure balanced we will apply the local rebuilding technique for augmented search trees as demonstrated (briefly) in Section 3.4. We choose the main structure T to be a BB[α]-tree. Hence rebalancing is performed by single and double rotations at nodes along the search path towards the inserted point (see Section 3.2.2.). We will only consider the case in which a single rotation is needed as double rotation can be treated similar. See figure 9.3.3. for the notations used. To perform a single rotation we have to build the list L that has to be associated with α and we

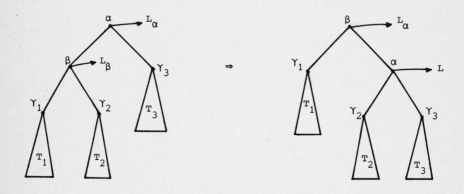

figure 9.3.3.

have to recompute the pointers lson and rson of the records in L_α that will be associated with β. Building L can be done by merging (and copying) the lists L_{γ_2} and L_{γ_3}. Recomputing the lson and rson values in L_α can be done during one simultaneous walk along the lists L_{γ_1}, L and the old L_α. It follows that when the size of L_α is N', the total amount of work needed for such a single rotation is bounded by O(N'). A similar result holds for double rotations. As the number of points below α is θ(N'), one can show, using a tedious argument of Lueker [Lu2] and Willard [Wi1,Wi2], that this O(N') work can be divided over some c.N' insertions that will be performed in the subtree rooted at α (now β) after the rotation, each time doing O(1) work on the construction of the lists, while, in the meantime, no rotation is needed at any of the nodes concerned. For query answering we still use information in the old lists or in the lists of some near descendants of α. It has been shown that in this way, augmented BB[α]-trees remain balanced while the query time does not increase in order of magnitude (see Lueker [Lu2] and Willard [Wi1,Wi2] for more details). It follows that with each insertion we have to do at most O(1) work on reconstruction for each node on the search path towards the inserted point and hence at most O(log N) work total.

Lemma 9.3.3. Insertions take at most O(log N) time each.

Proof

Aside from the recursive call (and BALANCE), the procedure INSERT takes at most O(1) time, and hence, because T is balanced and BALANCE takes O(log N) by the arguments above, INSERT takes O(log N) time. Also the updating of T_{root} takes O(log N) time.

□

Deleting a point p is much more easy than inserting a point. We only have to add a record with t_N to the list L_β associated to each node β on the search path towards p with numb of rec := numb of last(β) - 1. Filling in the other fields proceeds in the same way as in the case of insertions (step 1 and 2). Next we have to insert t_N in T_{root} and that is all. Because we do not actually delete p from T, the structure remains balanced.

Lemma 9.3.4. Deletions take at most O(log N) time each.

Proof

Follows from the proof of Lemma 9.3.3., ignoring the costs for the actual insertion and for BALANCE.

□

Lemmas 9.3.1. - 9.3.4. lead to the following result for k^{th} element/rank searching in the past:

Theorem 9.3.5. There exists a structure T for solving both the kth element and the rank searching problem in the past such that

$$Q_T(N) = O(\log N),$$
$$I_T(N) = O(\log N),$$
$$D_T(N) = O(\log N),$$
$$M_T(N) = O(N \log N).$$

Proof

The bounds on query, insertion and deletion time follow from Lemmas 9.3.1. - 9.3.4. With each update we add O(log N) records to lists. It follows that at time t_N, i.e., now, there are at most O(N log N) records. As both T and T_{root} take only linear storage, the bound on the amount of storage required follows.

□

Dobkin and Munro [DoM] use their structure for k^{th} element/rank searching in the past for solving certain polyhedra problems. As our (dynamic) structure has a query time of $O(\log N)$, while their (static) structure has a query time of $O(\log^2 N)$, most of the time bounds for their applications can be reduced by a factor of $\log N$, using the structure described above.

The structure can also be used for solving the 1-dimensional range counting problem in the past. Given a range [x:y], the number of points in it is equal to the number of points $\leq y$ minus the number of points $<x$, i.e., if x is not in the set rank y - - rank x and otherwise rank y - rank x + 1. Hence, we can solve the 1-dimensional range counting problem using the rank searching problem (and the member searching problem). So, to solve the in-the-past version of the 1-dimensional range counting problem we can use the structure described above, yielding a query and update time of $O(\log N)$.

To solve the d-dimensional range counting problem in the past, we use a super B-tree as described in Sections 2.3. and 3.4. except that we replace the 1-dimensional substructures by the structures described above. Queries are performed in the ordinary way until we come to the 1-dimensional structures on which we perform the queries in the way described above. Hence the moment of time at which the query has to be performed is only considered by the time we come to the 1-dimensional substructures. In this way, the query time is clearly bounded by $O(\log^d N)$. Insertions are performed in the same way as for ordinary super B-trees, until we come to the 1-dimensional substructures. For them we use the procedure INSERT described above. To delete a point p, we search for all 1-dimensional substructures the point is in and "delete" p from these structures in the way described above. Hence, the point is nowhere actually deleted. One easily verifies that updates performed in this way take $O(\log^d N)$ time each. This leads to the following result:

Theorem 9.3.6. There exists a structure S for solving the d-dimensional range counting problem in the past such that

$$Q_S(N) = O(\log^d N),$$
$$I_S(N) = O(\log^d N),$$
$$D_S(N) = O(\log^d N),$$
$$M_S(N) = O(N \log^d N).$$

Proof

This follows from the results known for super B-trees, Theorem 9.3.5. and the above discussion.

□

9.4. A very general approach.

In the previous two sections we devised in-the-past structures for two special
problems, making use of special properties of the problems. In this section we will
consider some very general techniques for transforming static or dynamic data structures for searching problems into structures for the corresponding in-the-past problems.

When only a static data structure S is known for the searching problem PR (and
no additional properties of S and PR are known) there seem to be only two ways of
transforming S into a structure for solving the in-the-past version of PR. A first
possibility is to build a static data structure S_i of all points currently in the set
after each update (at time moment t_i). To query the structure with object x at moment
t we first locate the last S_i such that $t_i < t$ and next perform a query with x on S_i.
This clearly yields a structure S' for solving PR in the past such that

$$Q_{S'}(N) = O(\log N + Q_S(N)),$$
$$I_{S'}(N) = O(P_S(N)),$$
$$D_{S'}(N) = O(P_S(N)),$$
$$M_{S'}(N) = O(N)M_S(N).$$

The query time of this structure is optimal (because $O(\log N)$ is always needed for locating the right moment of time and $Q_S(N)$ is always needed for querying the set) but
the update time and the amount of storage required are very bad. The second solution
works exactly the other way round. With each update we just list the point that is
inserted or deleted. When we want to perform a query we walk along all updates preceding the query moment t, in this way collecting the set of points present at moment
t. Next we build a structure of these points and perform a query on the structure.
It yields a structure S' such that

$$Q_{S'}(N) = O(N \log N + P_S(N) + Q_S(N)),$$
$$I_{S'}(N) = O(1),$$
$$D_{S'}(N) = O(1),$$
$$M_{S'}(N) = O(M_S(N)).$$

Hence, the update time is optimal, but now the query time is very bad.

When the data structure S known for the searching problem is dynamic, we can do
much better by, in some sense, mixing the two methods described. In this way we get
better trade-offs between update and query times. Rather than building another structure immediately after each update, we do so only every time after a number of updates
has occurred. With the updates in between two structures we only list the point that
has been inserted or deleted. To perform a query at some moment t, we start with the
structure nearest before t. On this structure we perform all updates up to t, next
we perform the query, and afterwards we restore the structure to its original shape.
This can be done easily by keeping a record of actions while we update the structure

and unwinding this record afterwards. When we make the gaps in between the structures broad, we will get a high query time and a low (average) update time, and when we make the gaps narrow we will get a low query time and a high (average) update time. Let f be a positive, nondecreasing, smooth integer function. Let $i_1 = 1$, and $i_{j+1} = i_j + f(i_j)$. We build a dynamic structure S_j of all points currently in the set after each time moment t_{i_j} (i.e., together with the i_jth update). Hence, between the structure after t_{i_j} and the structure after $t_{i_{j+1}}$ there are $f(i_j)$ updates at which we have done nothing but listing the points that were inserted or deleted. To be able to build a structure S_j after time moment t_{i_j} efficiently, we have to keep track of all points currently in the set. Therefore, we add to the structure a simple balanced search structure DICT of all points present. Updating DICT takes $O(\log N)$ time per update. So with each update we have to do at least $O(\log N)$ work, but some updates (those at moments t_{i_j}) are much more expensive. But, if the number of cheap updates is large (depending on the choice for f), the average update time will become reasonable.

Theorem 9.4.1. Let S be a dynamic data structure for a searching problem PR. For each positive, nondecreasing, smooth integer function f with $f(N) \leq N$ for all N, there exists a structure S' for solving PR in the past such that

$$Q_{S'}(N) = O(\log N + f(N)U_S(N) + Q_S(N)),$$

$$I^a_{S'}(N) = O(\log N + P_S(N)/f(N)),$$

$$D^a_{S'}(N) = O(\log N + P_S(N)/f(N)),$$

$$M_{S'}(N) = O(N/f(N))M_S(N),$$

where $U_S(N) = \max(I_S(N), D_S(N))$.

Proof

Let us consider the update time first. With each update we have to do $O(\log N)$ work on updating DICT. The amount of time needed to build S_j (after time moment t_{i_j}) is bounded by $P_S(i_j)$. Charging these costs to the $f(i_{j-1})$ updates that have taken place since the previous building of a structure makes for $P_S(i_j)/f(i_{j-1})$ steps per update. Because $f(N) \leq N$ for all N, $i_j \leq 2i_{j-1}$. Hence, because f is nondecreasing $f(i_j) \leq f(2i_{j-1})$ and because f is smooth $f(i_j) = O(f(i_{j-1}))$. It follows that

$$P_S(i_j)/f(i_{j-1}) = O(P_S(i_j)/f(i_j))$$

and, using also that P_S is at least linear, we can estimate this by $O(P_S(N)/f(N))$. The average update time follows.

When we want to perform a query at moment t, we first have to locate the structure S_j nearest before t. This can be done in $O(\log N)$ time using binary search. Next we have to perform at most $f(N)$ updates on S_j, which takes $O(f(N)U_S(N))$ time. Keeping the record of action can be done within the same amount of time. The query itself takes $Q_S(N)$. Undoing the updates, to restore S_j to its original form, using the record of actions, takes the same amount of time as the updates themselves. The query time follows.

In the same way as we charged building time to updates we can charge storage to updates. A structure S_j takes at most $M_S(i_j)$ storage. Sharing this over the $f(i_{j-1})$ updates that took place since S_{j-1} was built makes for $M_S(i_j)/f(i_{j-1})$ storage per update. We can estimate this by $M_S(N)/f(N)$. Hence the total amount of storage needed for the S-structures is bounded by $O(N/f(N))M_S(N)$. The amount of storage required for listing the updates and for DICT is bounded by $O(N)$. As $N \leq O(N/f(N))M_S(N)$, the bound follows.

□

The averages in update time appear because we build the S_j structures at once after the updates at t_{i_j}. Instead of doing so, we could spread the work over the next $f(i_{j-1})$ updates, each time doing $P_S(i_j)/f(i_{j-1})$ work on the construction. Because f is nondecreasing, it follows that S_j will be ready before we have to start building S_{j+1}. Hence, with each update we do at most $O(\log N + P_S(N)/f(N))$ work. Hence, we changed the average bounds on update time into worst-case bounds. It remains to be shown that this does not increase the query time in order of magnitude. (It clearly does not increase the bound on the amount of storage required.) When we want to perform a query at moment t, with $t_{i_j} < t \leq t_{i_{j+1}}$ it is possible that the structure S_j is not yet ready. But S_{j-1} surely is ready. Hence, we can start with S_{j-1}, perform the updates on it up to t, perform the query and restore S_{j-1} in its original form, Hence, we have to perform at most $f(i_{j-1}) + f(i_j) \leq 2f(i_j)$ updates. It follows that the query time remains of the same order of magnitude.

Theorem 9.4.2. Let S be a dynamic data structure for a searching problem PR. For each positive, nondecreasing, smooth integer function f, with $f(N) \leq N$ for all N, there exists a structure S' for solving PR in the past such that

$$Q_{S'}(N) = O(\log N + f(N)U_S(N) + Q_S(N)),$$
$$I_{S'}(N) = O(\log N + P_S(N)/f(N)),$$
$$D_{S'}(N) = O(\log N + P_S(N)/f(N)),$$
$$M_{S'}(N) = O(N/f(N))M_S(N).$$

As an example, consider the 2-dimensional convex hull searching problem. In Section 6.4.1. a dynamic structure was given with an update time of $O(\log^2 n)$, a query time of $O(\log n)$ and a preprocessing time of $O(n \log n)$, using $O(n)$ storage. Applying Theorem 9.4.2. with $f(N) = \lceil \sqrt{N}/\log N \rceil$, we obtain a structure S' for 2-dimensional convex hull searching in the past such that

$$Q_{S'}(N) = O(\sqrt{N} \log N),$$
$$I_{S'}(N) = O(\sqrt{N} \log^2 N),$$
$$D_{S'}(N) = O(\sqrt{N} \log^2 N),$$
$$M_{S'}(N) = O(N \cdot \sqrt{N} \log N).$$

Other trade-offs between query and update time (and storage required) can be obtained by different choices of f.

When the amount of storage required for the dynamic data structure S is smaller than the time required to build S, it is often possible to obtain better bounds for the update time by copying structures, rather than rebuilding them for scratch. Let $COP_S(n)$ be the time required to copy a S-structure containing n points. (In general we can take $COP_S(n) = O(M_S(n))$.) We will first show how better average update time bounds can be obtained. At the moment a structure S_{j-1} is ready, i.e., after the i_{j-1}th update, we copy the structure. Each time we perform an update, we perform it on the copy. It follows that when we come to the i_jth update S_j is ready. Next we copy this structure and perform the forthcoming updates on it until we come to the i_{j+1}th update etc. (Note that we do no longer need DICT.)

Theorem 9.4.3. Let S be a dynamic data structure for a searching problem PR. For each positive, nondecreasing, smooth integer function f, with $f(N) \leq N$, there exists a structure S' for solving PR in the past such that

$$Q_{S'}(N) = O(\log N + f(N) U_S(N) + Q_S(N)),$$
$$I^a_{S'}(N) = O(COP_S(N)/f(N) + I_S(N)),$$
$$D^a_{S'}(N) = O(COP_S(N)/f(N) + D_S(N)),$$
$$M_{S'}(N) = O(N/f(N)) M_S(N).$$

Proof

The bounds on query time and the amount of storage required follow from Theorem 9.4.1. The amount of time required for copying a structure S_j, we charge to the preceding $f(i_{j-1})$ updates. With an insertion we have to do $I_S(N)$ work for performing the update on a copy. Moreover we charged $COP_S(N)/f(N)$ work to it for copying. Hence, the average insertion time becomes $O(COP_S(N)/f(N) + I_S(N))$. Similar for the average deletion time.

□

It is again possible to change the average update time bounds into worst-case bounds, but the method is quite complex. (It is in some sense similar to the proof of Theorem 5.2.2.1.) We will only give a sketch of the method here. The interested reader is referred to [Ov6]. Rather than copying a structure S_{j-1} at once, we spread the work over the next $f(i_{j-1})$ updates. But these updates have to be performed on this copy. We cannot do this before the construction is finished. To have time left for performing the updates, we speed up the construction, doing with each insertion $I_S(i_j)$ extra work and with each deletion $D_S(i_j)$ extra work. When the construction is finished, we start performing the (buffered) updates in the right order, doing with each insertion $COP_S(i_{j-1})/f(i_{j-1}) + I_S(i_j)$ work and with each deletion $COP_S(i_{j-1})/f(i_{j-1}) + D_S(i_j)$ work. One easily verifies that the process overtakes itself before we come to the $i_j{}^{th}$ update. Hence, the structure will be available in time. This leads to the following result:

Theorem 9.4.4. Let S be a dynamic data structure for a searching problem PR. For each positive, nondecreasing, smooth integer function f, with $f(N) \leq N$, there exists a structure S' for solving PR in the past such that

$$Q_{S'}(N) = O(\log N + f(N)U_S(N) + Q_S(N)),$$
$$I_{S'}(N) = O(COP_S(N)/f(N) + I_S(N)),$$
$$D_{S'}(N) = O(COP_S(N)/f(N) + D_S(N)),$$
$$M_{S'}(N) = O(N/f(N))M_S(N).$$

As an example, let us again consider the 2-dimensional convex hull searching problem. As stated above $M_S(n) = O(n)$. It follows that $COP_S(N) = O(N)$. Applying Theorem 9.4.4. with $f(N) = \lceil \sqrt{N}/\log N \rceil$ we obtain a structure S' for solving the problem in the past such that

$$Q_{S'}(N) = O(\sqrt{N} \log N),$$
$$I_{S'}(N) = O(\sqrt{N} \log N),$$
$$D_{S'}(N) = O(\sqrt{N} \log N),$$
$$M_{S'}(N) = O(N.\sqrt{N} \log N).$$

9.5. Decomposable searching problems: a half-dynamic structure.

Let us now concentrate on decomposable searching problems. We will first show how static data structures can be transformed into half-dynamic in-the-past structures with low average insertion time bounds. When we look at the half-dynamic data structure for decomposable searching problems as described in Section 7.3.1. (the logarithmic method of Bentley [Be3]) it is clear that we never update blocks. We only build new blocks and throw old blocks away. It follows that when we do not destroy these "old" blocks, for any moment t in the past, there are structures of exponentially increasing size that together contain the point set as it was at moment t. Hence, the only real problem is to organize all structures in such a way that we can easily find the ones we need when we perform a query at some time moment t.

To this end we build all time moments t_i at which an insertion occurred, into a balanced binary (leaf-)search tree T. With each time moment t_i we associate a list

L_i of pointers to the blocks that together contain the point set after t_i. (This are at most $O(\log N)$ structures.) To insert a point p (at time t_N) we first insert t_N in T (at the right). Next we take the list of blocks associated with t_{N-1} and perform the insertion of p in the same way as we did in Section 7.3.1. except that we do not really throw blocks away. Next we associate with t_N a list L_N containing pointers to all blocks now "available" according to the insertion procedure. See figure 9.5.1. for an example. To perform a query with query object x at time t, we search with t in T to locate the last $t_i < t$. Next we perform a query with object x on all structures in L_i. This leads to the following result:

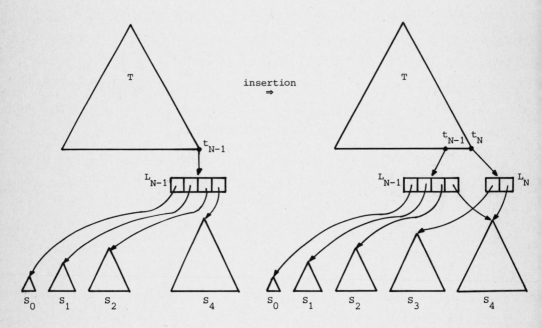

figure 9.5.1.

Theorem 9.5.1. Given a static data structure S for a decomposable searching problem PR, there exists a structure T for solving PR in the past such that

$$Q_T(N) = O(\log N)Q_S(N),$$
$$I_T^a(N) = O(\log N)P_S(N)/N,$$
$$M_T(N) = O(\log N)M_S(N).$$

Proof

For querying the structure we have to do $O(\log N)$ work for searching in T and next we have to perform queries on at most $O(\log N)$ blocks in the list. To perform

an insertion we have to do O(log N) work to perform the insertion in T. Next we have
to perform an insertion like in Section 7.3.1., which takes $O(\log N)P_S(N)/N$ average
time due to Theorem 7.3.1.1. and next we have to build L_N which takes O(log N) time.
The bound on the amount of storage required follows from the following observation.
Each point is in at most one structure of size 1, one structure of size 2, one structure of size 4 etc. It follows that all structures of size 2^i together need at most
$M_S(N)$ storage. As the largest structure has size $\leq N$, the largest i for which there
exist structures of size 2^i is at most log N. The bound follows.

□

Changing the average bound on the insertion time into a worst-case bound goes
easy. Rather than using the structure of Section 7.3.1., we use the method of Section 7.3.2., that yields worst-case bounds, for dynamizing the decomposable searching problem. Again we do not throw away any structures and we build all moments of
time at which an update occurred into a balanced binary search tree T and associate
with each t_i a list L_i in the way described above. In this way we clearly get the
bounds of Theorem 9.5.1. as worst-case bounds.

Theorem 9.5.2. Given a static data structure S for a decomposable searching problem
PR, there exists a structure S' for solving PR in the past such that

$$Q_{S'}(N) = O(\log N)Q_S(N),$$
$$I_{S'}(N) = O(\log N)P_S(N)/N,$$
$$M_{S'}(N) = O(\log N)M_S(N).$$

One easily verifies that $Q_{S'}(N) = O(Q_S(N))$ when $Q_S(N) = \Omega(N^\varepsilon)$ for some $\varepsilon > 0$, that
$I_{S'}(N) = O(P_S(N)/N)$ when $P_S(N) = \Omega(N^{1+\varepsilon})$ for some $\varepsilon > 0$ and that $M_{S'}(N) = O(M_S(N))$ when
$M_S(N) = \Omega(N^{1+\varepsilon})$ for some $\varepsilon > 0$. Hence we get essentially the same time bounds as for
the ordinary dynamization of decomposable searching problems except for the extra
factor of O(log N) in the amount of storage required.

Applications

a) Nearest neighbor searching.
   Applying Theorem 9.5.2. to the structure for nearest neighbor searching described
in Section 2.5., we obtain a structure S' for solving the nearest neighbor searching
problem in the past such that

$$Q_{S'}(N) = O(\log^2 N),$$
$$I_{S'}(N) = O(\log^2 N),$$
$$M_{S'}(N) = O(N \log N).$$

b) Range searching.

Applying Theorem 9.5.2. to the structure for d-dimensional range searching of Willard [Wi3] (see Section 2.3., Theorem 2.3.4.), we obtain a structure S' for the in-the-past version of the problem with

$$Q_{S'}(N) = O(\log^d N + k),$$
$$I_{S'}(N) = O(\log^d N),$$
$$M_{S'}(N) = O(N \log^d N).$$

9.6. Decomposable searching problems: a fully dynamic structure.

The method described in the previous section only allows for insertions. Performing deletions within the same framework seems to be difficult. Therefore, we will use a quite different approach to obtain efficient fully dynamic data structures for the in-the-past version of decomposable searching problems. From now on we assume that the given data structure S for the searching problem in mind is dynamic.

The approach is in some sense an extension of the method described in Section 8.3. for solving the batched dynamic version of decomposable searching problems. With each point in the set we associate an interval of time during which the point was present. When we want to perform a query at time moment t, we first locate all points whose existence interval contains t and next perform a query on these points. To this end, we again use a kind of augmented segment tree. The only problem is that we do not know all segments in advance. Hence, our structure has to be dynamic. But, no arbitrary updates can occur. We either insert a segment starting at t_N (i.e., at a moment of time larger than any moment in the tree) ranging up to infinity, or we change a segment $[t_i : \infty]$ into $[t_i : t_N]$. We will make use of these restrictions to describe a quite efficient structure for searching in the past.

As the main structure for the augmented segment tree we use a special balanced binary search tree that allows for efficient updates at the right.

Definition 9.6.1. A RI-TREE of depth 0 consists of one point. A RI-tree of depth h>0 consists of a root with a perfectly balanced binary left subtree of depth h-1 and a RI-tree of depth at most h-1 as a right subtree. Objects (moments of time in our case) are stored in the leaves of a RI-tree. (See figure 9.6.1.)

Note that there is exactly one way of storing N moments of time in a RI-tree. Clearly RI-trees are balanced (i.e., have a depth of $O(\log N)$).

To insert a new moment of time t_N in a RI-tree (at the right side) we first determine the deepest node α on the rightmost path with the depth of the right subtree of α strictly smaller than the depth of the left subtree of α. Let β be the rightson of α.

RI-tree of depth h:

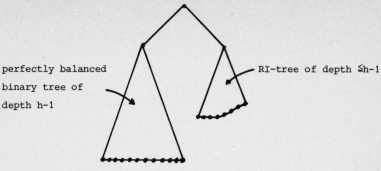

perfectly balanced
binary tree of
depth h-1

RI-tree of depth ≦h-1

figure 9.6.1.

It follows that the subtree rooted at β is perfectly balanced and hence, we can perform
the actions displayed in figure 9.6.2.a. If no such node α does exist, the whole RI-
tree is perfectly balanced and hence, we can perform the actions displayed in figure
9.6.2.b. Determining such a node α can clearly be done in $O(\log N)$ time. Hence, the
insertion of a new time moment t_N takes at most $O(\log N)$ time. It can even be shown
that insertions at the right side can be performed in time $O(1)$ but this is not important here, see [Ov6].

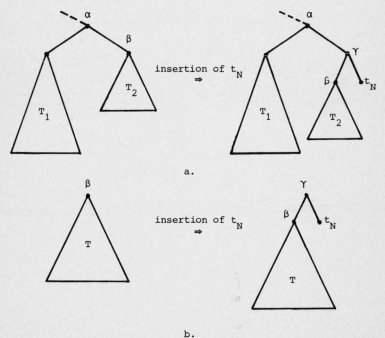

figure 9.6.2.

We will use the RI-tree T as the main structure for our augmented segment tree. To each internal node α we associate a S-structure of all points whose existence interval does contain the time interval below α but does not contain the time interval below the father of α.

To perform a query with query object x at time moment t we search with t in T to locate the last time moment t_i with $t_i < t$, and perform a query with x on the structures associated with the nodes passed on the search path and combine these answers using the composition operator of the decomposable searching problem.

To perform an insertion of a point p (at time t_N) we first insert t_N in the RI-tree in the way described above. Next we have to construct the S-structure S_{t_N} that has to be associated with t_N. This structure consists of the point p and those points that were inserted at time moments in T_2 and are not deleted yet. Moreover, the structure associated with β must now be associated with γ. The structure associated with β becomes empty. See figure 9.6.3. for the actions that have to be performed. Such an

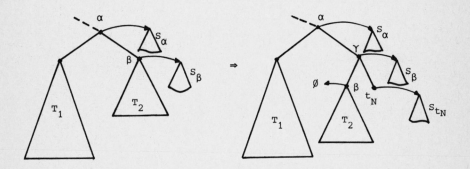

figure 9.6.3.

insertion sometimes takes a lot of time (when T_2 is large) but the average insertion time will be low.

Lemma 9.6.2. $I_T^a(N) = O(\log N)P_S(N)/N$.

Proof
        Clearly the insertion time is worse when no deletions are performed, because in that case the S-structures that have to be built are the largest. Consider all S-structures associated with nodes at some fixed depth h. There are at most 2^h such nodes, i.e., 2^h such S-structures, each of size at most $2^{\lceil \log N \rceil - h}$. Building these structures took $2^h . P_S(2^{\lceil \log N \rceil - h})$. It follows that the total building time is bounded by

$$\sum_{h=0}^{\lfloor \log N \rfloor} 2^h P_S(2^{\lceil \log N \rceil - h}).$$

One easily verifies that this is bounded by $O(\log N)P_S(N)$. As at least half of the
updates must have been insertions, it follows that the average insertion time is
bounded by $O(\log N)P_S(N)/N$.

□

It remains to be shown that we can perform deletions efficiently as well. To delete a point p we first insert t_N in the RI-tree as if we performed an insertion. Hence,
we build a structure S_{t_N} in the same way as for insertions except that we do not include the point p in the structure. Let α be the node on the rightmost path whose
S-structure contains p. (There exists exactly one such node α, assuming p was present.)
To be able to find α efficiently we add to the structure a balanced search tree DICT
in which we keep this information for each point in the set. Hence, with each insertion
and deletion we have to update DICT which takes $O(\log N)$. Moreover we have to update
DICT when we build and move structures, but the amount of time needed for this is domi-
nated by the building time. Hence the addition of DICT does not change the insertion
time bound of Lemma 9.6.2. After we have found the appropriate node α, we have to delete
p from S_α because p is no longer present during the whole interval of time below α.
But p was present during the intervals of time covered by nodes β that are leftson
of nodes on the rightmost search path from α to t_N. Hence we have to insert p in the
S-structure associated with these nodes. (See figure 9.6.4.)

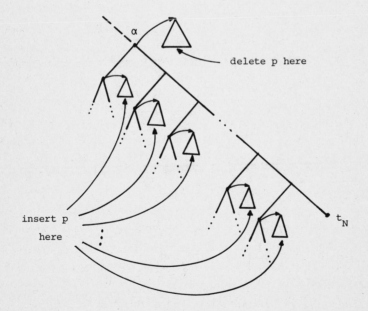

figure 9.6.4.

One easily verifies that in this way the structure is maintained correctly.

Lemma 9.6.3. $D_T^a(N) = O(\log N \cdot I_S(N) + D_S(N))$.

Proof
        Inserting t_N in the structure takes an average of $O(\log N)P_S(N)/N$ time. As $P_S(N)/N \leq I_S(N)$, this can be estimated by $O(\log N)I_S(N)$. Finding the appropriate node α takes $O(\log N)$. Deleting the point p from the structure S_α takes $O(D_S(N))$ and the insertion of p in the structures takes at most $O(\log N)I_S(N)$ because the depth of the tree is bounded by $O(\log N)$.

□

Now we can prove our result for in-the-past searching for decomposable searching problems:

Theorem 9.6.4. Given a dynamic data structure S for a decomposable searching problem PR, there exists a structure S' for solving the in-the-past version of PR such that

$$Q_{S'}(N) = O(\log N)Q_S(N),$$

$$I_{S'}^a(N) = O(\log N)P_S(N)/N,$$

$$D_{S'}^a(N) = O(\log N \cdot I_S(N) + D_S(N)),$$

$$M_{S'}(N) = O(\log N)M_S(N).$$

Proof
        The bounds on the average insertion and deletion time follow from Lemma's 9.6.2. and 9.6.3. To perform a query we have to search with t in T which takes $O(\log N)$. Moreover we have to perform at most $O(\log N)$ queries on S-structures of size at most N. The query time bound follows. To estimate the amount of storage required, consider all S-structures associated with nodes at some fixed depth h. These are at most 2^h structure that use at most $M_S(2^{\lceil \log N \rceil - h})$ storage each. Hence the total amount of storage is bounded by

$$\sum_{h=0}^{\lfloor \log N \rfloor} 2^h M_S(2^{\lceil \log N \rceil - h}),$$

which is bounded by $O(\log N)M_S(N)$.

□

One easily verifies that $Q_{S'}(N) = O(Q_S(N))$ if $Q_S(N) = \Omega(N^\varepsilon)$ for some $\varepsilon > 0$, $I_{S'}^a(N) = O(P_S(N)/N)$ if $P_S(N) = \Omega(N^{1+\varepsilon})$, $D_{S'}^a(N) = O(I_S(N) + D_S(N))$ if $I_S(N) = \Omega(N^\varepsilon)$ and $M_{S'}(N) = O(M_S(N))$ if $M_S(N) = \Omega(N^{1+\varepsilon})$.

Before giving some applications of the method we will give some indications of how the average time bounds can be changed into worst-case bounds. (Details can be found in [Ov6].) The average time bounds occur because of the insertion of t_N in T only. At this moment we have to build the structure S_{t_N} and this sometimes takes a lot of time. To avoid building this structure at once we use a technique similar to the method used for changing the average time bounds in the dynamization of decomposable searching problems into worst-case time bounds (Section 7.3.2.) We allow nodes on the rightmost path to have 1, 2 or 3 perfect binary left subtrees of the same depth. Again, we associate with each node α a structure S_α containing all points whose existence interval covers the whole time interval below α but not the whole interval below the father of α. At the moment a node α on the rightmost path would get a fourth left subtree we will take the first two left subtrees together and make one subtree out of them (by making them left and right subtree of a new internal node) and add this new subtree as a left subtree to the father of α. As a result of this change in the tree we have to reconstruct a number of associated S-structures (see figure 9.6.5. below). To obtain low worst-case update time bounds we will take care that these structures are available at the moment the change has to be made, and construct them during a number of preceding updates. Let T_1, T_2 and T_3 denote the three left subtrees a node α can get. As soon as a node α on the rigthmost path gets two left subtrees T_1 and T_2 we start building a S-structure S_1 of all points that were inserted during the time moments in T_1 and T_2 and that were not deleted by now, and the points in the current S_α. This structure S_1 will become the structure that has to be associated with α after we combine the two left subtrees T_1 and T_2 into one that will become left subtree one level higher in the tree. If the height of α is i, we will see to it that S_1 is ready within 2^i updates. To this end we do with each update $P_S(|S_1|)/2^i = O(P_S(2^i)/2^i)$ work on the construction. In the same way we start constructing a structure S_2 of all points that were present during T_1 (i.e., inserted before the first time moment in T_1) but were deleted in T_2 and a structure S_3 of points that were inserted during T_1 and not deleted in T_2 (see figure 9.6.5.). After exactly 2^{i-1} updates a third left subtree T_3 comes in (this follows from the method). At this moment we start building a structure S_4 of all points that were inserted during T_3 and are not deleted up to now, and a structure S_5 of all points that were present during T_3 but are no longer present. We will take care that both S_4 and S_5 are ready within 2^{i-1} updates, i.e., at the same moment as S_1, S_2 and S_3 are ready. This can be done doing $O(P_S(2^i)/2^i)$ work per update. There is only one problem. When the update is a deletion, it might be possible that in some of the structures S_i that are not yet ready, a point has to be inserted or deleted. To this end we add to each structure S_j a buffer BUF_j in which we store all updates that have to be performed on S_j when it is ready. To have time left for performing these updates we speed up the construction doing $I_S(2^{i+1})$ work when an insertion is put in the buffer and doing $D_S(2^{i+1})$ work when a deletion is put in the buffer. In this way all structures will be ready within 2^i updates. Exactly at this moment a fourth left subtree would come in but, we can now perform the action displayed in figure 9.6.5. to make room again, because all structures we need after the change are now ready. After this action α hàs only one leftson left. Hence there is room

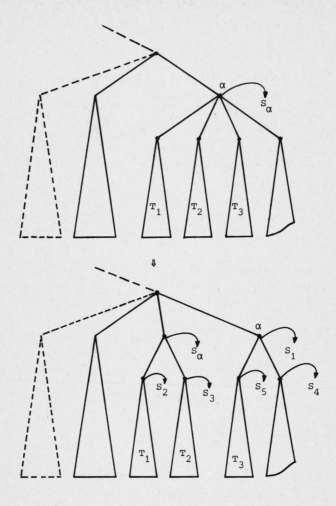

figure 9.6.5.

for the new one that comes in at this moment (because we performed the same action one level lower). This new one is the second left subtree of α and we again start the construction of S-structures. It follows that at level i of the tree we perform a change every 2^i updates and hence, every 2^i updates we add a left subtree to the father at level i+1, as we assumed.

It follows that with each update we have to do $O(P_S(2^i)/2^i)$ work for each level i of the tree. This is bounded by $O(P_S(N)/N)$ when $P_S(N) = \Omega(N^{1+\varepsilon})$ for some $\varepsilon > 0$ and by $O(\log N)P_S(N)/N$ otherwise. For an insertion this is all. When the update is a deletion we also have to perform a deletion in the S-structure of some node α on the rightmost path and we have to insert the point in all S-structures associated to leftsons of nodes on the rightmost path below α. Moreover we have to put the deletion in the buffer of the structure that will take over from α and we have to put an insertion in the buffers of structures we are constructing and that will become associated with leftsons of nodes on the rightmost path below α. This are at most $O(\log N)$ buffers. It follows that the total amount of time needed for these insertions and deletions is bounded by $O(D_S(N) + I_S(N))$ when $I_S(N) = \Omega(N^{\varepsilon})$ for some $\varepsilon > 0$ and by $O(D_S(N) + O(\log N)I_S(N))$ otherwise. This leads to the following result:

Theorem 9.6.5. Given a dynamic data structure S for a decomposable searching problem PR, there exists a structure S' for solving PR in the past such that

$$Q_{S'}(N) = \begin{cases} O(Q_S(N)) & \text{when } Q_S(N) = \Omega(N^{\varepsilon}), \ \varepsilon > 0, \\ O(\log N)Q_S(N) & \text{otherwise}, \end{cases}$$

$$I_{S'}(N) = \begin{cases} O(P_S(N)/N) & \text{when } P_S(N) = \Omega(N^{1+\varepsilon}), \ \varepsilon > 0, \\ O(\log N)P_S(N)/N & \text{otherwise}, \end{cases}$$

$$D_{S'}(N) = \begin{cases} O(D_S(N) + I_S(N)) & \text{when } I_S(N) = \Omega(N^{\varepsilon}), \ \varepsilon > 0, \\ O(D_S(N) + \log N.I_S(N)) & \text{otherwise}, \end{cases}$$

$$M_{S'}(N) = \begin{cases} O(M_S(N)) & \text{when } M_S(N) = \Omega(N^{1+\varepsilon}), \ \varepsilon > 0, \\ O(\log N)M_S(N) & \text{otherwise}. \end{cases}$$

Proof
    This follows from Theorem 9.6.4. and the above discussion.

$\square$

Applications

a) Nearest neighbor searching.
    In Section 6.4.5. a dynamic data structure S was given for solving the nearest neighbor searching problem with $Q_S(n) = O(\log n)$, $P_S(n) = O(n \log n)$, $I_S(n) = O(n)$, $D_S(n) = O(n)$ and $M_S(n) = O(n \log \log n)$. Applying Theorem 9.6.5. we obtain a structure S' for nearest neighbor searching in the past such that

$$Q_{S'}(N) = O(\log^2 N),$$
$$I_{S'}(N) = O(\log^2 N),$$
$$D_{S'}(N) = O(N),$$
$$M_{S'}(N) = O(N \log N \log \log N).$$

Other trade-offs between query and update time can be obtained by first applying the mixed dynamization method for decomposable searching problems to the structure (see Section 7.5.). A structure S for nearest neighbor searching was described in 7.5. yielding $Q_S(n) = O(\sqrt{n \log n})$, $P_S(n) = O(n \log n)$, $I_S(n) = O(\log n)$, $D_S(n) = O(\sqrt{n \log n})$ and $M_S(n) = O(n \log \log n)$. Applying Theorem 9.6.5. to this structure we obtain a structure S' for nearest neighbor searching in the past with

$$Q_{S'}(N) = O(\sqrt{N \log N}),$$
$$I_{S'}(N) = O(\log^2 N),$$
$$D_{S'}(N) = O(\sqrt{N \log N}),$$
$$M_{S'}(N) = O(N \log N \log \log N).$$

b) Range searching.

Applying Theorem 9.6.5. to the known dynamic data structure for d-dimensional range searching as described in Section 5.3.3., we obtain a structure S' for range searching in the past, with

$$Q_{S'}(N) = O(\log^{d+1} N + k),$$
$$I_{S'}(N) = O(\log^d N),$$
$$D_{S'}(N) = O(\log^{d+1} N),$$
$$M_{S'}(N) = O(N \log^d N).$$

(Compare Theorem 9.3.6. for range counting.) Similar results can be obtained for rectangle intersection searching.

9.7. Concluding remarks.

A number of general techniques have been given for turning data structures for searching problems into structures for solving the corresponding in-the-past searching problems. After giving two special purpose in-the-past structures, one for solving the member searching and the other for solving the kth element/rank searching problem in-the-past, to show what kind of in-the-past structures are possible, a general "brute force" method was given that can be used for solving the in-the-past version of any searching problem for which a dynamic data structure is available. Next decomposable searching problems were considered. For these problems much more efficient in-the-past structures were given.

The results in this chapter can be extended in a number of ways. Theorem 9.6.5. can easily be generalized to C(n)-decomposable searching problems (see Section 7.7.). The only change that has to be made is the bound on query time:

$$Q_{S'}(N) = \begin{cases} O(Q_S(N) + C(N)) & \text{when } Q_S(N) + C(N) = \Omega(N^\varepsilon), \ \varepsilon > 0, \\ O(\log N)(Q_S(N) + C(N)) & \text{otherwise.} \end{cases}$$

Also other trade-offs can be obtained by varying the number of sons nodes in the RI-tree may have, but this still has to be examined. It is also possible to obtain more efficient transformations for decomposable counting problems. Results can be found in [Ov6].

Bibliographical comments.

This chapter was based on Overmars [Ov5,Ov6].

CHAPTER X

FINAL COMMENTS AND OPEN PROBLEMS

    In this text a number of techniques have been presented and analysed for turning
static solutions to searching problems into dynamic solutions. Some of the dynamization methods given are applicable only to data structures that satisfy some special
properties and others are applicable to all data structures, provided the searching
problems they solve satisfy some constraints. The methods comprise most of the techniques that have recently been devised for dynamizing data structures for specific
problems. The results remedy the lack of flexibility as encountered particularly
in most data structures for multi-dimensional searching problems.
    The results are interesting both from a theoretical and a practical point of
view. The methods are a step into the direction of a uniform theory of searching problems and data structures. But they also serve as a tool-box for everyone who has to
devise dynamic data structures for specific problems in such fields as Computer Graphics, multi-attribute file searching and Databases. Not all methods are of the same
practical importance. The technique of balancing, described in Chapter 3, is often
used for obtaining dynamic data structures for simple searching problems. On the other
hand, the application of the technique to multi-dimensional data structures is hard
to implement. The partial rebuilding method of Chapter 4 can easily be implemented.
The techniques presented in Chapter 5 are of practical interest especially in the
average case, although one would probably not perform the clean-ups of the structure
at the moment the number of weak updates becomes large, but wait until the structure
is not used for some time (for example when no user is logged in). In this way the
structure can be used in an interactive environment, without the need for implementing
the complex mechanism of global rebuilding. The dynamization technique for order decomposable set problems (Chapter 6) gives a general solution that applies to all problems equally, but it is very well possible that for specific order decomposable set
problems easier (or even more efficient) dynamic solutions do exist. The general
method for dynamizing decomposable searching problems (Chapter 7) is particularly
interesting from the theoretical point of view. It shows what is achievable when dynamizing a particular searching problem. Only the simple methods (see e.g. Sections
7.2., 7.3.1. and 7.6.) can easily be implemented. The batched static and dynamic solutions presented in Chapter 8 are especially interesting for their way of reducing the
storage requirements of a problem. The structures for searching in the past (Chapter

9) are more of theoretical importance although there exist a number of practical applications (see Dobkin and Munro [DoM]).

Many unresolved questions remain that warrant a further study of dynamization.
We mention the following open problems and suggestions for future research in the
area of multi-dimensional data structuring and dynamization.

(i)   In Section 2.11. a number of searching problems were mentioned that have not
       been solved adequately. In particular it would be interesting to see whether
       the high amount of preprocessing needed for solving the (general) polygon inter-
       section searching problem can be reduced.

(ii)   In Section 2.12. it was shown how searching problems could be composed. It might
       be interesting to consider how and under what circumstances data structures for
       problems can be composed to obtain structures for the composed problems. Some
       work in this direction has been done, especially with respect to the addition
       of range restrictions ([Lu2]), but a more general theory is not available.

(iii) The partial rebuilding technique described in Chapter 4 yields only good aver-
       age time bounds. It is an interesting question whether these average bounds
       can be turned into worst-case bounds of a comparable order.

(iv)   As stated in Chapter 5, the global rebuilding technique can be generalized in
       a number of ways. Details still have to be supplied.

(v)   In Chapter 8 we presented a number of techniques for solving batched static
       and dynamic versions of searching problems. The techniques were mostly relevant
       only for decomposable searching problems. General techniques for obtaining
       batched solutions to other searching problems do not exist at the moment.

(vi)   The technique of "streaming" seems to be a powerful instrument in reducing the
       space requirements for solutions to problems. Other applications than the ones
       given in Chapter 8 might be interesting.

(vii) Like for ordinary dynamization of decomposable searching problems, other trade-
       offs can be obtained for batched dynamization. In [EdO2] some of these results
       were mentioned but others might exist.

(viii) It is possible to obtain other trade-offs between query and update time for
       the transformations presented in Chapter 9 by varying the number of sons nodes
       of the tree structure can have. The details are still open.

(ix)   A very general open problem concerns lowerbounds. Some results on lowerbounds
       do exist (see e.g. Fredman [Fr] for lowerbounds on the range searching problems,
       and see Mehlhorn [Me] for lowerbounds on the transforms for decomposable search-
       ing problems given in Chapter 7) but for most of the results presented there is
       still no indication that they are optimal in some way or another.

REFERENCES

[AdVL]   Adel'son-Vel'skii, G.M. and E.M. Landis, An information organisation algo-
            rithm, Doklady Akad. Nauk SSSR 146 (1962), pp. 263-266, transl. Sovjet
            Math. Dokl. 3 (1962), pp. 1259-1262.

[AhHU]   Aho, A.V., J.E. Hopcroft and J.D. Ullman, The design and analysis of computer
            algorithms, Addison-Wesley, Reading, Mass., 1974.

[AlMM]   Alt, H., K. Mehlhorn and J.I. Munro, Partial match retrieval in implicit
            data structures, Proc. 10th Symp. on Mathematical Foundations of Com-
            puter Science, 1981, pp. 156-161.

[Bar]   Barnett, V., The ordering of multivariate data (with discussion), J. Roy.
            Stat. Soc. (A) 139 (1976), pp. 318-354.

[Bay]   Bayer, R., Symmetric binary B-trees: data structure and maintenance algo-
            rithms, Acta Inform. 1 (1972), pp. 290-306.

[BayM]   Bayer, R. and E.M. McCreight, Organisation and maintenance of large ordered
            indexes, Acta Inform. 1 (1972), pp. 173-189.

[Be1]   Bentley, J.L., Multidimensional binary search trees used for associated
            searching, Comm. of the ACM 18 (1975), pp. 509-517.

[Be2]   Bentley, J.L., Multidimensional binary search trees in database applications,
            IEEE Trans. on Software Eng. SE-5 (1979), pp. 333-340.

[Be3]   Bentley, J.L., Decomposable searching problems, Inform. Proc. Lett. 8 (1979),
            pp. 244-251.

[Be4]   Bentley, J.L., Multidimensional divide-and-conquer, Comm. of the ACM 23
            (1980), pp. 214-229.

[Be5]   Bentley, J.L., Solutions to Klee's rectangle problems, unpublished notes,
            Dept. of Computer Science, Carnegie-Mellon University, 1977.

[Be6]   Bentley, J.L., Notes on a taxanomy of planar convex hull algorithms, Techn.
            Rep., Carnegie-Mellon University, 1980.

[BeF]   Bentley, J.L. and J.H. Friedman, Data structures for range searching, ACM
            Comput. Surveys 11 (1979), pp. 397-409.

[BeM1]   Bentley, J.L. and H.A. Maurer, Efficient worst-case data structures for
         range searching, Acta Inform. 13 (1980), pp. 155-168.

[BeM2]   Bentley, J.L. and H.A. Maurer, A note on Euclidean near neighbor searching
         in the plane, Inform. Proc. Lett. 8 (1979), pp. 133-136.

[BeSa]   Bentley, J.L. and J.B. Saxe, Decomposable searching problems I: static- to
         dynamic transformations, J. of Algorithms 1 (1980), pp. 301-358.

[BeSh1] Bentley J.L. and M.I. Shamos, Divide-and-conquer in multidimensional space,
         Proc. 8th Annual ACM Symp. on Theory of Computing, 1976, pp. 220-230.

[BeSh2] Bentley, J.L. and M.I. Shamos, A problem in multivariate statistics: algo-
         rithm, data structure and applications, Proc. 15th Annual Allerton
         Conference on Communication, Control and Computing, 1977, pp. 193-201.

[BeSh3] Bentley, J.L. and M.I. Shamos, Divide-and-conquer for linear expected time,
         Inform. Proc. Lett. 7 (1978), pp. 87-91.

[BeSt]   Bentley, J.L. and D.F. Stanat, Analysis of range searches in quad-trees,
         Inform. Proc. Lett. 3 (1975), pp. 170-173.

[BeW]   Bentley, J.L. and D. Wood, An optimal worst-case algorithm for reporting
         intersections of rectangles, IEEE Trans. on Computers C-29 (1980),
         pp. 571-577.

[Bl]   Blum, M., R.W. Floyd, V.R. Pratt, R.L. Rivest and R.E. Tarjan, Time bounds
         for selection, J. Comput. Syst. Sci. 7 (1972), pp. 448-461.

[BlM]   Blum, N. and K. Mehlhorn, On the average number of rebalancing operations
         in weight-balanced trees, Theor. Comp. Sci. 11 (1980), pp. 303-320.

[Br1]   Brown, K.Q., Fast intersection of halfspaces, Techn. Rep. CMU-CS-78-129,
         Dept. of Computer Science, Carnegie-Mellon University, 1978.

[Br2]   Brown, K.Q., Geometric transforms for fast geometric algorithms, Techn.
         Rep. CMU-CS-80-101, Dept. of Computer Science, Carnegie-Mellon Uni-
         versity, 1980.

[ChD]   Chazelle, B. and D.P. Dobkin, Detection is easier than computation, Proc.
         12th Annual ACM Symp. on Theory of Computing, 1980, pp. 146-153.

[CuOW]   Culik II, K., Th. Ottmann and D. Wood, Dense multiway trees, ACM Trans. on
         Database Systems 6 (1981), pp. 486-512.

[DoM]   Dobkin, D.P. and J.I. Munro, Efficient uses of the past, Proc. 21th Annual
         IEEE Symp. on Foundations of Computer Science, 1980, pp. 200-206.

[Ed1]   Edelsbrunner, H., Dynamic rectangle intersection searching, Techn. Rep.
         #47, Inst. f. Informationsverarbeitung, TU Graz, 1980.

[Ed2]   Edelsbrunner, H., Dynamic data structures for orthogonal intersection que-
          ries, Techn. Rep. #59, Inst. f. Informationsverarbeitung, TU Graz, 1980.

[Ed3]   Edelsbrunner, H., Complexity classes for dynamic on-line searching involving
          intervals on a line, Techn. Rep. #66, Inst. f. Informationsverarbeitung,
          TU Graz, 1981.

[Ed4]   Edelsbrunner, H., Intersection problems in computational geometry, Techn.
          Rep. #93, Inst. f. Informationsverarbeitung, TU Graz, 1982.

[Ed5]   Edelsbrunner, H., Optimizing the dynamization of decomposable searching
          problems, Techn. Rep. #35, Inst. f. Informationsverarbeitung, TU Graz,
          1979.

[EdKM]   Edelsbrunner, H., D.G. Kirkpatrick and H.A. Maurer, Polygonal intersection
          searching, Inform. Proc. Lett. 14 (1982), pp. 74-79.

[EdM]   Edelsbrunner, H. and H.A. Maurer, On the intersection of orthogonal objects,
          Inform. Proc. Lett. 13 (1981), pp. 177-181.

[EdMP]   Edelsbrunner, H., H.A. Maurer, F.P. Preparata, A.L. Rosenberg, E. Welzl and
          D. Wood, Stabbing line segments, Bit 22 (1982), pp. 274-281.

[EdO1]   Edelsbrunner, H. and M.H. Overmars, On the equivalence of some rectangle
          problems, Inform. Proc. Lett. 14 (1982), pp. 124-127.

[EdO2]   Edelsbrunner, H. and M.H. Overmars, Batched dynamic solutions to decomposable
          searching problems, Techn. Rep. RUU-CS-83-8, Dept. of Computer Science,
          University of Utrecht, 1983.

[EdOW]   Edelsbrunner, H., M.H. Overmars and D. Wood, Graphics in Flatland: a case
          study, Techn. Rep. #79, Inst. f. Informationsverarbeitung, TU Graz,
          1981.

[EdvL]   Edelsbrunner, H. and J. van Leeuwen, Multidimensional data structures and
          algorithms: a bibliography, Techn. Rep. #104, Inst. f. Informations-
          verarbeitung, TU Graz, 1983.

[FiB]   Finkel, R.A. and J.L. Bentley, Quad-trees; a data structure for retrieval
          on composite keys, Acta Inform. 4 (1974), pp. 1-9.

[Fr]   Fredman, M.L., A lowerbound on the complexity of orthogonal range queries,
          J. of the ACM 28 (1981), pp. 696-705.

[GaJ]   Garey, M.R. and D.S. Johnson, Computers and Intractability, Freeman, San
          Francisco, 1979.

[Go]   Gowda, I.G., Dynamic problems in computational geometry, M.Sc.Thesis, Dept.
          of Computer Science, University of British Columbia, 1980.

[GoK]   Gowda, I.G. and D.G. Kirkpatrick, Exploiting linear merging and extra stor-
           age in the maintenance of fully dynamic geometric data structures,
           Proc. 19th Annual Allerton Conference on Communication, Control and
           Computing, 1980, pp. 1-10.

[Gr]   Graham, R.L., An efficient algorithm for determining the convex hull of a
           finite planar set, Inform. Proc. Lett. 1 (1972), pp. 132-133.

[GuS]   Guibas, L.J. and R. Sedgewick, A dichromatic framework for balanced trees,
           Proc. 19th Annual IEEE Symp. on Foundations of Computer Science, 1978,
           pp. 8-21.

[Ha]   Hart, J.H., Optimal two-dimensional range queries using binary range lists,
           Techn. Rep. 76-81, Dept. of Computer Science, University of Kentucky,
           1981.

[Hu]   Huber, P.J., Robust statistics: a review, Annals Math. Statistics 43 (1972),
           pp. 1041-1067.

[Ki1]   Kirkpatrick D.G., Efficient computation of continuous skeletons, Proc. 20th
           Annual IEEE Symp. on Foundations of Computer Science, 1979, pp. 18-27.

[Ki2]   Kirkpatrick, D.G., Optimal search in planar subdivisions, SIAM J. Computing
           12 (1983), pp. 28-35.

[Kn]   Knuth, D.E., The art of computer programming, vol. 3: sorting and searching,
           Addison-Wesley, Reading, Mass., 1973.

[KuLP]   Kung, H.T., F. Luccio and F.P. Preparata, On finding the maxima of a set
           of vectors, J. of the ACM 22 (1975), pp. 469-476.

[LeP1]   Lee, D.T. and F.P. Preparata, An improved algorithm for the rectangle en-
           closure problem, J. of Algorithms 3 (1982), pp. 218-224.

[LeP2]   Lee, D.T. and F.P. Preparata, An optimal algorithm for finding the kernel
           of a polygon, J. of the ACM 26 (1979), pp. 415-421.

[LeW1]   Lee, D.T. and C.K. Wong, Worst-case analysis for region and partial region
           searches in multidimensional binary search trees and balanced quad
           trees, Acta Inform. 9 (1977), pp. 23-29.

[LeW2]   Lee, D.T. and C.K. Wong, Quintary trees: a file structure for multidimen-
           sional database systems, ACM Trans. on Database Systems 5 (1980),
           pp. 339-353.

[LeW3]   Lee, D.T. and C.K. Wong, Finding intersections of rectangles by range search,
           J. of Algorithms 2 (1981), pp. 337-347.

[Lu1]   Lueker, G.S., A data structure for orthogonal range queries, Proc. 19th
           Annual IEEE Symp. on Foundations of Computer Science, 1978, pp. 28-34.

[Lu2]   Lueker, G.S., A transformation for adding range restriction capability to
          dynamic data structures for decomposable searching problems, Techn.
          Rep. #129, Dept. of Inform. and Computer Science, University of Cali-
          fornia, 1978.

[MaO]   Maurer, H.A. and T.A. Ottmann, Dynamic solutions of decomposable searching
          problems, in: U. Pape (ed.), Discrete structures and algorithms, Hanser
          Verlag, Wien, 1979, pp. 17-24.

[Mc]   McCreight, E.M., Priority search trees, Techn. Rep. CSL-81-5, XEROX Palo
          Alto research centre, 1981.

[Me]   Mehlhorn, K., Lowerbounds on the efficiency of transforming static data struc-
          tures into dynamic structures, Math. Syst. Theory 15 (1981), pp. 1-16.

[MeO]   Mehlhorn, K. and M.H. Overmars, Optimal dynamization of decomposable search-
          ing problems, Inform. Proc. Lett. 12 (1981), pp. 93-98.

[MeT]   Mehlhorn, K. and A. Tsakalides, AVL-trees, refined analysis and application
          to sorting presorted files, Techn. Rep. A-82/05, Fachbereich Informatik,
          Universität des Saarlandes, 1982.

[NiR]   Nievergelt, J. and E.M. Reingold, Binary search trees of bounded balance,
          SIAM J. Computing 2 (1973), pp. 33-43.

[Ol]   Olivié, H., A study of balanced binary trees and balanced one-two trees,
          Ph.D.Thesis, Dept. of Mathematics, University of Antwerp, 1980.

[Ov1]   Overmars, M.H., The equivalence of rectangle containment, rectangle enclosure
          and ECDF searching, Techn. Rep. RUU-CS-81-1, Dept. of Computer Science,
          University of Utrecht, 1981.

[Ov2]   Overmars, M.H., Dynamization of order decomposable set problems, J. of Algo-
          rithms 2 (1981), pp. 245-260.

[Ov3]   Overmars, M.H., General methods for "all elements" and "all pairs" problems,
          Inform. Proc. Lett. 12 (1981), pp. 99-102.

[Ov4]   Overmars, M.H., Transforming semi-dynamic data structures into dynamic struc-
          tures, in: J.R. Mühlbacher (ed.), Proc. 7th Conference on Graphtheoret-
          ical Concepts in Computer Science (WG81), Hanser Verlag, Wien, 1982,
          pp. 173-182.

[Ov5]   Overmars, M.H., Searching in the past I, Techn. Rep. RUU-CS-81-7, Dept. of
          Computer Science, University of Utrecht, 1981.

[Ov6]   Overmars, M.H., Searching in the past II: general transforms, Techn. Rep.
          RUU-CS-81-9, Dept. of Computer Science, University of Utrecht, 1981.

[Ov7]   Overmars, M.H., The locus approach, in preparation.

[OvL1]   Overmars, M.H. and J. van Leeuwen, Maintenance of configurations in the
           plane, J. Comp. Syst. Sci. 23 (1981), pp. 166-204.

[OvL2]   Overmars, M.H. and J. van Leeuwen, Dynamically maintaining configurations
           in the plane, Proc. 12th Annual ACM Symp. on Theory of Computing, 1980,
           pp. 135-145.

[OvL3]   Overmars, M.H. and J. van Leeuwen, Dynamic multi-dimensional data structures
           based on quad- and k-d trees, Acta Inform. 17 (1982), pp. 267-285.

[OvL4]   Overmars, M.H. and J. van Leeuwen, Two general methods for dynamizing decom-
           posable searching problems, Computing 26 (1981), pp. 155-166.

[OvL5]   Overmars, M.H. and J. van Leeuwen, Worst-case optimal insertion and deletion
           methods for decomposable searching problems, Inform. Proc. Lett. 12
           (1981), pp. 168-173.

[OvL6]   Overmars, M.H. and J. van Leeuwen, Some principles for dynamizing decompos-
           able searching problems, Inform. Proc. Lett. 12 (1981), pp. 49-53.

[OvL7]   Overmars, M.H. and J. van Leeuwen, Dynamization of decomposable searching
           problems yielding good worst-case bounds, in: P. Deussen (ed.), Theo-
           retical Computer Science (5th GI-Conf.), Lect. Notes in Comp. Sci. 104,
           Springer Verlag, Berlin, 1981, pp. 224-233.

[Pr]   Preparata, F.P., A new approach to planar point location, SIAM J. Computing
           10 (1981), pp. 473-482.

[PrH]   Preparata, F.P. and S.J. Hong, Convex hulls of finite sets of points in two
           and three dimensions, Comm. of the ACM 20 (1977), pp. 87-93.

[PrM]   Preparata, F.P. and D.E. Muller, Finding the intersection of n halfspaces in
           time O(n log n), Theor. Comput. Sci. 8 (1979), pp. 45-55.

[ReND]   Reingold, E.M., J. Nievergelt and N. Deo, Combinatorial algorithms, Prentice-
           Hall, Englewood Cliffs, 1977.

[Sam]   Samet, H., Deletion in two dimensional quad trees, Comm. of the ACM 23
           (1980), pp. 703-710.

[Sax]   Saxe, J.B., Decomposable searching problems, Ph.D.Thesis, Dept. of Computer
           Science, Carnegie-Mellon University, to appear.

[SaxB]   Saxe, J.B. and J.L. Bentley, Transforming static data structures to dynamic
           structures, Proc. 20th Annual IEEE Symp. on Foundations of Computer
           Science, 1979, pp. 148-168.

[Sh1]   Shamos, M.I., Computational geometry, Ph.D.Thesis, Department of Computer
          Science, Yale University, 1978.

[Sh2]   Shamos, M.I., Geometry and statistics: problems at the interface, in: J.F.
          Traub (ed.), Recent results and new directions in algorithms and com-
          plexity, Acad. Press, New York, 1976, pp. 251-280.

[ShH1]   Shamos, M.I. and D. Hoey, Closest-point problems, Proc. 16th Annual IEEE
          Symp. on Foundations of Computer Science, 1975, pp. 151-162.

[ShH2]   Shamos, M.I. and D. Hoey, Geometric intersection problems, Proc. 17th Annual
          IEEE Symp. on Foundations of Computer Science, 1976, pp. 208-215.

[SiF]   Silva-Filho, Y.V., Average case analysis of region search in balanced k-d
          trees, Inform. Proc. Lett. 8 (1979), pp. 219-223.

[Su]   Supowit, K.J., Topics in computational geometry, Techn. Rep. R-81-1062,
          Dept. of Computer Science, University of Illinois, 1981.

[Sw]   Swart, G.F., An O(log n) time algorithm for finding bridge points of convex
          arcs, Techn. Rep., University of Washington, 1980.

[To]   Toussaint, G.T., Pattern recognition and geometrical complexity, Proc. 5th
          International Conference on Pattern Recognition, 1980, pp. 1324-1347.

[ToA]   Toussaint, G.T. and S.G. Akl, The convex hull problem, Plenum Press, to
          appear.

[ToB]   Toussaint, G.T. and B.K. Bhattacharya, On geometric algorithms that use the
          furthest-point Voronoi diagram, Techn. Rep. 813, School of Computer
          Science, McGill University, 1981.

[Tu]   Tuckey, J.W., referred to in [Sh2], p. 267.

[Va]   Vaishnavi, V.K., Computing point enclosures, IEEE Trans. on Computers C-31
          (1982), pp. 22-29.

[VaW]   Vaishnavi, V.K. and D. Wood, Rectilinear line segment intersection, layered
          segment trees and dynamization, J. of Algorithms 3 (1982), pp. 160-176.

[vLM]   van Leeuwen, J. and H.A. Maurer, Dynamic systems of static data structures,
          Techn. Rep. #42, Inst. f. Informationsverarbeitung, TU Graz, 1980.

[vLO1]   van Leeuwen, J. and M.H. Overmars, Stratified balanced search trees, Acta
          Inform. 18 (1983), pp. 345-359.

[vLO2]   van Leeuwen, J. and M.H. Overmars, The art of dynamizing, in: J. Gruska and
          M. Chytil (ed.), Mathematical Foundations of Computer Science 1981
          (Proc. 10th Symp.), Lect. Notes in Comp. Sci. 118, Springer Verlag,
          Berlin, 1981, pp. 121-131.

[vLW]   van Leeuwen, J. and D. Wood, Dynamization of decomposable searching problems,
         Inform. Proc. Lett. 10 (1980), pp. 51-56.

[Wi1]   Willard, D.E., Predicate-oriented database search algorithms, Garland Pu-
         blishing Company, New-York, 1979.

[Wi2]   Willard, D.E., The super B-tree algorithm, Techn. Rep. TR-03-79, Aiken Com-
         putation Lab., Harvard University, 1979.

[Wi3]   Willard, D.E., New data structures for orthogonal queries, Techn. Rep.
         TR-22-78, Aiken Computation Lab., Harvard University, 1978 (revised
         version to appear in SIAM J. Computing).

[Wi4]   Willard, D.E., Polygon retrieval, SIAM J. Computing 11 (1982), pp. 149-165.

[Wi5]   Willard, D.E., Balanced forests of k-d* trees as a dynamic data structure,
         TR-23-78, Aiken Computation Lab., Harvard University, 1978.

INDEX